Aristotle

Aristotle

The Collected Papers of Joseph Owens

edited by
John R. Catan

State University of New York Press
Albany

For my son, Paul

Published by
State University of New York Press, Albany

© 1981 State University of New York

For information, address State University of New York Press, State University Plaza, Albany, N.Y., 12246

Library of Congress Cataloging in Publication Data

Owens, Joseph.
    Aristotle, the collected papers of Joseph Owens.

    Companion vol. to the author's St. Thomas Aquinas on the existence of God.
    "Complete bibliography of Joseph Owens, C.Ss.R.":
    Includes bibliographical references and indexes.
    Contents: Aristotle, teacher of those who know—
Aristotle on categories—The Aristotelian conception of the sciences—[etc.]
    1. Aristotle—Addresses, essays, lectures.
I. Catan, John R. II. Title.

B485.082   185   81-7602
ISBN 0-87395-534-X AACR2
ISBN 0-87395-535-8 (pbk.)

Contents

Foreword

Interest in Aristotle seems to maintain a steady pulse. True, the reasons for the persistent attention to his writings may vary widely. Great philosophers as well as great artists have the gift of inspiring profoundly different conceptions and meaning in the individuals who contemplate their work. The Greek commentators, the Islamic intellectuals, the medieval Scholastics, the Renaissance humanists, the nineteenth-century philologists, the twentieth-century analysts, and numerous other scholarly movements, have all shown an absorbing fascination in Aristotle in spite of the differences in their respective viewpoints. This history would in itself be ample testimony to the breadth of the Aristotelian achievement. It would augur intellectual profit for any type of reader who approaches the Stagirite, and would make manifest the propriety of Dante's characterization of him as the teacher of those who know.

The breadth of universal interest and the openness to the various fields of scholarly engagement may have their explanation, partly at least, in Aristotle's own conception of human intellectual endeavor. For him all human knowledge is solidly grounded in the things experienced in the course of everyday life. These things are obvious and accessible to all inquirers. They are what a person becomes and is cognitionally in ordinary sensation and understanding. In that way they form the common basis for all subsequent reasoning by individuals or groups. Their qualitative and quantitative aspects give rise to the far-reaching penetration of the natural and life sciences. Of the mathematicized sciences Aristotle knew only astronomy, optics, harmonics and mechanics, and only in the stage of development they had reached in his day. But his philosophical views about them are still enlightening. His understanding of the world of nature, moreover, went beyond the domain of the qualitative and the quantitative. It gave a further explanation of sensible things in terms of their substantial principles, matter and form. This is a different but in no way rival account of visible things through the philosophy of nature, and it answers its own set of questions about the universe.

Still further, for Aristotle the investigation of those same tangible things from the viewpoint of their being opens on the world of supersensible things, in the discipline that later came to be known as metaphysics. But in spite of the necessitating causation that prevails throughout the visible universe and in its links with the immaterial substances, Aristotle's ethics shows the way to proceed in practical science from a radically new starting point, free choice, while at the same time keeping human life and human conduct within the same real world studied by the other sciences. Causation and liberty walk side by side, neither excluding the other. Correspondingly his conception of the arts and crafts, as working into external things some forms already existent in the mind, brings out strongly the humanizing aspect of those activities.

In all these domains Aristotle still broadens our intellectual outlook. Even after the terrific tensions and the undermining erosions of twenty-three centuries his thought has much to offer. The following papers of mine aimed to investigate some aspects of it that have been notably influential. The project of publishing these papers collectively, the selection of them and their arrangement in the volume, are all due to the enterprise and industry of Professor John Catan. May I express my trust that his confidence and that of Mr. William Eastman of SUNY Press in the ongoing demand for discussions about Aristotle will prove justified. Other writers from Plato to Heidegger may be much more brilliant, and quicker to stir enthusiasm. The adrenalin they pour into western thinking has its important function. But for basic solidity, breadth of vision, reassuring balance and quiet penetration of thought, there is good reason to believe that Aristotle will continue to play a role all his own.

J. Owens
January 22, 1981

Editor's Preface

This book is a companion to the recently published *St. Thomas Aquinas on The Existence of God: The Collected Papers of Joseph Owens* (Albany: SUNY Press, 1980) whose main emphasis is Saint Thomas Aquinas. A cursory reading of that book also reveals the presence throughout of references to and lengthy explanations of Aristotle's teachings. The present book, then, brings together articles by Father Owens which have been influential in changing current scholarly opinion on Aristotle. The main emphasis in this book is on the theory of knowledge, embracing the logical works as well as the *Physics*, the *de Anima*, and associated cognitive problems in moral philosophy. Father Owens has written, of course, on the *Metaphysics* of Aristotle in his well-known *Doctrine of Being in the Aristotelian Metaphysics* (Toronto: Pontifical Institute of Mediaevel Studies, 1978), 3rd edition revised. I have therefore not included any articles concerned with the *Metaphysics* that essentially reproduce material in *The Doctrine of Being in the Aristotelian Metaphysics*, I leave to the reader the pleasure of consulting Father Owens' most recent survey of scholarly opinion on the *Metaphysics* to be found in his Introduction to *The Doctrine of Being* etc. I have also presented a complete bibliography in chronological order up through the beginning of 1981 as well as a short biography of Father Owens.

It is my pleasure once again to thank Father Owens for his cooperation in my editing, although I am responsible for the final arrangement and choices. I would also like to thank the following publishers, journals, and their editors for permission to reprint: *Editio Bellarmin* (Montreal, Canada); *The Review of Metaphysics*; *Notre Dame University Press*; *International Philosophical Quarterly*; *Studia Moralia* (Rome); *The American Philosophical Quarterly*; *Herder* (Germany); *The Monist*; *State University of New York Press*; *Man and World*; *Canadian Journal of Philosophy*; *Eidos Press*; *Phoenix*; *Martinus Nijhoff, Inc.*; *D. Reidel, Inc.*

J.R.C.

Brockport, New York
Spring 1981

1. Aristotle—Teacher of Those who Know *

I

The now rather pompous title *maestro di color che sanno* did not seem at all out of place at the time it was given by Dante (*Inferno*, IV, 131) to Aristotle. Not only in philosophy but also in science and theology the Stagirite's concepts and methods dominated university teaching at the beginning of the fourteenth century. His logic provided the categories and the norms that guided organized human knowledge during the epoch. Later the humanistic trends of the Renaissance, the Biblical emphasis of the Reformation, and the mathematical penetration of modern science played havoc with this dominating reputation of the ancient Greek thinker. Nevertheless his works continued to be studied and used, especially by the nineteenth century philologists and the Neoscholastic philosophers and theologians, and in a lively modern tradition developed notably at Oxford but spreading to the major centers of culture throughout the world. The world-wide interest finds expression in the *Symposium Aristotelicum* held in a different country every third year, and in a continued output of books and articles that keep enriching present-day knowledge of Aristotle. This mentality seems crystallized in the observation that "the wisdom of Aristotle grows on the mind as one ponders upon it, and the future will be all the better if it continues to digest his wisdom."[1]

There is, of course, opposition. An existentialist may decry the effort "to impose on Gothic evangelical inspiration the deforming tyranny of Aristotelianism."[2] A theological writer may call for the complete dehellenization of Western culture, in the interests of a new religious spirit. A devotee of belles-lettres may be inclined to look upon the Aristotelian tradition as "dry as dust" Peripateticism. A modern

---

*Originally published: "Aristote—Maitre de ceux qui savant", *La Philosophie et les philosophes* (Montreal, Bellarmin and Desclée, Paris-Tournai, 1973) translated from the English by Bernard and Roger Càrriere, pp. 45-68. The inclusion of the essay in the present volume is its first publication in English. The English version here is that of Father Owens.

JRC.

philosophical critic may regard the Stagirite's thinking as naively realistic. Someone immersed in laboratory techniques may assess Aristotle's whole accomplishment as antiquated science. Yet his thinking continues to thrive in spite of all these severe attacks, just as it has withstood the inroads of adverse criticism down through the centuries.

Surely a way of thinking that has survived so much deeply rooted opposition and continues to flourish amid so much hostility deserves serious consideration. Its history alone would make it part of the intellectual concern of a truly educated person. Its presumed potentialities for service to the ongoing development of Western civilization make advisable a fairly profound acquaintance with its basic principles and workings. It is, whether one likes it or not, a long built-in feature of the Western mentality. It should accordingly be understood in sufficient depth by anyone who claims to take a rational part in present-day intellectual life. An educated person today should be in a position to form his own considered judgment on the merits and shortcomings of Aristotle's thought, on the role it has actually played in shaping Western culture, on its possibilities for influence on the future, and upon the sources of the multiple adverse criticism against it that have been perennial from the time of its origin in the fourth century B.C. Only in this way is one equipped to make a balanced assessment of the role the Stagirite has played and continues to play in the Western world.

II

Aristotle is regularly associated with Stagira, in eastern Macedonia. There his father, though resident at the Macedonian court as royal physician, had his property. At the age of seventeen, or almost seventeen, Aristotle went to Athens. He remained there till he was nearly thirty-seven. During that time he was closely associated with Plato's Academy. Practically nothing is known with certainty of his personal relations with Plato, though his writings show a profound grasp and throughgoing influence of Plato's thought. Nor is anything known definitely about his motives for leaving Athens around the time of Plato's death in 347 B.C. A wave of anti-Macedonian sentiment is the most likely guess. During the next three years he was at the court of Hermias, who ruled the coastal towns of Atarneus and Assos in Asia Minor and who was an admirer of Plato. Then he lived for a short time at nearby Mytilene. A year or so later he was called to Macedon to act as a tutor to Alexander for the next eight years. A short time after Alexander's accession to the throne he returned to Athens for a second stay, of about twelve years. After Alexander's death anti-Macedonian feeling forced him by the early spring of 322 B.C. to leave for Chalcis on the island of Euboea, where he owned property. By mid-fall he had died of stomach trouble, a little over sixty-two years in age.[3]

From the time of his first Athenian period Aristotle had engaged in both teaching and writing. He taught rhetoric, in accord with the popular demand of the time, and also the philosophy contained in his treatises. His writings were voluminous. The surviving works are in the form of school *logoi*, a traditional Ionian literary genre. They are neither mere lecture notes nor writings given a format for presentation to the general public, but carefully written and condensed coverages of philosophical topics that were meant to serve as the basis for lively discussions within highly specialized circles of "hearers." For purposes of citation the treatises allowed themselves to be grouped in narrower or wider collections, according to the viewpoint of the moment. Each grouping had an appropriate title. But besides the treatises, other works of Aristotle were read and quoted in antiquity, and under very different titles. Only the quotations have survived, with some brief references and descriptions. These are now published under the heading of *Fragments*.[4] The fragments often show an ornate style, indicating that the works were meant for the general literary public and not precisely for school activity.

Very little about their chronological order can be deduced from these writings. Extensive efforts have been made to arrange them chronologically on the basis of passages that are alleged to show doctrinal proximity to or distance from Plato's thought. But there is no general agreement. Read in one way, the texts labelled "Platonic" are interpreted as revealing a docile pupil who accepted Plato's teaching without question. Other texts then present Aristotle as gradually maturing towards independent thought, while the passages that show him a fulfledged "Aristotelian" come last in order of time (Jaeger). Read in the opposite direction, the same passages reveal a brash young student who opposed his master on point after point, but in mature life began to see that the old man was not so stupid after all, and then finally became to a notable extent a "Platonist."[5] Actually, the indications are far too tenuous to give firm support to any general chronology. A few works, such as the *Topics* and the *De Caelo*, may for various reasons be placed comparatively early. But for most, any dating remains uncertain. Moreover, the nature of the treatises as school *logoi* would allow additions or changes at any time in Aristotle's teaching career.

According to a sufficiently reliable account (Strabo, XIII, 1, 54; Plutarch, *Sylla*, XXVI, 1-2), the treatises were taken to Skepsis in Asia

Minor after the death of Aristotle's pupil Theophrastus. There they lay buried in an underground hiding place till early in the first century B.C. Yet the ancient lists as well as other evidence indicate the copies of many of the treatises were in use during that period along with the works meant for general circulation. However, after the Skepsis find the treatises were edited and published by Andronicus of Rhodes in the first century B.C., and became the subject of commentaries in Greek down to the fourteenth century A.D., while the works meant for the general public were allowed to perish. In this tradition five logical works (*Categories, De Interpretatione, Prior Analytics, Posterior Analytics, Topics* and *De Sophisticis Elenchis*) were grouped together as the *Organon* or instrument for learning. Then followed the works on the philosophy of nature, the *Physics* covering the overall considerations of nature while *De Caelo, On Generation and Corruption, De Anima, Parva Naturalia*, and several detailed works on the animals, dealt with particular areas. Fourteen treatises had gradually been gathered into the collection called the *Metaphysics*, focusing ostensibly on things that are "beyond nature."[6] Further, there were three sets of ethical treatises called the *Nicomachean Ethics*, the *Eudemian Ethics*, and with division of modern opinion on its authenticity the *Magna Moralia*. There were also the *Politics*, which was meant as a continuation of the ethical doctrine, and the *Rhetoric*, and a work on literary criticism called the *Poetics*. Together these are known as the *Corpus Aristotelicum*, and in the nineteenth and twentieth centuries the fragments from the lost works have been added. Some unauthentic works had slipped into the collection with the course of time, but these are now carefully distinguished from the others in any good modern edition or translation. Suitable English translations are readily available in *The Works of Aristotle* (ed. W. D. Ross), the *Loeb Classical Library*, and in many particular renditions of individual works.

III

In general, the traditionally accepted order of Aristotle's writings tries to reflect his doctrinal assessment of the various disciplines. Logic, though called a science by him and conforming to the procedure he requires for a science, is not included by him in his formal divisions of the sciences (*Metaph.*, E 1,1025b22-1026a23; K 7,1063b36-1064b6). It is regarded as something that has to be learned first, something that is required before one is able to deal scientifically with reality or truth, (*Metaph.*, Γ3,1005b2-5). With the role of logic so understood, the truly basic division marking the general types of sciences is located between the theoretical sciences on the one hand, and the practical and productive sciences on the other. The reason for this basic division lies in the nature of their respective starting points. These are either independent of the mind or else a result of its activity. The starting points for theoretical sciences are found in things, those for practical sciences are found in human choice, and those for productive sciences are found in human ideas or plans. Since the practical and productive sciences are always for the sake of something else, namely the action or the product, they are regarded as of lesser worth than the theoretical sciences, which in principle are for their own sakes and not necessarily for the sake of anything else. Hence the traditional approach to the Aristotelian treatises reflects this doctrinal division. Logic comes first, as a prerequisite. Then come the theoretical sciences, as superior in nature, to the practical and productive sciences. As able to command the productive sciences, practical science in the form of ethics or politics comes next. Rhetoric and poetics, as productive sciences, conclude the extant Aristotelian entries in the general schema.

The Aristotelian logic divides simple objects of thought into "categories." The longest list, given only twice by Aristotle himself (*Cat.*, 4, 1b25-27; *Top.*, I 9,103b22-23), has ten. Of these the first and basic is substance, for instance a man. The other nine, called "accidents", presuppose and are dependent on substance. The most important are the qualitative, the quantitative, and the relative - for instance the ways in which a man is educated, is six feet in height, and is a husband or father. Elsewhere Aristotle gives shorter lists, according to his purposes at the moment. The things that go in the categories are regarded as univocal when they come under the same concept in being designated by a common name, as for instance Socrates and Plato are each called a man in the sense that the identical notion "man" is found in each. On the other hand things are equivocal when the concepts are different even though the designating name is identical, as when the instrument for writing and the place to keep pigs are each called a pen. Aristotle does not give examples of this extreme or pure equivocality. He is interested rather in cases where the difference in concept is only partial, as when the notion "being" is applied to a man and to a color, or to any of the other accidents. All are said to be, but what is meant for the substance is being in itself, while for the accident what is meant is being in something else, namely in a substance. The combined sameness and difference are found in the things themselves, and both have to enter into the concept by which these things are understood. In this way the most important Aristotelian concepts keep in close touch with reality. Since the concepts are basic in logic, their flexible correspondence to reality will ground a logic that is not restricted in grasp to any single category, such as the quantitative or mathematical. It likewise allows the same existent to be known individually as Socrates, specifically as a man, generically as an animal or a living thing or a corporeal thing, and supergenerically as a being or as good.

Neither truth nor falsehood is found in these simple objects of the categories, objects that are designated by mere names. Only when the objects are joined with or separated from one another as expressed in the complexity of a proposition or sentence do truth and falsity arise. When the conjunction or separation can be observed immediately by the mind in things, as for instance that one thing is not another, that the whole of a thing is greater than any one of its parts, that Socrates is pale, and so on, the proposition is immediately known. Where a proposition is not immediately known, it may become known through the mediation of other propositions, and in this way is mediately known. The process by which human knowledge thus increases is called reasoning, or to use the Greek term, "syllogism". What is contained is neither of two propositions independently known, is cognitionally engendered through their union in the syllogism. Aristotle illustrates the workings of the syllogism by an example of ancient knowledge about the relative distances of celestial bodies from the earth. A modern counterpart will make the point much clearer today. An astronomer observes in the spectroscope the shift towards red in the spectra of the outer galaxies. Independently he has the other proposition that a shift to the red means that the body is receding at great speed. He draws the conclusion, present in neither of the propositions taken separately, that the outer galaxies are receding with tremendous velocity. Knowledge genuinely new has been attained by the reasoning or syllogistic process. Aristotle's *Analytics* consist in working out the norms by which reasoning is able to function correctly and avoid errors. The basic propositions or premises have to be immediately known as true, the proper universality of the mediating term or concept that brings the two premises together has to be assured, and the new proposition or conclusion follows in an arrangement or "figure" in which this universality becomes operative. Where only probability is had in one or both of the premises, only probability can be expected in the conclusion.

As in its concepts so in its propositional phase this logic is obviously regulated by close correspondence with reality. The propositions are true if the objects are united in reality as they are synthesized in the mind. The further the reasoning proceeds from immediate observation the more intricate and difficult will the concepts become, but the ultimate criterion of truth will always be the immediately observed reality on which the reasoning was basically grounded. The Aristotelian logic is accordingly a propositonal as well as a predicate or class logic. It may sometimes be found contrasted with Stoic logic or modern logic precisely from this class viewpoint. But just as it is impossible to draw an exact line between formal logic and material logic, since both have to use matter as well as form, so any logic has to make both concepts and propositions operative. The difference lies in relative degree.

Almost everywhere today Aristotelian logic has been replaced in school teaching by modern mathematical logic. Because of its essentially mathematical character and the marvelous advances it has made in the last century, the mathematical logic is eminently adapted to the quantitative procedures of the experimental and statistical sciences. Whether or not Aristotelian logic is open to profitable development in this direction, it has not in point of fact been elaborated in the mathematical area and could hardly achieve any useful purpose in attempting to duplicate or rival the achievements of the mathematical logicians. On the other hand many modern philosophers, though sufficiently acquainted with mathematical logic, have not found it very helpful for work in philosophical disciplines such as metaphysics or ethics. The Aristotelian logic is much better suited to deal with the polyvalent concepts of metaphysics and the flexible and ever varying notions in moral and political philosophy. It still has advantages of its own.

The different logical frameworks also enable one to understand the contrasts in the acceptation of the notion "science". Science, from the Aristotelian viewpoint, includes any organized body of knowledge obtained by proceeding from premises, originally accepted as true, to their logically drawn conclusions. Accordingly metaphysics, philosophy of nature, and ethics come under the Aristotelian division of the sciences. They are sciences in his logical framework, just as astronomy, optics, harmonics and mechanics likewise were sciences. Modern use of the term, quite in accord with the framework of mathematical logic, tends to restrict the notion "science" to the experimental, mathematical, and social sciences, excluding metaphysics and ethics. However, the terminology "philosophical sciences" as well as "theological sciences" has never quite been lost, and is understandable against the background of the Aristotelian logic. Against this background it is not at all strange to find metaphysics regarded not only as a science but as the highest of sciences, and to find ethics in spite of its flexible character ranged as a prominent and genuine kind of science. It is this approach that has to be kept in mind in assessing the various disciplines that Aristotle regarded as sciences.

Sensible things, one should always remember, are the origin of human cognition for the Stagirite. In their concrete totality they are dealt with by the philosophy of nature, which analyzes them into their basic principles of matter and form in order to explain their observable changes. The reasoning in the philosophy of nature concludes that their movement is eternal and ultimately caused by the eternal rotatory movements of the heavenly bodies. In the course of these general discussions in the *Physics,* many problems of time, place, the void, chance, movement and nature are dealt with, but always from the viewpoint of the basic principles matter and form. The treatment does not correspond to any procedure used in modern science. Nor is it meant to be a philosophy of science, since it deals not with science but directly with nature, though on a level different from that of the experimental sciences.

Particular areas of the natural world are dealt with in other works, though on the same philosophical plane that receives its general development in the *Physics.* The stars and planets are treated of in the *De Caelo* (*On the Heavens*). Comets, meteors, and other phenomena considered intermediate, are discussed in the *Meteorologica.* Terrestrial changes are studied in *De Generatione et Corruptione.* Corporeal living beings constitute the subject matter of *De Anima* (*On the Soul*), though one part of the human soul, namely the mind, presents an aspect that seems to call for study by the science that transcends the natural order, namely metaphysics. But particular vital phenomena, such as sensation, recollection, respiration and sleep continue to be treated on the level of the philosophy of nature in a group of rather short treatises that since medieval times has been called the *Parva Naturalia.* Five longer and detailed works, *History of Animals, Parts of Animals, Generation of Animals, Progression of Animals* and *Movement of Animals,* survey the then known animal kingdom. The exact and painstaking research of the *Parts of Animals* drew from Darwin the admiring comment: "Linnaeus and Cuvier have been my two gods, though in very different ways, but they were mere schoolboys to old Aristotle."[7] However, even in this field Aristotle's viewpoint remained that of his philosophy of nature. Anything in the world of nature should be studied scientifically by taking the thing's basic form as the starting point. From that form the properties and characteristics of the thing are deduced, just as the details of a house may be learned by studying its blueprint: "For elsewhere, as for instance in house building, this is the true sequence. The plan of the house, or the house, has this and that form; and because it has this and that form, therefore is its construction carried out in this or that manner . . . Thus we should say, because man is an animal with such and such characters, therefore is the process of his development necessarily such as it is; and therefore is it accomplished in such and such an order, this part being formed first, that next, and so on in succession; and after a like fashion should we explain the evolution of all other works of nature" (PA, I 1,640a15-b4; Oxford tr.). This is the conception of natural science actually projected in the *Parts of Animals*. Elsewhere (e.g., *De An.,* I 1,402b16-25) Aristotle acknowledges the necessity of reaching essence through properties. But a Greek optimistic confidence in the power of the human intellect to penetrate natural essences seemed to blind him to the fact that the qualitative aspects of material things do not give the mind any objective manifestation of the inner nature.

On the other hand, quantity does manifest its own nature, with the result that on the mathematical level the situation is different. Aristotle delights in using mathematical examples, for here his conception of scientific procedure works perfectly. From the nature of a triangle one can without added evidence deduce its properties. He was sufficiently familiar with the arithmetical and geometrical knowledge of his time, but there is no evidence that he worked at advancing it. His bent lay rather in showing how it grounded a distinct level of scientific investigation. It was able to take things "in abstraction" from their sensible qualities, and thereby enjoy a strictly quantitative object whose nature is penetrated by the human mind and serves as the basis for the demonstration of properties. On this level function also "the more physical branches of mathematics, such as optics, harmonics, and astronomy" (*Ph.,* II 2,194a7-8), with mention elsewhere of mechanics and, in its own way, of medical science. These are regarded as mathematical sciences. They formed the subject of Aristotelian works now lost. They had their qualitative counterparts, such as "acoustical harmonics", but the qualitative aspects did not furnish grounds for cogent and positive deductive demonstration, as the quantitative aspects do (*APo.,* I 13,78b35-79a16).

Here one may make some observations of one's own. The Aristotelian conception of corporeal things finds a basis for scientific reasoning in their extension and quantity, because the nature of quantity is penetrated by the human mind. Correspondingly, however, the substance of these corporeal things is penetrated by the mind insofar as the substance is something extended. The substance remains specifically the same thing, water or gold for instance, while it is extended through quantitative parts without any formal difference occurring. It thereby manifests itself as a nature consisting of specifying form and non-specifying matter, as its substantial components. By them it is constituted a mobile being and provides the basis for cogent reasoning about corporeal substances in their generic grade as bodies. Only on that generic grade is the Aristotelian philosophy of nature valid as a science in the epistemological framework in which it was developed. It is barred from scientific penetration into the qualitative aspects and corresponding particular natures of things. These can be penetrated *only* on the mathematical level. One's own reflective awareness of the successive grades of vegetative, sentient, and intellectual life is no exception, for the reflexive awareness, while sufficient to distinguish the substantial grades as constituting different genera, does not make manifest any specific natures.

Aristotle himself does not make these observations. In the sixteenth century his scientific method found itself pitted stubbornly against the surging quantitative conceptions of modern science. In the nature of his doctrine there was no ground whatever for this deplorable opposition. Sciences like astronomy and mechanics had fitted neatly into his divisions. Chemistry and modern physics and all the new experimental and statistical sciences should likewise have appeared as normal developments of his quantitative approach to things of nature. His broad view allows amply for all the laborious research and exact measuring and cataloguing that keep achieving magnificent triumphs. The neat Aristotelian synthesizing, it is true, may seem thrown ludicrously out of balance by the vast preponderance of the modern experimental sciences. But may not this reflect the overall paradox that the area in which the human mind is by far most proficient fails to provide the answers to its deepest aspirations and most agonizing problems?

The third and highest kind of theoretical science deals with what is beyond nature but reached through the findings of the philosophy of nature. The eternally unchanging movements of the heavens, as these have been established in the *Physics*, require as their ultimate cause a type of substance that has no potentiality whatever for change. This type is without matter, since matter is potentiality for change. It exercises its causality through being loved and desired. In number it corresponds exactly to the number of original celestial movements observed by the astronomers (*Metaph.*, Λ 6-8, 1071b3-1074a17). In the *De Anima* (II 12,424a17-24; III 4,429a15-18), form received without matter causes cognition. Accordingly Aristotle without hesitation regards form existent without matter as existent cognition. The result is that separate substance is a cognition and a life far higher than the human counterparts: "And

God *is* in a better state. And life also belongs to God; for the actuality of thought is life, and God is that actuality; . . . for this *is* God" (*Metaph.*, Λ 7,1072b26-30; Oxford trans.). Lacking potentiality to anything else, this subsistent thinking can have only itself as its object: "Therefore it must be of itself that the divine thought thinks (since it is the most excellent of things), and its thinking is a thinking on thinking" (9,1074b33-35; Oxford trans.). The science that deals with this primary instance of being will thereby treat universally of all beings: ". . . if there is an immovable substance, the science of this must be prior and must be first philosophy, and universal in this way, because it is first. And it will belong to this to consider being *qua* being" (E 1,1026a29-31; Oxford trans.). Hence "first philosophy" and "theological philosophy" (a19) designate indifferently for Aristotle the highest theoretical science, later called "metaphysics."

Philosophy of nature, mathematics, and metaphysics are accordingly the three kinds of theoretical philosophy for Aristotle. Contradistinguished from them is practical philosophy, which unlike them does not start from objective things but from human choice: "The origin of action - its efficient, not its final cause - is choice" (*E N*, VI 2,1139a31-32: Oxford tr.). Each man chooses the ultimate end to which he directs all his actions. Some locate it in pleasure, others in honor and reputation, others in the life of thought. Wealth, though it might seem most sought after, is obviously pursued for something else, namely for what it will bring. The purpose of moral philosophy is to make people good by enabling them to choose correctly both as regards the ultimate end and as regards each individual action. Cultivation of the virtue of practical wisdom or prudence, and of the moral virtues of temperance, courage and justice, provides the means for this purpose. These virtues are interdependent, each requiring all the others. They are cultivated by life and under good laws and by proper education (*paideia*) from earliest childhood. As an aid, Aristotle projected an extensive collection of the laws of Greek city-states. Only one of these studies, the *Constitution of Athens*, is extant, having been recovered in the last decades of the nineteenth century on Egyptian papyri. Aristotle himself locates the ultimate goal of human endeavor in the life of contemplative thought. To enable people to attain that life all individual and social or political activity should be directed. Political life in this way provides a secondary type of happiness, in subordination to the primary type, contemplation. In this setting moral philosophy and political philosophy obviously coincide, since their object is the same. Yet so profound and universal are the Aristotelian moral principles that they offer a method open "to *any* social and cultural materials, to *any* set of institutions and standards, to *any* cultural heritage."⁸ Perhaps for this reason is the *Nicomachean Ethics* usually found to be the most fascinating of all Aristotle's works.

Of the "productive" sciences, that is, those that have their starting point in some idea or plan in the human mind, only two are found developed in the *Corpus Aristotelicum*, namely rhetoric and literary criticism. The *Rhetoric* studies persuasive arguments and how they are to be used in literary compositons (III, 8) and in speeches. The *Poetics*, which from the sixteenth century on has found use as a basic text in literary criticism, still excites interest through its conceptions of *Mimesis* as the explanation of fine art, and of *Catharsis* as a purification in tragedy of either events or emotions.

IV

Such is the tableau of the sciences that constitute philosophy as Aristotle envisaged it. Though the practical and productive sciences have radically different starting points from those of the theoretical, nevertheless all three function in the same real world. The world that people know through the theoretical sciences is the world in which they live and work. This Aristotelian approach is very hard to appreciate today. The stark and uninhibited protrusion of reality throughout the philosophical sciences lies open now to radical misunderstanding. Descartes' intellectual asceticism had isolated human thought and made it serve as the starting point for subsequent Western philosophy. Mid-twentieth century procedure has focused upon the interpersonal phenomenon of language as the starting point. Through language and thought one has to make one's way to the real. To this mentality the Aristotelian attitude can hardly appear as anything else than a claim, utterly absurd, to a "hot line" for communication with the real world. It would bypass language and thought.

Epistemologically, however, there is no "line" of any kind involved in the immediate Aristotelian grasp of reality. The forms of sensible things are received in the percipient without their matter (*De An.*, II 12,424a17-24). So received they cause the percipient, whose soul is potentially all things, to be actually the things perceived or known (III 7-8,431b16-432a10), just as the same forms received in matter cause the things to be absolutely. Only by becoming the other things cognitionally, moreover, is the human mind able to know itself (4,429b5-10). Only concomitantly in the cognition of something else is there any awareness of the perception or intellection (*Metaph.*, Λ 9,1074b35-36). This means that cognitionally the mind is first and foremost the thing that is other than itself. It does not require any mediation or "line" to reach the real object that it perceives or knows. It *is* that thing, more fundamentally even than it is itself, in the cognitional order. Language and thought, though objects of immediate awareness, are so only concomitantly in the basic awareness of the thing. Here the thing functions as the *message*, and likewise is the *medium* in which language and thought, though attained immediately, are represented and probed. Far from appearing as a naive realism, this understanding of cognition is not even a "moderate realism" or any other authentic type of realism, for "realism" as used by people to characterize their own epistemologies implies a procedure from thought to the justification of real, external things. This procedure is not only lacking in Aristotle, but is rendered superfluous and impossible by his understanding of human cognition.

So assessed, the innate potentiality of the human mind to be all things leaves it open to every kind of knowledge and to indefinite expansion of its vision. This natural openness of the human mind finds vivid expression and fertile development in Aristotelian philosophy. Throughout the centuries people who have used Aristotle's principles have come to very different conclusions from those he reached. By becoming immersed in his philosophy they learned to think for themselves. Like Stagira itself, set deeply within a horseshoe formation of mountains that opens out into the broad expanses of the sea, Aristotle's conclusions are adapted to his times while flowing from principles that offer indefinite possibilities of fruitful application in other climes and eras. Not only his ethical conceptions,[9] but also his procedures in theoretical philosophy remain open to the problems of today's world. Aristotle does not give the answers, but his philosophy equips the mind to think out and as far as possible solve those problems as they arise.

Answers are needed in philosophy as in everything else. They should be the right answers. In the technological atmosphere of today right answers are required everywhere, and they are wanted fast. In philosophy, however, a fast answer usually turns out to be a wrong answer. Long and painstaking exploration is necessary. Only at one's peril may one neglect the wisdom that has endured down through the centuries. The answers have not been handed on ready made by Aristotle. He does not think for any other age. But he does introduce the readers of other ages, including the present, to profound philosophical thinking that opens marvelously on their own problems and guides them to right answers in the pursuit of requisite knowledge. In that way he continued to be, in Dante's words, the teacher of those who know.

2. Aristotle on Categories

A recent article makes the following statement: "One must first realize that a definition of category construction is an arbitrary procedure. . . Ryle has set up his own arbitrary test for categorizing words." [1] From Ryle to Aristotle seems a far cry back through the centuries. Yet the notion of categories does as a matter of historical fact originate with the Stagirite. From his time on, it has had an uninterrupted descent through the Scholastics and Kant down to the present day. Since recessive as well as dominant traits keep recurring in any strain, a thoroughgoing study of the topic should hardly incur the charge of "philosophical paleontology" for taking into account the doctrine of categories as found in its original Aristotelian habitat. In particular, the present paper would inquire whether the notion of category construction was intended in its beginnings to be an *arbitrary* procedure, whether it was meant to categorize *words*, and how it stands up to later examples of category mistakes. The paper, accordingly, will first examine briefly the doctrine of categories in its original Aristotelian setting; secondly, it will try to determine the type of treatment found there; and finally it will confront the Aristotelian doctrine with some irritant instances of category mistakes.

I

The Greek term "category," as is well known, signified in all its pre-Aristotelian instances either an accusation in general or in particular a charge laid against some one in the courts. [2] It was a legal term. The corresponding verb, however, had in popular usage also the senses of show, reveal, prove, signify, declare, and so on. It was used by Plato [3] in the sense of "assert." Along this groove it appears fullfledged in the Aristotelian treatise *Categories* [4] in the technical signification of "predicate." The linguistic development would indicate that the basic meaning of the noun as it passed over into its philosophical sense was "that which is asserted" of something else. Correspondingly, the verbal form in its technical use would mean "to assert something" of something else.

The opening chapter of the *Categories* fails to reveal whether it is introducing a grammatical, a logical, or a metaphysical treatise. It deals with equivocals and univocals ⁵ and ends with a definition of paronyms. The definition of paronyms is given in purely grammatical terms. Paronyms derive their name from an identical source with a difference only in case ending, as bravery and the brave, grammar and the grammarian. ⁶ The second chapter, however, proceeds to state that an *expression* (*tôn legomenôn*) can be either complex or simple—complex like "a man runs," or simple like "man" or "runs." Then it immediately passes over to beings (*tôn ontôn*). Of the things that are, it states, some are asserted (*legetai*) *of* a subject, but are not *in* any subject. The example given is that "man" is asserted of a particular man.⁷ To supply for Aristotle a current instance of what is here meant, one might use the sentence "Bertrand Russell is a man." This type of statement, to take the Aristotelian text literally, is dealing with beings and is asserting something of a subject. What is asserted, "man," is not *in* any subject even though it is asserted *of* a subject. In other words, the logically proper name "Bertrand Russell" denotes (of course from the Aristotelian viewpoint!) a substance and not an accident.

Is this logic or metaphysics? It reads like a mixture of both. It has quite patently left the grammatical field. What immediately follows sounds more positively metaphysical: "Other things are *in* a subject, but are never asserted *of* a subject."⁸ The example given is an individual instance of grammatical knowledge, or an individual bit of whiteness. Strange as such an example may sound to modern ears, its meaning is not hard to grasp. An individual instance of grammatical knowledge has to be *in* some one's mind (*psychê*); and an individual instance cannot be asserted *of* anything else—nothing but itself can be the individual instance of grammatical knowledge. But is not the positive side of this description entirely metaphysical? To be "in a subject," the *Categories*⁹ goes on to explain, means to be in something not as a part but as incapable of existing in separation from the thing in which it is. The positive description is wholly in terms of being—being in a subject. Only the negative part is in the logical terms of assertion—things never asserted of a subject. The mode of existing is the only positive factor used in the description.

The text of the *Categories* then rounds out the possibilities. Other things, it shows, are both asserted of a subject and are in a subject. "Knowledge," for instance, is asserted *of* a subject like grammar, when one says "Grammar is knowledge." But knowledge is likewise *in* a subject, namely in the mind. Other things, finally, are neither *in* a subject nor are ever asserted *of* anything else. Examples are an individual man and an individual horse.¹⁰ The meaning again is clear. An individual man, like President Eisenhower, is never *in* anything else, according to this Aristotelian use of the preposition "in"; nor is he ever asserted *of* anything else. The meaning, indeed, is clear. But the seemingly strange mixture of metaphysics and logic persists.

On the basis of these fundamental and presumably self-evident distinctions, Aristotle proceeds in the next six chapters of the *Categories* (3,1b10-8,11a38) to treat of what in other works he calls the *schemata* or columns[11] of predication. Without any explanation he uses the term "category" technically in the sense of predicate.[12] The verbal form occurs regularly in this section in a meaning that corresponds to the notion "assert" in the preceding chapter of the treatise.[13] The advantage of category construction is first made manifest. When one thing is predicated of another, Aristotle shows, all its own predicates may be asserted of that subject. "Man," for instance, is predicated of an individual. Since "living thing" is predicated of man—man is a living thing—so "living thing" may be predicated of that individual.[14] Here emerges the notion of a *schema* of predication, that is, a column of predicates in which the lower predicate is always subordinate to the higher. This is category construction, or "category" in the sense that will become traditional.[15] In whatever category you place something you thereby assure for it all the superior or more general predicates pertaining to that category. The superior differentiae contained in any predicate, accordingly, are all applicable to the subject of which that predicate is asserted. Hence arises the purpose of correctly locating any subject in its proper category.

The first of these Aristotelian *schemata* or category constructions has been traditionally known as "substance."[16] "Substance" is far from a literal translation of the Greek term for this first category. *Ousia*, the Greek designation, is an abstractive form of the participle "being." If the form "beingness" were permissible in English, it would convey the required notion.[17] "Substance," as a name for the Aristotelian category, denotes the fundamental type of being that is found in anything. Without this basic kind of being there could be no other type of being in the thing. In the *Categories* it is described negatively as that which is *in* nothing else. Contrasted with it are a number of *schemata* containing things that have to be in something else, in the sense of entitative dependence on substance. These other categories are called, in general, accidents. The most important *schemata* of accidental predicates are quantity, quality, relation, place, time, action and passion.[18] Two others, position and what is rendered broadly in the Oxford and Loeb translations as "state" are added on a couple of occasions.[19] There is no reason for thinking that the number (ten or under) of categories given on any occasion in Aristotle is meant to be exhaustive.[20]

The distinction between substance and accidents is based solely on being. It is the difference between being in a subject and never being in a subject. The distinction of the accidents from one another seems to be based upon natures both as they exist in reality and as they are conceived in the mind. Quantity and quality are irreducible to each other both in reality and in conceptualization, relations are different from absolute characteristics, place from time, and so on. The category constructions seem applicable to both the logical and the metaphysical orders. Nor is the grammatical aspect entirely forgotten. In the category of substance, the Aristotelian treatment mentions, both word and definition are predicated in the same way. With accidents, however, while the definition is never predicable of the subject in which they exist, the word is sometimes predicable and sometimes not predicable. You may say that body is white. But you may never say that body is "whiteness" or that it is the definition of a color white (5,2a19-34).

II

The preceding survey should furnish enough data to approach the query concerning the type of investigation contained in the Aristotelian *Categories*. Is the treatment grammatical, logical, or metaphysical? Or is it a combination of different types of treatment? If so, are the different types coordinate, or is one basic and the other or others subordinate? Quite obviously, it is not fundamentally a grammatical treatment. There are indeed a few grammatical considerations involved, but these are quite minor and patently incidental. Nor is there anything surprising that grammatical considerations should have been included in a logical discussion in ancient Greece. It was common practice in Megarian and Stoic logic.[21] No less an authority than Trendelenburg, however, attempted to show that the Aristotelian categories were based upon grammatical considerations. He achieved little success, as he was not able to produce any plausible evidence in support of his view. It would serve no purpose to reconsider the attempt.

Does the treatment in the *Categories*, then, belong to the domain of logic? This view is supported by the undoubtedly logical character of much that has just been seen in the Aristotelian inquiry, such as predication of species in regard to individuals, and genera in regard to species. But how will it account for the equally apparent metaphysical aspects of much else in the treatise, such as the explanation of substance and accident in terms of being? Moreover, the categories are presented in the Stagirite's *Metaphysics* as determinations of being[22] and as ways in which being is expressed. Is the doctrine of categories for Aristotle, then, basically metaphysical with logical aftermaths? Or, vice versa, is it fundamentally a logical growth that blossomed into a metaphysics? Or is it a loose combination of logical and metaphysical doctrines? Or is there an historical development and change in Aristotle from one viewpoint to the other? Or does the doctrine of categories pertain to a twilight zone between logic and metaphysics?

All these views have had their advocates, with different shadings and different grades of emphasis. They have all been thoroughly discussed,[23] and there is no need of reopening the controversies and re-emphasizing the difficulties that each encounters. One result, however, may be considered as established. The discussions have left unassailable the *fact* that both logical and metaphysical features are involved in Aristotle's presentation of the categories. In explanation I would suggest that the natures upon which the categories bear are *common* to both logic and metaphysics. They are the property of neither, but rather the communal pasture land of both. The common natures of man, horse, extension, color,and so on, are what the categories envisage in both their logical and their metaphysical function. It is the nature of man that is predicated of the individual man, it is the nature of man that calls for all the superior predicates in the category, it is the nature of man not to be in a subject, and it is also the nature of man to exist in reality as an individual. It is the nature of color to be in a real body, and to be predicated of a particular color.

This doctrine of the common nature does not, it is true, appear in any dominant way in Aristotle's own writings. In mediaeval times, however, it was widespread.[24] But there is enough in Aristotle, I think, to allow it the status of a recessive characteristic in his conception of the categories. The same object, according to the Stagirite, is known in two different ways. In so far as it is known actually, it is individual. In so far as it gives knowledge that can be applied to other individuals, it causes the indefinite and potential way of knowing that is called the universal.[25] It is the same nature that is found in both ways, namely as individual and as universal, and so is common to both. There is little difficulty, therefore, in seeing the common nature as latent in the Aristotelian doctrine, and as bound to come to light in one way or another with the course of time.[26]

The acceptance of the common nature need not mean setting up any twilight zone between thought and reality, between the subject of logic and the subject of metaphysics.[27] Rather, it means that the same common nature has a twofold being, being in reality and being in the human mind. As it exists in the real world, it is found only in individuals and exhibits the characteristics that allow it to be treated of by the physical sciences and by metaphysics. As it exists in the mind it presents in its intelligible aspects the specific and generic grades, the higher grades predicable of the lower, and all predicable of the individual substance. In this way it offers a subject for logical treatment like that found in the *Prior* and *Posterior Analytics*.

The Aristotelian doctrine of categories, accordingly, is grounded upon the natures of things. It is not based upon linguistic usage, and is not concerned primarily with words. Because category construction has to follow the natures of things and not human caprice, it is not at all an arbitrary procedure. Wholehearted respect for natures that are not subject to human whims will deliver the logician from what he fears most of all, a situation in which anything can be said of anything. In both the real and the cognitional orders such respect will serve as a reasonable deterrent from the gay uninhibited life in a wonderland of nonsense. Those natures are common territory to both logic and metaphysics. A thoroughgoing treatment of categories, therefore, has to include both the logical and metaphysical aspects. It is a mark of Aristotle's philosophical acumen to have treated of them in this twofold way.

III

Since the natures of things can exist both in reality and in the mind, one obvious type of category mistake would be to apply to a nature existent in reality predicates that belong to it only as it exists in the mind. And *ad hoc* example would be: "Khrushchev is a man; man is a species; therefore Khrushchev is a species."[28] An actual and by no means innocuous instance, as far as the understanding of Aristotle is concerned, is the oft repeated notion that the concrete individual is primary substance for Aristotelian metaphysics. In Aristotelian logic the concrete individual is indeed the primary substance. It is the basic subject of all predication. From the logician's viewpoint, accordingly, it is the primary being (*ousia*). But that does not at all mean that the concrete individual is primary being or primary substance in the real order. In the *Metaphysics*, Aristotle's doctrine to the contrary is explicit. Form is the primary substance.[29] The concrete individual and the matter are only secondary instances of substance in the real world. Yet this category mistake has resulted in a common misconception—the Aristotelian metaphysics is believed to give primacy to the concrete individual, in contrast to the Platonic primacy of form! Further, from the logician's standpoint the species and genera in the first category are substances. They are universals; and from the point of view in the *Metaphysics*, no universal can be substance.[30] Confusion of the two standpoints has provided an argument that the *Categories* is in conflict with the teaching of the *Metaphysics*.[31] Does not this situation indicate rather the category mistake of confusing logical and metaphysical predicates in their application to the same subject?

Moreover, what are distinct categories from the logician's viewpoint need not be so for the metaphysician. Action and passion seem clearly enough to be two logically different classes of predicates, asserted of a subject in ways that are irreducible to each other.[32] Yet from the standpoint of the metaphysician they seem to express, according to Aristotle, but one and the same reality. Action is located in the patient. Along with passion, it seems identified with the motion that the patient undergoes.[33] Action, passion, and motion seem to constitute only one new reality. This teaching is difficult and is far from satisfactory. But it is clear enough to show that the nature of action was categorized for Aristotle in different ways when it was regarded from a logical and when it was regarded from a metaphysical viewpoint. Correspondingly, disposition and "state" are accepted as categories in the *Organon*.[34] That need not at all mean that from a metaphysical standpoint they form new and distinct categories.

Within one and the same category, then, a mistake may be made by confusing logical with real predicates. Within the same category, likewise, a mistake may be made by directly categorizing the principles of things that belong to that category. The Aristotelian substantial form, for instance, is the principle of intelligibility in everything that is placed directly in the category of substance. If you attempt to place the form directly in that category, what happens? In the case of a man you are conjuring up a ghost (if not in a machine for Aristotle at least in some kind of a receptacle)[35], and in the case of bodies other than human, one might say a gremlin in the clod. It is the man or the stone that is directly categorized. The Aristotelian substantial form, whether in man or brute or plant or clod, cannot be categorized in itself, but only as the intelligible and active principle of a substance that can be categorized. To categorize the form for itself is to commit the category mistake of the ghost in the machine. Aristotle is well aware of the difficulties in regard to intellection that are encountered by the soul as a corporeal form, but such is his doctrine.[36]

Correspondingly, any attempt to categorize directly the other principle of sensible things, the Aristotelian matter, would fly into contradiction with the Aristotelian descriptions. The underlying matter of bodies is expressly described as "not something."[37] To categorize it for itself would be to regard it as a clod, as "something." It would be making this second type of category mistake. A mathematical point is not in itself extended, even though it belongs reductively to the category of quantity. It is not categorized directly as quantity, but reductively as a principle of quantity. The reduction of a thing's principles to its own category may not appear as a dominant feature in the Aristotelian doctrine on categories, but it is implicit in the Stagirite's teaching on the nature of sensible things and of abstract quantity.[38]

There is, finally, the most obvious type of category mistake. The two types just considered occur within one and the same category, either by confusing predicates of the cognitional order with predicates of the real order, or by directly categorizing the principles of a thing as though they were things in their own right. The third type is made by placing something not in its proper category at all, but in an alien one. For instance, to conceive the sensible qualities or sense data as there in themselves, as given or as existent or as knowable in themselves, is to *substantize* them, according to the Aristotelian category construction. It means giving them being in themselves, no matter how one cares to explain that being. The fantasy of an elephant carrying them like baggage is as much the result of a category mistake as is the abusive notion of the ghost in the machine. It is putting them in the category of substance instead of quality. To conceive faculties or powers or any other accidents as though they were little souls, according to the Cartesian interpretation,[39] is merely a more pronounced and patent instance of the ghost in the machine or the gremlin in the clod. To reduce killing to a relation,[40] even for the purposes of logic, seems another instance of such a category mistake. It would hardly make legal sense to hang a man merely for being related to his victim. He is hanged for what he did to him, for his *action* and not for his *relation* to him, even though the relation of "murderer" follows upon the action of murdering. It may well be that the mathematical logician is interested only in the relation that follows upon the killing, but that hardly justifies him in designating the nature of the killing as a relation. It is a nature that should be categorized, logically or metaphysically, as action. Similarly, the attempt to conceive mind as a relation is in the Aristotelian context an evident category mistake. Mind is a knowing or a faculty of knowing, and so belongs in the category of quality. The laudable purpose of getting along with a few categories as possible is driven to an intolerable extreme when all possible objects of human cognition are reduced to qualities and a few kinds of relations.[41] The other categories will sooner or later drastically insist on their rights.

This brief glance at the Aristotelian doctrine of categories and its confrontation with instances of category mistakes will indicate, it is hoped, some pertinent features of the earliest explicit category construction. It was based upon the natures of things and not upon the use of language. Because it was concerned with natures and not primarily with words, it was not at all an arbitrary procedure. The natures of things resist the manipulations of human whims, and keep the universe from becoming a world where everything is nonsense. But these natures exist in two ways, in reality and in cognition.[42] Some predicates will belong to the nature just of itself, no matter where it is found. Other predicates will belong to a nature only in real existence. They are those concerned with its real history in some individual. Still other predicates will belong to it only as it exists in intellectual cognition, for instance that it is a species or a genus. These considerations show why categories are the concern of both the metaphysician and the logician, and why confusion in the three ways in which predicates apply will necessarily give rise to category mistakes. The Aristotelian doctrine likewise shows why the intrinsic principles of things cannot be placed directly in a category. Its basic grooves of category construction, along with this warning, still serve quite well as dissolvents for such category mistakes[43] as the ghost in the machine, the elephant with the baggage, or murder a relation. The category doctrine as found originally in the Stagirite's works is open to a great amount of development and elaboration, both to smooth out its own difficulties and to meet problems of current discussion. It offers a solid basis for profitable philosophic construction. It is far from complete, but what is there is very good.

3. The Aristotelian Conception of the Sciences

Perhaps the time is favorable for a reassessment of Aristotle's role in the formation of the western scientific mentality. True, memories of bitter opposition between degenerate Aristotelian tradition and emerging experimental science still hang heavily enough over the issue. Are not the experimental sciences now, however, far too well established to be in any real danger of contamination through a renewal of contact with the authentic Aristotelian tenets? On the other hand, has not the present era become increasingly conscious of the need to understand itself through its historical roots? In the intellectual order, are not these roots sunk deeply in the Greek thought that reached its bloom in the century of Plato and Aristotle?

When mentioning racial excellences in the *Republic* (IV, 435E-436E), Plato was quite willing to concede preeminence in warlike virtues to the northern nations, and in money-making to the Phoenicians and Egyptians. As the special characteristic of his own country he reserved the love of learning. Is this but another instance of a race at the height of its culture flaunting a self-assigned vocation to provide the rest of mankind with intellectual light? Or is there more than national vanity at stake in the Greek claim? Is it hard to show historically, that the intellectual side of western civilization was in fact given definite shape by the Greeks?

The tremendous achievements of European science and art have without doubt quite generally grown from seeds planted in ancient Hellas. In important instances, nevertheless, the developments have been along lines unforeseen by the Greeks and at first sight perhaps opposed to some of their notions, when the notions are taken as frozen and final. But were these notions really static or finished? Should they not rather be viewed as transitory phases in the unfolding of basic insights? In this relevant perspective, may it not be worthwhile to reconsider the general conception of scientific knowledge that emerged among the Greeks and was given relatively fixed contours in the philosophical treatises of Aristotle?

The Universal as Object of Scientific Knowledge

From Socrates through Plato to the Stagirite there is a marked development in the notion of scientific knowledge, a development that in one notable respect is unilinear. This is the tenet that scientific knowledge somehow deals with the universal. The universal, no matter how much its functions and capacity have been watered down by subsequent theoricians, is in some way or other an indispensable condition for any scientific inference.[1] It is what allows a truth established in observable instances to be applied to other instances not immediately observed. With Socrates the notion of universality received its first expression as the search for what a virtue is, in contrast to the individual instances of the virtue. At least, if one can judge from a brief account in Xenophon's *Memorabilia* (I, 1, 16), from the portrayal of Socrates' methods in the earlier Platonic dialogues, and from Aristotle's precise descriptions, Socrates, in opposition to the rhetorical education of the Sophists, strove to ground human conduct not on this or that example of the virtue, but upon an all-embracing knowledge of the virtue itself. A particular example, no matter how rhetorically it was driven home by vivid illustration and emotional appeal, might hold for one set of circimstances only. It could easily turn into an opposite vice if imitated slavishly in other circumstances. The courage that binds a soldier to his post becomes stupid and costly rashness where circumstances require retirement to a more favorable position.[2] Socrates strove rather to ground human action on knowledge of the virtue itself, a knowledge that would hold for all instances of the virtue, regardless of the varying circumstances. As far as can be seen through the obscurity that hides the historical Socrates, does not this seem to have been the import of his message and the lead that was followed out in the Platonic Idea and the Aristotelian universal?

In Plato, of course, the picture is much clearer. The sensible world is in a thoroughgoing condition of flux. The only stability is through the Ideas reflected by sensible things. In linking a sensible occurrence to an Idea, you have tied it by the bond of causality[3] to its eternally stable ground. You thereby have scientific knowledge of it, in contrast to the ever fleeting glimpse furnished by the sensible appearance, a glimpse that could give rise only to opinion. In knowing the Idea you have knowledge that is enduring and that will hold for every instance. Why? The reason is that through the Ideas you have knowledge of a thing in the light of the thing's causes.

This development of the notion of universality reaches its climax and acquires its name with Aristotle. Yet the Platonic Idea, described as both immanent and transcendent in Plato's own writings, is interpreted dogmatically by the Stagirite as transcendent only. As such the Platonic Idea is emphatically rejected. Nevertheless, in regard to scientific knowledge, are not the combined universal and causal features stressed in the Idea retained by Aristotle and brought by him to the highest development reached in the ancient world?

With the Aristotelian treatises, in point of fact, the notion of the universal appears full-fledged from the start. It is made the basis of predication and reasoning. It thereby grounds the science of logic. Knowledge in the universal and knowledge through cause are understood, as in Plato, to coincide. To know the cause of a thing is to known the reason why it always happens, why it must so happen. Knowledge of cause distinguishes the methods of the trained physician from the hit or miss tactics of the amateur. The amateur may happen to hit upon the right cure, but he does not know why. He may be entirely wrong when he applies his remedy to a second case. Scientific knowledge, however, gives the cause and holds for all cases where the same cause is recognized.[4]

Aristotle's equating of cause and universal may, perhaps, be more readily grasped if a modern example is supplied. Before Pasteur's discoveries, only hit or miss methods of preventing infection were available. Once the cause of infection was discovered, the killing of the germs by effective sterilization could be expected to hold for any case whatsoever. Knowledge of the cause extends it to all instances.

With Aristotle, the reason for equating cause and universal in regard to knowledge was the reduction of the causes ultimately to formal cause. The formal cause is what makes a number of singular things coincide in the one species. The form is the reason for the species. The one Greek term (*eidos*) for form and species, which was likewise an alternate designation for the Platonic Idea, made this relation of individual form and universal species easily felt. Knowledge of a universal, in fact, was knowledge of a thing through its form, a knowledge that was potential[5] in the sense that it was applicable to all other singulars of the species. Instead of cognition of a supersensible Idea outside a thing, knowledge of the universal was for Aristotle knowledge of the sensible thing itself under its formal aspects. It was knowledge of a thing in terms of the basic type of cause.

Logic Not a Science

In Aristotelian logic, accordingly, all strictly demonstrative processes, because based on universal aspects, are based upon the thing's causes. If the cause used for the explanation is the proximate or fully commensurate cause of the thing, it gives rise to the most perfect kind of mediate knowledge. This was called by Aristotle τοῦ ϑιότι ἐπιστήμη and is rendered in English by the Oxford translation as "knowledge of the reasoned fact." If on the other hand the means of demonstration is an effect or only a remote cause, then, although the cause of one's knowledge, it does not give the exactly fitting cause of what is demonstrated. The demonstration, though cogent and holding universally, is not completely demonstrative, because it does not make manifest the thing's proximate cause. It is called by Aristotle demonstration of the ὅτι, and is rendered in the Oxford Translation as "knowledge of the fact." Instances given by the Stagirite are the different kinds of astronomy and harmonics. Nautical astronomy—apparently a descriptive knowledge of the stars sufficient to guide pilots—comes under "knowledge of the fact" (ὅτι). It is patently on the level of qualitative procedure, based on the color, brightness, and configurations of the stars. Mathematical astronomy, on the other hand, is "knowledge of the reasoned fact" (διότι). The same contrast is found between acoustical harmonics and mathematical harmonics.[6]

According to these examples, Aristotelian logic maintains that a merely qualitative procedure in any natural science gives only "knowledge of the fact" (ότι). Qualitative cognition does not reveal the fully commensurate reason but rather just the fact of what it establishes, though universally. Quantitative procedure in the study of nature, on the contrary, gives "knowledge of the reasoned fact" (διότι). It makes manifest, in the accidental order of quantity, the exactly fitting reason for each of its conclusions.

Logic, as developed by Aristotle, satisfies its own norms for scientific status. It proceeds universally in dealing with the processes of human reasoning, and treats of them in function of their causes. The syllogism, for instance, is shown to give a necessary conclusion because of the respective relations of the major and minor terms to the middle. Yet Aristotle, though referring to logic as a science,[7] does not list it in his formal divisions of the sciences. He regards it as a necessary propaedeutic for the sciences proper.[8] In consequence the Peripatetics traditionally refused to grant logic the status of a science, though the Epicureans and Stoics and in the middle ages the Scholastics experienced no hesitation in giving it its rightful place among the sciences. Even as late as the closing decades of the sixteenth century, Zabarella continued in the obstinate Peripatetic mentality of maintaining that logic was not a science because its objects came and went with human cognition. They were contingent things, lacking the character of necessity required by the subject of a science.[9]

Theoretical and Practical Sciences Distinguished

Be that as it may, in his formal grouping of them in the *Metaphysics*, Aristotle divides the sciences according to various kinds of causes that all lie outside the logical order. If these causes are in the thing that is studied, they give rise to theoretical or speculative sciences. Theoretical sciences deal with things already present before the mind's gaze, and not with things that come into being as a result of the intellect's activity. In this regard the words "theoretical" and "speculative" have to be kept free from modern connotations of uncertainty, as in the expressions "mere theory" or "mere speculation." The term "theoretical" in an Aristotelian context has its Greek sense of contemplation. It means that something before the mind is being contemplated. Likewise the causes by which the thing is being explained are contemplated, either immediately or mediately, in reality itself. There is no note of uncertainty implied. The term is compatible with the highest certitude and with the most rigorous type of scientific knowledge. All the mathematical sciences, for instance, came under the designation "speculative" or "theoretical" for the Stagirite. As regards purpose, theoretical or speculative knowledge was simply for the sake of knowing.

Contradistinguished from the theoretical sciences are the practical and the productive. These have as their purpose something apart from knowledge itself. Practical science aims at guiding human conduct or action (*praxis*), while productive science is meant for turning out a product. These sciences find in the agent or producer the causes from which they proceed. Unlike the theoretical scienes, they do not find the causes in the thing itself. The thing, in their case, is something that does not yet exist. It is something still to be done or produced.[10] In these ways the line of cleavage between the theoretical sciences on the one hand, and on the other the practical and productive, is radical and clear-cut.

Like Plato,[11] Aristotle sees the practical and productive sciences embedded in the activities of the agent or producer. Carpentry, for instance, is an art worked into the actions and capacities of the carpenter. These sciences, accordingly, cannot be detached from operative power. They find their first principles in a training and habituation of human capacities in regard to operation. In the productive sciences knowledge of the forms to be produced plays a basic role in this habituation.[12] Today such sciences would be called arts and crafts. Aristotle devoted special treatises to two of them, rhetoric and literary criticism.

The practical sciences, as contrasted with the productive, have deliberate choice as their principle. Their purpose is the guiding of human conduct, considered apart from any further product. They are concerned with the way a man should guide his own actions, not in respect to an ulterior product but in regard to his own perfection as a man. Their norm is the difficult mean between excess and defect. The mean has to be determined in each particular case by the man of practical wisdom.[13] There is no rigidly fixed plan, as in the case of the productive sciences. To judge the moral mean correctly, lifelong habituation is required.[14] In ethical matters, the situation is new in every case. It is influenced by ever changing circumstances. Hence long and careful habituation from earliest youth is necessry for man to be able to make the correct decision in each instance and attain consistently the ethical mean. The habituation envisaged by Aristotle was the complex and highly nuanced Greek *paideia*.

Because the correct mean is consistently attained, the universality required for a science is present in moral reasoning. No matter how much the mean keeps shifting its position as circumstances incessantly change, it always remains at the middle point between the extremes of excess and defect. In this way it is universally the mean and necessarily the mean, even though such universality and such necessity are highly fluid. It gives rise to premises that hold only roughly and for the most part, and these premises in turn engender conclusions of the same general type.[15] But they are truly premises and truly conclusions. They constitute a science in the Aristotelian sense. The notion that a science can find its principles in the habituation of the doer or producer may seem rather strange to present-day conceptions, but it offers a fruitful solution to difficulties arising from notions of ethics as a theoretical science of norms or as a purely statistical investigation.

In contrast to the practical and productive, the theoretical sciences see their principles in the things that are studied. In solidarity with the Greek tradition that goes back through Plato to the *doxa* of Parmenides, Aristotle regards sensible things as characteristically mobile or changeable. Change or motion, he finds, means that a subject loses one form and acquires another. Every sensible thing, therefore, is basically composed of two substantial principles, matter and form. Each of these Aristotle calls *nature*. In them he finds a means of explaining things scientifically on a level that is accordingly called *natural* philosophy. It is an explanation in terms of a thing's material and formal causes. Natural philosophy, therefore, gives its ultimate explanation through a thing's substantial principles, for the basic matter and the first form are the constituents of a sensible thing's substance, requiring efficient and final causes for change.

Mathematics

Besides the substance, however, there is one accident in sensible things that furnishes principles for scientific explanation. This is the thing's quantity. Quantity, when considered in abstraction, offers as principles points and lines and surfaces and three-dimensional figures as well as all the different numbers and their relations. This is the level of the mathematical sciences. It is attained by abstraction. What is meant by abstraction in Aristotle? "Abstraction" and "things taken in abstraction" (τὰ ἐξ ἀφαιρέσεως) seem reserved by him for the mathematical order. [16] Abstraction refers to quantity taken apart in the mind's consideration from what accompanies it in reality. But from what can quantity be abstracted? Certainly it can be considered apart from sensible qualities like hardness and color, and also from real place and time and other accidents that follow upon quantity. But can quantity ever be abstracted by the intellect from substance, which is prior to it in notion? [17] This would be impossible according to the Aristotelian conception of the relation of accident to substance. In its very notion, quantity like any other accident is a modification of a substance. Take away the notion of substance from its definition, and the notion of quantity itself is destroyed. The regular Aristotelian term is τὸ πόσον the quantitative. [18] It has to be a quantitative something. That "something" is a substance. The Aristotelian term *ousia* brings out the conception much more clearly. The substance is what gives being to quantity. Take away substance from the definition of the quantitative, then, and you remove quantity from being. You destroy the notion of quantity itself.

Moreover, Aristotle requires a certain type of matter in the mathematicals. He calls it intelligible matter. [19] Just as physical matter enables the specifically same form to be extended and to be found in different individuals, so intelligible matter, presumably, allows the quantitative abstract form to be extended in lines, surfaces and geometrical solids. It makes possible many individual twos, and threes and all other numbers, and the many points, individual lines, and individual figures. But what is intelligible matter? Aristotle does not spell its notion out. It seems to be matter in relation to quantity only, leaving out of consideration its relations to the sensible qualities and to place, time, and the other accidents. Just as physical matter permits sensible substance to be spread out in real parts and in a multiplicity of real singular things, so when considered solely in relation to quantity, that is, in abstraction, it allows the abstract quantitative form to be spread out in parts and to be individuated. That seems to be what Aristotle had in mind when speaking of intelligible matter, though he has left no detailed explanation.[20] Examined in the light of their quantitative principles, sensible things can be treated of by what Aristotle calls the more physical of the mathematical sciences.[21] As examples, he mentions astronomy, acoustics, optics, and mechanics. This should mean that any science of nature whose procedure is quantitative, like modern physics or chemistry, would come under the mathematical sciences and not under natural philosophy.

Metaphysics

Finally, the highest of the theoretical sciences is primary philosophy, or, in Aristotle's understanding of the term, theological science. This is what subsequent Peripatetic tradition called metaphysics. In it things are treated of from the viewpoint of their being. Again, the Parmenidean contrast of being with becoming is operative. Being meant the unchangeable and abiding, in contrast to the ever changing sensible world. In the sensible world, however, Aristotle believed he had demonstrated the presence of one abiding feature, the eternity of cosmic motion.[22] From it he reasoned to the existence and nature of supersensible forms as separate substances. These were being only. They had no principle of becoming, that is, no matter or potency. From them, through final causality, being was derived to the sensible world. Being, therefore, was present in that way in the sensible universe, and accounted for the stability of the formal elements in sensible things.

Against this background, the three types of theoretical science were contrasted with one another in terms of mobility and immobility and relation to matter. Natural philosophy dealt with mobile things that had physical matter in their constitution. Mathematics treated of things that contained matter—now intelligible matter only—but which had been rendered immobile by the intellect's abstraction. Primary philosophy had as its subject things separate from all matter and immobile in reality.[23]

Natural Philosophy

The gradation here might seem to reflect the three higher divisions of Plato's divided line.[24] Yet in giving the above schema of the theoretical sciences, Aristotle sets aside any such close parallelism with his predecessor. He declares expressly that if there were no separate substances, natural philosophy would be the highest science. That places natural philosophy on a higher level than mathematics or the mathematical treatment of sensible things. The reason, from the viewpoint of the general framework of Aristotelian metaphysics, is not hard to see. Natural philosophy explains things by their substantial principles, matter and form. Mathematical treatment explains them through quantitative principles, principles that belong to an accidental category. As substance is prior to the accidental, so the science that explains things by substantial principles will have to be prior to the science that explains them by principles located in one of the categories of accident.

But does not Aristotle in the *Posterior Analytics* (I, 13, 78b32-79a16) regard the mathematical sciences of things as more perfect than the corresponding physical sciences? These physical sciences, he maintains, yield only knowledge of the fact (ὅτι), while their mathematical counterparts give "knowledge of the reasoned fact," or commensurately demonstrative knowledge (διότι). The examples of physical science that Aristotle brings forward in making this comparison, however, are all qualitative treatments like nautical astronomy or acoustical harmonics. They are explanations through accidental principles. Unlike quantity, these other accidents do not make manifest the exactly fitting reason for what they demonstrate. To supply an illustration, a color is green because of the mixture of blue and yellow pigments. The mixture of these pigments is sufficient to establish the fact that the resultant color will be green. But they do not show the reason why it is so and must be so, in the way a pair of twos make manifest the reason why they are and must be a total of four. Since Aristotle makes the study of the *Analytics* precede the study of all theoretical science of reality, is he in any position to assume in his hearers an acquaintance with his own natural philosophy? He can credit them only with knowledge of the already accepted sciences, like astronomy and harmonics. He nowhere speaks as though he had his own natural philosophy in mind when making the comparisons between the mathematical and the corresponding physical sciences in the *Analytics*. In the examples used, he has not compromised the position given to natural philosophy in the *Metaphysics*. He has said nothing against the rank of natural philosophy as a completely demonstrative science on a higher level than mathematics.

At the same time, the status of mathematical investigations of nature as completely demonstrative (διότι) is unhesitatingly acknowledged. As far as their manner of demonstrating is concerned, the mathematicized physical sciences belong to the most perfect type of scientific procedure. The reason they rank lower than natural philosophy is not any lack of thoroughness in demonstration. The reason, rather, is the priority of substance over accident. The demonstrative processes of the mathematicized sciences are fully commensurate in making manifest the cause of the things with which they deal. But in this case the cause itself, since it pertains to the category of quantity, has, in terms of being, a lower grading than principles in the category of substance, as the order of the categories makes plain.

Sterility of the Peripatetic Tradition

In spite of this basic Aristotelian framework, however, the long Peripatetic tradition neglected to develop the explanation of nature along quantitative lines, and, as is well known, in the early stages of modern physics and chemistry even set itself strongly against that development. Must Aristotle himself bear the blame for this? In the *Parts of Animals* he models the study of nature on the lines of a productive science. Just as the plan in the mind of the builder is the cause of the materials becoming a house, so in all the works of nature the form is the final cause of the composition and of the arrangements of the parts.[25] To understand any natural thing, for instance man, you take first the thing's form, identified with its final cause, and through the form you learn all about the arrangement and functioning of its parts.[26] In a word, the procedure in the study of natural things is equated with the study of artificial things. As the builder knows all about the house from the blueprints, so the investigator of nature is expected to learn all about natural things by studying their forms.

This procedure works perfectly where man himself is the producer, as in the case of artifacts. But what justifies him in using this method in regard to things of which he is not the cause? What allows him to think that he has prior knowledge of nature's plan in making an elephant or a horse, or even water or earth or air or fire? Has human intellection really enough insight into the nature of the heart, for instance, to say on simple inspection that because the heart is the source of arteries and veins and the producer of blood, it has to be made of materials similar in kind? Yet that is the way Aristotle himself proceeds.[27] The many subsequent centuries of sterile endeavor made it abundantly clear that the human intellect has no such antecedent knowledge of natural things. Any attempt to grasp the form of a natural thing in this fashion is just as liable to complete error as was Aristotle's view in this instance. The only way that has proven fruitful for specific knowledge of natural things has been careful, prolonged observation of detail with elaborate experiment, carried out through exact measurements and submitted to involved mathematical treatment.

Yet Aristotle seemed satisfied that a simple insight into natural things revealed what they were for, and thereby made manifest their final cause. This knowledge of their final cause was for him knowledge of their form, because the final cause and the formal cause of a thing were identical. The specific properties of a natural thing, therefore, could be deduced from what was known of the form. The study of the specific traits and composition and functions of sensible things was but a continuation of the Aristotelian natural philosophy. Through centuries the Peripatetic tradition stubbornly refused to acknowledge that the specific forms of natural things are impenetrable to human intellection, and that only a generic knowledge of them as corporeal and living and organic is accessible to natural philosophy. What Maritain has called the "philosophic optimism of the ancients"[28] seemed to leave Aristotle himself content with an exaggerated confidence in the power of mere intellectual intuition to penetrate into the deepest recesses of nature. His own procedure in treating of natural things was of a kind that gave rise to the belief that the proper way of investigating specific natures was through their final cause, a cause that coincided with their form. The result centuries later was a legacy of tension between the Aristotelian tradition and the modern physical sciences, a tension that has not yet been completely overcome.

General Aristotelian Schema and Modern Science

Nevertheless, the general Aristotelian schema allows ample room for the inclusion of all the modern physical sciences. According to the Aristotelian conception of the sciences in its theoretical pattern, as distinguished from actual Peripatetic practice, no tension with modern sciences should arise. Sciences whose procedure is by measurement come under Aristotle's mathematical order, and not under his natural philosophy. In the realm of quantitative procedure lay the widest opportunities for detailed expansion of the scientific mentality inaugurated by the Greeks. Yet Aristotle himself gives no inkling of having foreseen the vast possibilities in this direction. None of the Greeks did, except perhaps vaguely the Pythagoreans. It is sometimes said that the Greek conception of the free mind was a barrier to the banausic tasks of close experiment and detailed tabulation. But Aristotle gives no sign of nausea in the detailed labor of collecting and arranging the encyclopedic store of data on the animals. He regards as childish the objection that the study of the animals is a disgusting pursuit or unworthy of the philosopher's attention.[29] The reason for his blindness to the tremendous possibilities open to mathematical treatment of nature may lie at least partly in his attitude that an educated man can have sufficient general knowledge to hit upon well-grounded opinions in all subjects, while he can have strictly scientific knowledge in only limited spheres.[30] Aristotle's own natural bent was for the spheres that today are called properly philosophical. This seems to have rendered him content to leave the mathematical explorations to others. Were not centuries of slow progress still required to make apparent to the man of general education the astounding future that was in store for the quantitative study of natures?

In any case, has not Aristotle in his overall conception of the sciences provided a solid groundwork upon which the future development of experimental investigation could have been based, instead of being forced into opposition to his heritage? His notions, moreover, are broad enough to place under genuinely scientific knowledge a satisfying range of human intellectual activities. They bring under it the cognition of the supersensible in metaphysics. They include in it the study of nature through substantial as well as quantitative aspects. They approach the study of human conduct on neither a purely statistical nor a rigidly theoretical basis, but by an authentically practical method that is in essence scientific and yet allows full play for human freedom and creativity. Through this wide and varied range of application, is it not also apparent how Aristotle's conception of the sciences allows for the blossoming of a thorough-going philosophy of man,[31] out of its combined metaphysics and natural and practical and productive philosophies, even though no such unitary study was undertaken by the Stagirite himself? If science "comprises what we know, that is to say, everything we 'really' know,"[32] is not this truly open vision of scientific knowledge a requisite for intellectual life today?

May it not be said, then, that Aristotle has laid foundations broad enough and solid enough to carry the burden of subsequent developments in western civilization? His was a global conception of scientific knowledge that cannot well be forgotten. Its influence is ineradicable, no matter how much it may have fallen into the human subconscious in the present era. Brought back to explicit consciousness, will it not help western culture to understand itself better in terms of historical roots? Viewed in this perspective it seems to furnish, in one instance at least, some ground for what looks at first sight like over-fervent eulogy in an unquestionably modern presentation of the Stagirite's thought: "Clearly Aristotle did not say everything; though without what he first said, all words would be meaningless, and when it is forgotten they usually are."[33]

4. Matter and Predication in Aristotle

Introduction

In describing the basic matter of things, Aristotle removed from it all determinations and so all direct intelligibility. Yet he regarded the basic matter just in itself as a subject for predication. You can say things about it. You can say, for instance, that it is ingenerable and indestructible, and that it is the persistent substrate of generation and corruption. Still more strangely, Aristotle means that a substance or substantial form, like that of a man, of a plant, of a metal, can be predicated of matter.[1] How can this be, if matter is in itself wholly undetermined and entirely unintelligible? How can matter even be indicated, if it exhibits nothing that can halt the gaze of the intellect?

The above observations envisage two ways in which characteristics may be predicated of matter. One is essential (*per se*) predication. Matter is of itself ingenerable and indestructible, somewhat as man is animal and corporeal. The other way is through added forms. Matter is metallic, bovine, human through the forms of a metal, a cow, a man. But these forms are substantial, not accidental. Yet their predication in regard to matter resembles accidental predication, just as the specific differentia in the category of substance is predicated of the genus as though it were a quality. As changes within the category of substance are called by Professor Fisk in the present volume "qualified-like changes", this type of predication may correspondingly be designated "quality-like" predication. It is one type of the medieval *predicatio denominativa*.

In ordinary predication, as treated in Aristotelian logic, the ultimate subject is always actual and concrete. The universal, from a metaphysical viewpoint, is potential (*Metaph.*, M 10, 1087a 15-22). The concrete singular always retains its actuality as its various features are universalized and made potential. It cannot be treated as an undetermined residue that remains after its predicates have been removed. Logical analysis of predication, therefore, leads ultimately in Aristotle to the actual, and not to something wholly potential like matter. Ultimate matter is arrived at through the reasoning of the *Physics*. So reached, it poses problems for metaphysics. How does it have being, and how are forms predicated of it? The Stagirite had here to grapple with a refined concept attained by his scientific thinking and established to the satisfaction of that technical procedure itself, but which broke through the systematized logic presupposed by him for every theoretical science.

The solution reached by Aristotle in this question may or may not provide light for other disciplines when in the course of their reasonings they arrive at concepts that cannot fit into the grooves of the logic they have been using. Such new concepts may well appear self-contradictory when stretched on the Procrustean bed of a closed logical system. Certainly in metaphysics pertinent help for understanding the notion of essence can be obtained from studying Aristotle's procedure in establishing the notion of matter. Whether or not such help may be extended to other disciplines has to be left a question for investigators who specialize in them. But the contingency is one that can be encountered when any discipline pushes its concepts far past the experiences in which human thought commences. Concepts taken from immediate experience sometimes have to be refined in peculiar ways if they are to function in very remote areas of inquiry. The procedure of a first-rate thinker in meeting such a contingency belongs to the common treasury of achievements in the history of thought, and hardly deserves to be forgotten. Aristotle's method in this problem seems, then, *prima facie*, a subject worthy of investigation and critique.

The Subject of Predication

First, what is the basic subject of predication in Aristotelian logic? As is well enough known, this ultimate subject of predication is the highly actual concrete singular thing. It is the individual man, or the individual horse, or the individual tree, according to the examples used in the Aristotelian *Categories*.[2]

This doctrine of predication functioned without special difficulty when applied throughout the world of common sense thought and speech. Quite obviously the ultimates with which ordinary conversation deals are shoes and ships and sealing-wax and cabbages and kings, individual pinching shoes and flat-tasting cabbages and uncrowned office kings, as one meets them in the course of everyday life. These are all concrete individual things or persons. Aristotelian logic, it should be kept in mind, was expressly meant as a propaedeutic to the sciences. It did not presuppose knowledge of any theoretical science. Rather, it had to be learned before any theoretical science could be approached.[4] There should be little wonder, then, that Aristotelian logic was not geared to function smoothly in situations brought into being solely through the results of scientific analysis and construction. Yet those situations have to be expressed in concepts and in language. Logic has to be applied to them as they occur. Aristotle, as may be expected, could not go very deeply into any theoretical science without encountering situations that broke through logical norms presupposed in his hearers. Was he prepared to meet such situations? Was he able to adapt his logic to them as they presented themselves in the course of his scientific investigations?

The Problem of Matter

An instance that could hardly be avoided was that of matter. Matter quite obviously did not come under the notion envisaged for an ultimate predication in a logic where that ultimate subject is the concrete singular thing. In the everyday universe of discourse the material or stuff out of which things are said to be made is always of the concrete individual stamp. The wood of which a house is constructed consists of individual pieces. The bronze in which a statue is cast is a piece of bronze in definite dimensions in a definite place at a definite time. In the later Scholastic vocabulary these concrete materials out of which more complex things were made received the designation, '*materia secunda*', or 'secondary matter'. Bronze and wood and stone were indeed matter, in the sense that things were made out of them. But they were not the basic or ultimate matter out of which those things were made. That was signified by calling them secondary matter. The designation implied that there was a still more basic matter that was not concrete nor individual. Aristotle had not finished the first book of his *Physica* or philosophy of nature before he had established in sensible things a subject still more fundamental than the concrete individual. A visible, tangible, or mobile thing, the Stagirite showed, was necessarily composite. It was literally a *concretum*. It was composed of more fundamental elements. These ultimate constituents of sensible things, according to the Aristotelian reasoning, were form and matter. Matter played the role of ultimate subject, and a form was its primary characteristic.

The absolutely basic matter of the Aristotelian *Physics* became known in Scholastic terminology as *materia prima,* "primary matter". By Aristotle himself it was simply called matter. However, Aristotle uses the term 'matter' regularly enough to designate the concrete materials out of which artifacts are made, materials like bricks and stones and wood. So there was ground for the Scholastic insistence on the use of two expressions, 'primary matter' and 'secondary matter,' to mark the important distinction. For convenience in the present study the term 'materials' or 'material' will be used wherever possible to denote what the Scholastics called "secondary matter", and the term 'matter' without any qualification will be used regularly for the absolutely basic substrate of things as established in the Aristotelian *Physics*. By "matter", then, will be meant what the mediaeval vocabulary designated as "primary matter".

With matter in this sense established as subject, and form as its immediate though really distinct characteristic, you may readily expect to hear that the form is considered to be predicable of matter. You will not be disappointed, Aristotle actually does say that substance, in the sense of substantial form, is predicated of matter: "... for the predicates other than substance are predicated of substance, while substance is predicated of matter."[5] That is his express statement. What does it mean? At the very least, it means that matter is the ultimate subject with which predication is concerned. Everything other than substance you can predicate of substance. But what is intelligible about substance can in turn be predicated, denominatively of course, of matter. The principle of intelligibility in a substance is its form, and its form is the primary characteristic of its matter, from the "quality-like" viewpoint.

At first sight, perhaps, nothing could seem more natural than to predicate a form of its corresponding matter. Characteristics are regularly predicated of subjects. A new subject has been unearthed by the Aristotelian philosophy of nature. The substantial characteristic of that subject has been isolated. What is more normal, then, than to say that here as in other cases the characteristic is predicable of its subject?

Yet as soon as one tries to express this type of predication in any definite instance, linguistic and conceptual difficulties arise. How would you word a sentence in which a substance, or a substantial form, is predicated of matter? The first part of Aristotle's assertion was clear enough: "Predicates other than substance are predicated of substance." The predicates other than substance are the accidents. They are quantity, qualities, relations, activities, time, and place. They are predicated without difficulty of a concrete, individual substance. You may indicate a particular tree and say without hesitation that it is large, green, near to you, growing in the yard at the present moment. Each of these accidents is obviously predicated of a substance, the individual tree. But, the Aristotelian text continues: "the substance is predicated of matter". How would you express this in the case of the tree? You would have to say that matter is this particular tree. You would have to say that matter is likewise Socrates, or is Plato, or is this particular table or that particular stone. Such predication is unusual, and requires considerable explanation even to make sense.

Some light may be obtained from the way in which for Aristotle a thing may be defined in terms of the materials of which it is composed. If asked what a house is, you may answer that it is "stones, brick, and timbers".[6] If that may be called a definition, it is surely the least perfect type of definition possible. But Aristotle does refer to it as a definition in terms of the materials that are able to be made into a house. From that viewpoint the house is the materials that constitute it, and conversely the materials are the house insofar as definition and thing defined are convertible. In general, then, in the way in which a thing may be said to be its materials, the materials themselves may be said to be the thing. Awkward though this predication is, what prevents it from being applied in the case of the basic matter of which things are composed? In each particular case it should allow you to say that matter is this individual man, this individual stone, this individual tree. Substance, even the individual substance, would in this way be predicated of matter.

The context in which the present doctrine occurs is one of the central books of the Aristotelian *Metaphysics*. In a metaphysical context, the universal is not substance. When in this context substance is said to be predicated of matter, it can hardly mean just another instance of universal predicated of particular. From the viewpoint of logic, the secondary substance or the substance taken universally is predicated of the particular substance. Even though present as a condition, that logical doctrine can scarcely be what Aristotle meant in saying in the *Metaphysics* that substance is predicated of matter. It is not just another case of predicating universal of singular, as in the assertion: 'Socrates is a man'. Subject and predicate are really the same when a universal substance is predicated of a particular substance. If you say: "Matter is a man", however, you have a different type of predication. Matter does not coincide in reality with a man in the way Socrates does. A really distinct principle, the form of man, is added. From this viewpoint the predication resembles rather the assertion of an accidental form in regard to substance, as when one says that a man is pale, or fat. The accidental form is really distinct from the substance, as the substantial form is really distinct from its matter. Such predication will be of the "quality-like" type.

That indeed is the way in which Aristotle presents the situation. As an accidental form, for instance quantity, is predicated of substance, so substance is predicated of matter. What is predicated of matter, accordingly should be the substantial form or act, and not the composite. Later in the same part of the *Metaphysics* it is stated in exactly that manner:". . . as in substances that which is predicated of the matter is the actuality itself, in all other definitions also it is what most resembles full actuality."[7] As accidental forms are predicated of substances, then, so the substantial form is what is predicated of matter within the category of substance.

The doctrine clearly enough is that form in the category of substance may be predicated of its matter as of a subject. You may accordingly apply the form of man to matter, the form of iron to matter, and so on, and call it predication. But how can you express this in ordinary language? It can hardly be done. Ordinary language has not been developed to meet this contingency. The best you can do, perhaps, is to say that matter is humanized, equinized, lapidified, and so on, as it takes on forms like those of man, horse, and stone. To say that matter is human, equine, lapideous, or that it is a man, a horse, a stone, may be true enough in this context; but with all its linguistic oddity the way of speaking hardly brings out the full import of the situation. It tends to give the impression that matter is of itself these things. The Aristotelian meaning, on the contrary, is that matter is not of itself any of these things, but becomes them by receiving the appropriate substantial forms. As their real subject it remains really distinct from them, somewhat as a substance remains really distinct from its accidents. The assertion that matter is humanized, equinized, lapidified by the reception of different substantial forms expresses the predication with less danger of being misunderstood, though with still less respect for linguistic usage.

The linguistic difficulties, however, turn out to be mild in comparison with the conceptual. The immediate context of the Aristotelian passage that gave rise to this discussion is enough to cause doubts about the very possibility of the predication. Matter had just been defined as "that which in itself is neither a particular thing nor of a certain quantity nor assigned to any other of the categories by which being is determined".[8] Matter is not anything definite. It is not a "what" nor at all an "it". It exhibits nothing that could provide a direct answer to the question "What is it?" It has in itself none of the determinations by which a thing can be or be recognized or indicated or known or understood. The text states explicitly that it has no quantitative nor other categorical determination. Of itself, therefore, it has no length nor breadth nor thickness nor number nor parts nor position. It cannot at all be conceived in the fashion of the Cartesian concept of matter. In this concept, matter was identified with extension.[9] Nor can the Aristotelian matter be represented as anything capable of detection by means of a pointer-reading. There is nothing about it, in itself, that could register in quantitative terms. It belongs to a level on which neither quantitative nor qualitative physics has any means of functioning. It eludes quantitative and qualitative and other accidental determinations, as well as all substantial determinations.

Yet it cannot be expressed by negations of known characteristics, as for instance non-being is expressed negatively in terms of being.[10] The nature of matter cannot be represented in terms of what it is not. The same Aristotelian text continues:

> Therefore the ultimate substratum is of itself neither a particular thing nor of a particular quantity nor otherwise positively characterized; nor yet is it the negations of these, for negations also will belong to it only by accident.[11]

All categorical determinations are first denied to matter. They are outside its nature, and in that sense "belong to it only by accident". This has been expressed in the preceding paragraphs of the present study by saying that the forms are really distinct from matter somewhat as accidents are really distinct from substances. But, the Aristotelian text insists, the negations of all the different determinations are just as accidental to matter. None of them can express its nature, as the term 'nature' is used of matter in the *Physics* (II *1*, 193a 28-30; 2, 194a 12-13). It eludes even negations. You can indeed say that matter is not something, or better still, that it is a "not-something". What you say is true. But you have not thereby expressed the nature of matter, even negatively. Negations are just as accidental to it as are the determinations it takes on in the actual world. You are still only skimming its accidental manifestations. You have not penetrated to its proper nature. Its nature eludes the negations.

In a word, matter as reached by Aristotle escapes in itself both determinative and negative characterizations. It cannot be conceived or described in any direct fashion, either determinatively or negatively. It is not even a "what" nor an "it" that is capable of being indicated. In terms of modern logic, it is not the "referent" of any "demonstrative" (i.e. monstrative) symbol, because it cannot be presented directly to one's cognition. Nor can the referent be any property or set of properties, because such determinations are lacking to matter in itself.[12]

How, then, is the Aristotelian matter to be conceived and represented? How can it be set up as a subject for predication? Quite obviously, from the above considerations, no direct method, either affirmative or negative, is capable of grasping what Aristotle meant in this regard. The concept will have to be that of a positive subject, able to receive predication. No negation is able to express the nature of matter. Yet from that notion of positive subject every determination will have to be removed, even, or rather especially, the determination expressed by "something".

Matter is explicitly not a "something" nor a "what" nor an "it". All determination, even the most elementary, has to be drastically eliminated from the notion of the positive in this concept. The concept that expresses the Aristotelian notion of matter will have to be the concept of a positive object that is wholly indeterminate. Is the human mind able to form such a concept? If so, upon what referents will it be based?

Presumably Aristotle could not have spoken so cogently about matter if he had not worked out its concept to his own satisfaction. The most likely way to learn how the concept is formed, accordingly, should be to follow the steps by which the originator of the concept reasoned to the presence of matter in sensible things. In this context, of course, the referents will be sensible things in themselves, and not Kantian phenomena.

Substance and Change

How, then, did Aristotle arrive at the notion of matter as a real subject, and as a subject denominatively characterized by forms that remained really distinct from it? In the first book of the *Physics*, the Stagirite surveyed the teachings of his philosophic predecessors on the basic principles of natural things. Things in the world of nature were known by observation to be capable of motion or change. In the course of his survey, attention is focused upon the universal requirements for change. Any change whatsoever needs three principles. It has to have a subject that loses one form and acquires another. The three principles necessarily involved are therefore the form that is lost, the form that is acquired, and the subject that undergoes the loss of the old form and the acquisition of the new.[13]

The Aristotelian examples meant to illustrate this doctrine are clear enough. They are concrete individual materials that lose and acquire different forms. Bronze is the subject that becomes a statue. At first the bronze has a nondescript form or shape. Then it is cast into the form of a statue, say of the Greek god Hermes. It is the subject that changes from one form or shape to another. The notion of form in this example is readily understood from its ordinary English use. It is the external shape of the bronze. Another Aristotelian example, however, uses 'form' in a more esoteric way. A man from an uneducated state comes to be educated. The man is the subject that changes from uneducated to educated. 'Uneducated' describes the quality of the man who has not had proper schooling. 'Educated' means the quality of adequate instruction and cultural training. Both 'educated' and 'uneducated' mean qualities; and in the Aristotelian vocabulary qualities are forms.

As can be seen in these examples, the original form from which the subject changes is more properly regarded from the viewpoint of a privation of the form to be acquired in the change. It is expressed in a privative way, as in the term '*un*educated'. Any of the Aristotelian categories, like the thing's quantity, its place, its time of occurrence, or any of its relations, is a form in this technical Aristotelian sense. Change can take place in any of the categories of being.[14] But in its very notion, as has emerged from the foregoing analysis, it involves indispensibly the three principles—a subject that changes, a form that is lost, a form that is acquired.

This essential notion of change is reached from the changes that are observed in the accidental categories, like change from place to place, from size to size, from color to color. But the analysis of the notion establishes it as a general concept that will hold wherever change is found, regardless of the particular category. It is accordingly applied to Aristotle in the category of substance. In all other categories the subject of the change is observable. You can see the man who changes from uneducated to educated. You can touch the bronze that is cast from a nondescript form into a statue. You can handle the wood that is made into a bed. But with change in the category of substance you cannot observe the subject that changes, even in principle. This means that you cannot observe the subject changing. Change in the category of substance is accordingly not observable, even in principle.

There need be little wonder, then, that Aristotle is sparing in examples of change in the category of substance. Without too much enthusiasm he accepted the tradition of the four Empedoclean elements as the basic simple bodies, and admitted as generation the change of any one of these bodies into another.[15] But he is very circumspect in determining just where substance is found. Earth, air, and fire, three of the traditional elements, do not seem to him to have sufficient unity in their composition to be recognized as substances. Living things seem to have that unity, yet just where the unity is cannot be located to easily.[16] The one instance that he does mention definitely, though only in a passing way, is the change to plants and animals from seed.[17]

Today this Aristotelian example may not seem any too happy an illustration of substantial change. Without having to call the fertilized ovum of a rhinoceros a little rhinoceros, one may argue either for or against the position that an embryo is the same substance as the fully developed animal. To say that a tadpole is not a frog does not commit you to the stand that the one is a different substance from the other. In general, it may be easy enough to claim that the change from something non-living to something alive is a change in substance. But in regard to pinpointing the change from non-living to living substance, or even to showing definitely that there was change from the truly non-living, are we today in any noticeably further advanced position than was Aristotle? Similarly, with modern chemical knowledge, it is easy to show definitely that air, fire, and earth are not substances in the Aristotelian sense. We no longer share the Stagirite's hesitations in that regard. With respect to water, however, can a definite decision be given? In the higher kinds of living things, Aristotle's criterion was a unity that distinguishes the complex organism from a heap. It is the same criterion that enables us now to consider the ant a different thing from the sandpile. In man, consciousness adds a still more profound criterion of unity. Every man considers himself a different being from other men, a different being from the substances he absorbs in nutrition and from those into which he will be dissolved when he dies. Apart from preconceived positions arising out of conclusions in metaphysics or in modern physics, and illegitimately transferred to the domain of natural philosophy, the difference of one being from another and the change of one sensible being into another may in general be admitted. *The evidence of pertinent bearing either for or against, though, is scarcely any greater now than it was in Aristotle's day.*

However, the plurality of things in the universe will hardly be contested any more today in a properly physical context than in the Stagirite's time.[18] As long as a plurality of beings in the sensible universe is admitted without subjecting the term 'beings' to intolerable strain, the plurality of substances required for the Aristotelian demonstration of matter is present. 'Substance' in Aristotle's terminology meant the entity or *ousia* of things. Wherever you have a being, simply stated, you have an *ousia*, a substance. Nor should there be too much difficulty about the change of one thing, macroscopically speaking, into another. Molecular compounds are changed into other compounds, transmutation of the elements is no longer a dream. The one real difficulty might lie in the proposal to locate the individuality of things in sub-atomic particles. In that case might not all the changes taking place in the physical universe be merely new combinations of the particles, as in Democritean atomism? There would be only accidental change, not substantial change.

The denial of any unifying principle in things over and above the sub-atomic particles would leave the behavior of every particle wholly unrelated to that of the others. A cosmic puppeteer would have to cause the regularity of the world processes. A principle of unity in each thing itself, on the other hand, would have to be deeper than the division into particles and into quanta, and indeed would have to be of a different order. It would have to function on a more profound level, in order to dominate the polarity of the sub-atomic particles and to maintain the statistical regularity of the quanta. Such a principle would function exactly as the Aristotelian substantial form. It would be the deepest principle of unity in a thing, and so would make a thing "a being" simply and without qualification. It would be the principle that rendered the thing intelligible. It would be the thing's basic determinant, making the thing one kind of thing and not another. It would be deeper than the entire qualitative and quantitative or measurable orders in the thing, and so would enable the thing to exist and function as a unit in spite of the common patterns of atomic and sub-atomic motion that it shares with other things. When this formal principle gave way was to its successors in changes like nutrition or death, a radically new thing or things would come into being, in spite of common spectra before and after the change and in spite of the equality of the total weight before and after. It would enable the thing to function as a nature and not just artifically at the hands of a cosmic puppeteer. In a word, this principle would coincide entirely with the Aristotelian form in the category of substance.

The argument for the change of one substance into another, accordingly, seems neither stronger nor weaker in any notable way than it was in fourth century Greece. If you grant that you are a different thing or a different being from the food you absorb in nutrition and from the substances into which you will dissolve in death, you have recognized the data necessary to understand the Aristotelian demonstration. When one substance changes into another, what disappears is the most basic principle of determination and knowability, the principle that most radically made food one thing and man another thing. Without it, nothing in the thing could be knowable or observable. It is of course immediately succeeded by the form of the new thing. But the change of the one thing into the other requires a common subject, according to the very notion of change. Such a common subject will be unobservable both in principle and in fact, because it is what loses and acquires the most basic of forms and so of itself has not even the most rudimentary principle of knowability or observability. It has to be known in virtue of something else. That "something else," quite naturally, will be the observable subject in accidental change, like the wood that becomes a bed or the bronze that becomes a statue. Some corresponding subject has to be present for substantial change. In that analogous way, then, the subject of substantial change, namely matter, is indirectly known. It is known as the conclusion of scientific reasoning in the Aristotelian sense of 'scientific'. In Aristotle's own words:

The underlying nature is an object of scientific knowledge, by an analogy. For as the bronze is to the statue, the wood to the bed, or the matter and the formless before receiving form to any thing which has form, so is the underlying nature to substance, i.e. the "this" or existent.[19]

The presence of matter is proven stringently from the requirements for change, while the nature of matter is established through analogy with the subject of accidental change. The demonstration presupposes the universal notion of change and the two terms, but not the substrate, of substantial change.

The original referent upon which the Aristotelian concept of matter is based is therefore the subject of accidental change, like wood or bronze. From that notion of "subject", however, all determinations are removed, with the proviso that the negations as well as the determinations are accidental to it. In its own nature, then, this refined notion of subject remains as positive as ever. It was a positive notion from the start, as seen in a positive subject like wood or bronze, and all determinations were denied it under the express condition that none of these pertained to its own nature. In this way the notion *positive* is shown to be independent of *determinate*. For Aristotle, 'actual' was a synonym for 'determinate'. What lacked actuality, or in technical language the potential, could therefore be positive. By establishing the concept of the potential as positive even though non-actual or indeterminate, Aristotle has been able to set up matter as a positive though entirely non-actual subject of predication. Because the potential is positive without being determinate, this concept of matter is possible to the human mind. Its referent is any sensible thing considered potentially as substance. It is the concept of a principle wholly undetermined, yet necessarily posited in reality by any form that is extended, multiplied in singulars, or terminating substantial change.

Conclusion

As should be clear from the foregoing considerations, matter in the category of substance can be an object of scientific inquiry only on the level of natural philosophy. It cannot at all be reached by qualitative or quantitative procedures like those of chemistry and modern physics. What is predictated of it, in itself, does not belong to the order of the measurable or the directly observable, even in principle. Its predicates are notions like *purely potential, unknowable of itself, incorruptible,* and so on. Its presence is still necessary to explain substantial change, if such change is admitted. In any case, its presence is absolutely required to account for the extension of a formally identical characteristic in parts outside parts, and for the multiplication of the characteristic in a plurality of individuals, without any formal addition whatsoever. The Aristotelian matter has not been superseded nor even touched by the stupendous progress of modern physics. Nothing that is measurable can perform its function in explaining the nature of sensible things, and by the same token it cannot be brought forward to account for anything that requires explanation in measurable terms. Any type of matter dealt with by chemistry or modern physics would in comparison be secondary matter, and not matter that is a principle in the category of substance. "Matter" in the basic Aristotelian sense is therefore in no way a rival of the "matter" that can be measured or of the mass that can be transformed into energy, but is rather a very different means of explanation for sensible things on another scientific level, the level of natural philosophy.

In distinguishing his two tables, the solid one he wrote on and the "nearly all empty space" table he knew as a physicist, Eddington failed to stress that his knowledge of his scientific table was constructed from his knowledge of the ordinary table.[20] The scientific construct was the result of understanding the ordinary table in quantitative terms. The same ordinary table can also be understood scientifically (in the traditional sense of knowledge through causes) in terms of substantial principles, form and matter, as is done in natural philosophy. It can also be understood in terms of entitative principles, essence and being, as is done in metaphysics. They are all different accounts of the same thing, given on different levels of scientific (again, in the centuries-old meaning of "scientific") investigation. All these different accounts are necessary for a well-rounded understanding of sensible things. None of these accounts can afford to despise any of the others, nor seek to substitute for any of them, nor to interfere with any of them. Each has its own role to play, a role that only itself can play. The Aristotelian matter is a principle for explaining things on the level of natural philosophy. On that level it has its own predicates, predicates that still have to be used today in the properly balanced explanation of nature.

5. The Grounds of Universality in Aristotle

As a philosophical term, "universal" (*katholou*) seems clearly enough to originate with Aristotle. It does not occur in a technical sense prior to the Aristotelian treatises;[1] and is used regularly throughout their pages. Its precise meaning, moreover, stems definitely from Aristotelian philosophy, though with a deep background in Socrates and Plato. A glance at the background should help make clear on the one hand the continuity of the trend that culminated in the Aristotelian universal, and on the other hand the distinctiveness and the originality of the conception of the universal in the Stagirite's own thought. A sufficient grasp of what the universal meant for him, and how he saw it functioning in scientific knowledge, is an obvious preliminary requirement for an investigation into its grounds.

With Socrates the notion of what something is, in contrast to the particular instances in which it is found, had been stressed consistently against the teaching of the Sophists. In Plato this notion was carried over into the Idea, separate from and participated in by the particular sensible things. For both Socrates and Plato the all-pervading concern with the topic arose from the need to base human thought and human conduct upon scientific knowledge, rather than upon the traditional doxastic conceptions inculcated so successfully by the Sophists and by the flourishing school of Isocrates.[2] In the struggle for scientific knowledge, Aristotle was continuing the trend inaugurated by Socrates and Plato. As with his two predecessors, his interest lay in grounding human knowledge and activity upon the permanently stable, instead of locating it in a collection of moment-to-moment opinions upon an ever-changing flux. In the Aristotelian noetic, however, only particular sensible things could be the original objects of human cognition.[3] They alone provided the data for all further knowledge. Of their nature they were changeable. Yet within them, somehow, had to lie the stability and permanence demanded by scientific knowledge.

This situation gave birth to the notion of the universal. It required that a particular sensible thing, changeable by its very nature, should at the same time be stable and abiding object of knowledge. It had to find in the sensible thing itself an object with necessity[4] sufficient for scientific knowledge, that is, something that holds for all the particulars. The many and changing singulars had to be contained in a unitary *whole* that was unchanging, abiding, and all-embracing. Knowledge in terms of this unitary whole was knowledge *katholou*, knowledge bearing upon all the singulars as upon a distinctive whole. In that way the unitary whole was conceived as a "universal."

Since the universal, in the Aristotelian noetic, could not be an object outside the sensible thing, it had somehow to coincide with each of the singulars in which it was exemplified.[5] Though a unitary whole, it had to be identical with each of the singulars in turn, and accordingly be predicable of each. This feature gave the universal its distinguishing characteristic within the general notion of "whole." The universal, consequently, was listed by Aristotle as one of the various meanings of that notion. It was "a whole in the sense that it contains many things by being predicated of each, and by all of them, e.g., man, horse, god, being severally one single thing, because all are living things."[6]

The universal, upon which scientific knowledge is based, is therefore for Aristotle something that is identical with each of the singulars in turn. That is why it can be predicated of each of them. That is why you may say, for instance, that Socrates is a man, and Callias is a man, and Coriscus is a man, and every other human individual is a man. Each of them is severally a "man," and "man," while a unitary whole, is each of them in turn. Each of the singular things instantiates one and the same universal. In each instantiation there is, each time, but one real object, able to be regarded in two different ways. In one way it is regarded as singular, in another way it is regarded as universal.

Because of this identity of the singular with the universal in each instance, both the formal and the material elements that compose the singular sensible thing are also found in the universal: "But man and horse and what are thus applied to singulars but universally, are . . . something composed of this particular formula and this particular matter, treated as universal."[7] Like the sensible thing with which it is identical, the universal consists of the two contrasted constituents, matter and form. The only difference is that both thing and constituents are now regarded in a different way. In the one case they are regarded as singular, in the other case as universal.

This conception of the universal is spelled out in further detail in the immediately following chapter of the Aristotelian treatise: "It is also clear that the soul is the primary substance and the body is matter, and man or animal is the compound of both taken universally."[8] Here the soul, that is, the physical form,[9] is mentioned as one constituent and is contrasted with the other constituent, the matter. The universal is characterized as the compound of both, regarded in universal fashion. The really existent man, "Socrates" or "Coriscus," is the compound of both constituents, and as such is a singular. The universal is also the compound of both, but of both as taken universally.

Universal and particular, accordingly, denote the same real thing,[10] regarded in different ways. How is this possible? What grounds are there, either in the particular sensible things from which all human cognition originates for Aristotle, or in the human way of regarding them , that makes possible this conception for the universal? The difficulty is not brought out explicitly in the texts just considered. It is rather a problem that arises from them. But these texts do sketch in its general lines the Aristotelian notion of the universal. They allow one, therefore, to introduce a few preliminary points of precision that are necessary for clarity in a present-day discussion.

First, the Aristotelian universal is what is expressed by the predicate "man" in a sentence like "Socrates is a man." The same predicate "man" can likewise be united by the copula with any other individual such as "Callias" or "Coriscus." Callias is a man; Coriscus is a man. The predicate is one and the same in all the cases and is identical with each particular instance in turn. Each *is* the predicate, though the predicate itself as a universal remains a unit. The Aristotelian universal, accordingly, is a unitary whole that is expressed by a predicate like "man."

Second, the universal is clearly distinguished from the form that unites with the matter in both singular and universal. The form is only a part of the universal, just as it is only a part of the singular. The universal includes matter in its notion, while the form is the constituent that is distinguished from the matter. The form is a "this" (*tode ti*),[11] while the universal is regularly contrasted with a "this." The form is *ousia*, in fact primary *ousia*,[12] in the context of the *Metaphysics*, while the universal is not *ousia* from its viewpoint. Though "Form" and "Idea" coincide in Plato, in Aristotle form and universal are divergent. To conceive the Aristotelian universal as a Platonic Idea now functioning as an inherent form in matter would clash with the patent meaning of these Aristotelian texts.

Third, the Aristotelian universal, in its ordinary instances, is not what is represented by words like "humanity" or "whiteness."[13] The universal is predicated of each individual in such a way that each one in turn is the universal. You say 'Socrates is a man, Coriscus is a man, Callias is a man.'' But you do not say"Socrates is humanity, Coriscus is humanity,

Callias is humanity." You may say "The wall is white, the snow is white, the metal is white," but not that each or any of them is "whiteness." "Humanity" or "human nature" is something composed of both matter and form, and is therefore obviously different from the form or soul of man. But how does it differ from the universal? Aristotle does not seem to have any interest in delving into this problem.[14] Whatever his explanation might have been, however, notions like "whiteness" and "humanity" do not in their ordinary use correspond to his description of the universal.

The texts just considered, then, pinpoint the Aristotelian universal to what is expressed by a predicate like "man." They distinguish it definitely enough from what is expressed by notions like "humanity," and by the technical Aristotelian conception of "form" in contrast to matter. So determined, the universal, although a unit, is identified in reality with each of many singulars in turn. For this reason it is predicable of each of them. The functioning of the universal, so understood, emerges readily enough from the structure of Aristotle's logic. The syllogism, that is, the process of reasoning, depends for its validity upon a middle term: ". . . if the universal goes, the middle term goes with it, and so demonstration becomes impossible."[15] Because the middle term is universal with regard to the minor, and the major term is universal with regard to the middle, what is known independently of the major term becomes known thereby of the minor term. In this way human knowledge is increased through reasoning. Without the factor of universality, therefore, scientific knowledge would not be possible. As knowledge through conclusions inferred from premises, science for Aristotle depends upon the universal.[16]

II

It is one thing, however, to show from the logical structure of reasoning that science depends upon the universal, and to require identity of universal and singular in order that scientific knowledge bear upon reality. It is quite another thing to show how this is possible. The sensible thing, from which all human knowledge takes its rise, is in every case singular. It is not a universal. It is something changeable. Yet it alone is what is directly attained in human cognition. How can knowledge of it provide knowledge of anything universal?

Obviously, where the knowledge is of the universal and the thing known is a singular, knowledge cannot be conceived as a mere replica of what is known, as a photographic reproducing or a cataloguing or a calculation of things. The mind is a life. It is a vital activity, and may be expected to elaborate its object, to work upon it, to represent it in a manner different from the here-and-now manner in which it exists in the real world. Can it do that without distorting or misrepresenting the thing known? Is there something about a sensible thing that enables it to be known in a way different from and wider than the way in which it actually exists in the real world?

These reflections suggest that two different sources have to be probed to determine the grounds of universality in Aristotle. One is the sensible thing that is known. What is the structure of the sensible object itself? Does its composition provide a basis for knowledge of it in universal fashion? Is there something about it, in its real existence, that allows it to be known as a universal? The other possible source is the mind's own activity. What type of cognitional activity can encounter a singular thing and know it as universal, without distorting or falsifying the object? Even though mind against an Anaxagorean background[17] be granted a status above material mixture, is it thereby equipped to free a sensible object from the limitations of here and now? In saying that mind or soul is in some way all things,[18] that the knower and the thing known are one in the actuality of cognition,[19] does Aristotle mean that the knower confers his own way of being upon the thing known? But would that help in the present difficulty? The knower is an individual substance. He is not a universal. How could the knower's way of being help at all to explain universality?

These considerations, nevertheless, suggest an examination first of the sensible thing's structure, then of the activity of the human intellect, for the purpose of bringing to light any grounds for universality that may lie in each.

III

First, what is the structure of sensible things for Aristotle? The opening books of the *Physics* show that every sensible substance is composed of two principles, matter and form. The matter, unknowable in itself, becomes knowable through analogy. As the bronze is to the statue and as the wood to the bed, so is the underlying nature in any sensible substance to its corresponding form.[20] The notion of an underlying nature within every sensible substance has resulted in the *Physics* from a long inquiry into the principles of change. The general conception of change, reached by analysis of observable instances like wood becoming a bed or bronze a statue, requires a subject to pass from one form into another. Change in substance, accordingly, means that an appropriate subject loses one form and acquires another. This subject is "the primary matter underlying each of the things that have in themselves the principle of motion or change.''[21] The matter, though in itself formless and in consequence entirely indeterminate and knowable, has therefore become intelligible under the general notion of "subject," a notion acquired from observable substrates of change such as bronze and wood. But just in itself the matter contributes no intelligibility to the thing.

The other principle reached by the *Physics* is the form, in the sense of the first or basic formal principle. It is the fundamental knowable content of the thing, in contrast to the unintelligible matter and to the accidental characteristic. Through it are present the determinations that render a sensible thing knowable: "For only the form, or the object as having form, can be expressed in the concept; whereas the material element by itself cannot be expressed in the concept.''[22]

By actuating matter the form constitutes the singular thing. It can never be found in reality except as informing matter, that is, as in a singular thing and as physically repeated and physically distinct in each new instance of the singulars. But in itself is it singular? As a "this,''[23] it does stand in definite contrast to the universal. Yet in its own aspect as form it does not seem immediately to distinguish one sensible instance from another. Rather, the sameness of the form in all the many singulars is stressed:

> . . . the begetter is adequate to the making of the product and to the causing of the form in the matter. And when we have the whole, such and such a form in the flesh and in these bones, this is Callias or Socrates; and they are different in virtue of their matter (for that is different), but the same in form; for their form is indivisible.[24]

The use of the one Aristotelian term *eidos* for both "form"—which is a real physical principle—and for "species"—which is universal—may give rise to caution regarding the Oxford translation of *eidos* throughout this passage as "form." Yet in the passage *eidos* definitely means the form that is achieved in the matter through physical causality. The effect of the causality is undoubtedly a physical form. The concern is with a product that is made, that is begotten, in the real world. The passage does not bear upon a universal that is known in the mind. The *eidos* in question is a form "in this flesh and in these bones," and it constitutes singulars, namely Callias and Socrates. It is one constituent of the compound that is the real physical man.

The universal, on the other hand, is not one of the two physical constituents. It is the composite of both, taken universally. On account of one constituent, their matter, Callias and Socrates differ from each other.

But in the *eidos* that has just been described, they are the same. Their form, under its own aspect of form and as expressly contrasted with matter, is not divisible. A sudden and unexplained change in the meaning of *eidos* from "form" to "species" in this passage could hardly be accepted, even though sameness in form results in sameness of species and is expressed in the Greek by exactly the same phrase.

The passage indicates that the form just as form does not immediately distingush one singular from another. Human form (the soul), insofar as it is form alone, is the same in all instances of men. It serves to render all the instances human, to give them all the one specific nature. The distinction of the singular instance from one another follows upon the matter. Yet the form in itself is not a universal but a "this." To be in the real world the form of a sensible thing has to be singularized by matter. That is its essential requirement. When real it has to constitute a particular man like Socrates or Callias. As the cause of being,[25] it imparts individuality to the matter and to the composite; for, unlike an absolutely separate form, it calls for realization solely in singular individuals. It requires that the thing of which it is the form be a singular.

In the real singular, accordingly, the form is the principle of determination and the principle that renders the thing knowable, though just of itself it does not immediately distinguish one singular from another. It is the immediate origin, rather, of the features common to them all. Has it not, therefore, the requisite condition for functioning as the ground of a knowledge of things that does not differentiate one singular from another, of knowledge applicable to them all? In its formal role it provides the source for common specific content and not immediately for discernment of singulars. This content extends equally and indifferently to all the singulars of the species. It makes knowable the composite, the entire thing. When a sensible thing is known in the way in which it is characterized by its form, it is indeed known as an object that includes matter. What is known is something composed of both principles, matter and form. Otherwise not the thing itself, but only its form, would be known. Yet the composite sensible thing is the origin of human cognition.

An object is characterized and made knowble by a form that just in itself does not distinguish its singulars. Has not the sensible thing, therefore, within its structure a principle that may readily serve as a ground for universal knowledge? Why may not the form characterize the matter in the *known* object in a way that leaves the object a composite with a knowable content common to all the singulars? This will require elaboration through the activity of the knower, for here the cognition does not reflect the way in which the matter singularizes the object in the real world. But it does retain the knowable content given the object by the form. As long as no new content is added by the mind's activity, the object will remain the same thing.[26] Only the universal way in which it is known will be new. The mind, in fact, has no natural tendency to attribute universality to the real things themselves, even when conscious that it is knowing them in universal fashion. In the object known there need be no falsification or distortion.

The universality, then, understood in this way, is not actually present in the real sensible thing. But it may be regarded as potentially present, because the intrinisic ground that allows it to be attained, the physical form, is actually present in the thing. Because of the form, the sensible thing can be known universally and can be defined.[27] The unitary character of sameness of the form as form in all the singulars will permit a common definition that gives expression to the total composite and will allow its content, matter as well as form, to be applied as a universal to all the singular instances.

This conception of the universal is not, of course, without difficulties. How, for instance, does it counter the thrust of Plato's *Parmenides* (131B): "If so, a Form which is one and the same will be at the same time, as a whole, in a number of things which are separate, and consequently will be separate from itself" (tr. Cornford)? Aristotle does not seem to feel the impact of this objection. The form is not a thing existent in itself. To ask if it is separate from itself is to place it first as existent in itself, instead of in matter. Perhaps the Stagirite could have answered that in the impossible supposition of a sensible form existing without matter it would allow only one individual in a species, since there would be nothing to multiply it.[28] Where being is explained ultimately by form,[29] as in Aristotle, the difficulty that each act of being means existential distinction is not felt. Within its own metaphysical framework, therefore, his notion of sameness in form does not seem to run into self-contradiction. But it can hardly hope to prove complete or satisfactory when questions in terms of existence are encountered.

Another difficulty is that in the Aristotelian universal the material principle functions sufficiently to leave the object a composite of matter and form, but not sufficiently to render it singular. For Aristotle, however, matter may function in cognition differently from the way it functions in the sensible world. In the objects of mathematics it plays the role of intelligible matter, in contrast to sensible matter.[30] Within the Aristotelian framework, then, there need be no internal inconsistency in the stand that matter in a known object like the universal does not exercise all the functions it performs in the real sensible world. This consideration, however, throws the problem into the activity of the human intellect in its cognition of sensible things.

IV

A further ground for universality, then, has to be sought in the mind's activity. Through the well-known rout simile in the concluding chapter of the *Posterior Analytics*,[31] Aristotle describes how cognition of the universal is attained. Attention is focused upon one among a number of indiscriminate particulars. For instance, the individual Callias is seen and understood as a man, as a unitary object under which all the other singulars may be brought, as "a single identity within them all." (100a7-8; Oxford tr.) The one explanation given is: "The soul is so constituted as to be capable of this process." (a13-14; Oxford tr.) The Stagirite speaks as though he is observing human cognition, noting the facts, and then saying that because as a fact the activity is taking place, the soul is accordingly capable of it.

Nor does the *De Anima* provide any further explanation of this capability on the part of the soul. In the soul there is a passive intellectual principle, and a corresponding active principle: "And in fact mind as we have described it is what it is by virtue of becoming all things, while there is another which is what it is by virtue of making all things: this is a sort of positive state like light; for in a sense light makes potential colours into actual colours."[32] The passage is extremely enigmatic. But on one point at least it is definite. In addition to becoming all things through cognition, the mind has a different phase of activity in the course of its grasping them. It is an activity illustrated by the simile of light making colors actually visible. The surfaces of sensible things, this would mean, are regarded as potentially colored. In the dark or the dusk, no differentiated colors appear. The light shines upon them, and the distinct colors become actually visible. Like light, this phase of mind is its unitary self (a22-23) and nothing more. But by its actual presence and activity it makes actual what was previously only potential in things.

The mind, then, is described as active insofar as in its knowing things it brings into actuality what was present in them only potentially. Does this consideration help in regard to universal knowledge? By reason of the form, what the sensible thing is offers a ground for universality. Can the activity of the intellect, bearing upon it like light, make it known in a way which, though actually individual,[33] is applicable to any other singular instance? The account is only by way of a simile. It does not seem to penetrate intrinsically into the workings of the intellect. Can it be regarded as anything more than the observation in the *Posterior Analytics* that such is the nature of the soul? The results of intellectual activity are carefully observed, and because they are found to be of this kind the intellect is declared to be of a nature able to effect them. The point is merely driven home with an illustration from the activity of light.

In particular, the Aristotelian account does not show how the mind is able to view an object in a way that allows matter to remain in the object's constitution without rendering it singular. The Stagirite stresses the fact that sensation, imagination, and intellectual cognition[34] receive the forms of sensible things without their matter. In this rising scale of cognition there is obviously a question of degree.[35] In the real sensible world, matter limits the thing to a definite here and now. In external sense-perception it keeps the thing singular, but allows the one singular thing to be found in the cognitive activity of a number of different percipients. In the imagination it permits the things to be freed also from restrictions of time. In the specific universal it gives rein to knowledge above the limitations of space and time and above the conditions of contingence. In the more generic universals it opens out over a gradually increasing range. Aristotle, accordingly, sees differences in the way matter functions in the real world and in the various grades or types of cognition. In the cognitive activity of the knower the matter is observed to function in a manner appropriate to each grade. But this remains an observation. It is hardly a satisfactory explanation. Yet it is enough to show that for Aristotle the universal depends upon the activity of the human intellect as well as upon the form of the sensible thing.

V

The grounds for universality in Aristotle, therefore, are twofold. First, in every sensible thing there is a basic formal principle that, though individual, brings each instance into formal identity with all the other instances. Secondly, in human intellectual cognition there is an active principle that raises knowledge above the status of photographing or registering or cataloguing and actualizes what was only potential in the real thing. The unity indicated by the formal principle of sensible things is not something actual in the real world. In the real world each sensible thing is something apart from the others, and the form of each is physically distinct from the forms of the rest. But in knowing sensible things universally, the human intellect is able to grasp the concrete physical thing as characterized distinctively by its formal nature, to know it in a way that holds equally for all other instances of the form.

Aristotle has penetratingly observed the facts made manifest in the phenomena of scientific knowledge. He has analyzed them in his logic and thereby shown the functioning of the universal in human reasoning processes. The universal is there, as a datum. It is observable through reflection. To find in the Aristotelian treatises an adequate account of it in terms of its causes or grounds, however, becomes a disappointing endeavor. The physical form of the sensible object and the active phase of human intellection seem to be the grounds offered in the text. These are solidly based on careful observation. They avoid internal contradiction and offer a framework in which subsequent investigations have been carried on and in which future inquiries may be profitably pursued. But in their own location in Aristotle they can hardly be expected to prove satisfactory. The protracted controversies on the universals throughout the middle ages, the continuing attacks from Nominalists in later centuries, the more recent approaches from the analysis of language instead of from the natures of things, as well as the widely divergent conceptions of soul and intellect in the long tradition of Aristotelian thought, all bear eloquent witness of the inconclusive status of the theme in the Stagirite's own text. Yet it would be rash to say that his account has lost its relevance. In point of fact, it still commands attention. Though incomplete, it remains a beacon light pointing out a way of inquiry, inviting further study, and providing a clearly defined framework in which fruitful discussions may continue to be carried on.[36] It is still a challenge.

6. The Universality of the Sensible in the Aristotelian Noetic

I

As is well enough known, all human cognition originates for Aristotle in sensible things. The closing chapter of the *Posterior Analytics* (II 19, 100a 1-b 5) and the seventh and eighth chapters of *De Anima's* third book (431a 1-432a 14) make this role of sensible objects in human intellection indisputably clear. The wording of *De Anima*, however, is that "the soul never thinks without an image" (III 7, 431a 16-17; Oxford tr.), that "the objects of thought are in the sensible forms" (II 8,432a 4-5), that "when the mind is actively aware of anything it is necessarily aware of it along with an image" (a 8-9), and that while concepts are not phantasms they are not had without phantasms (a 14-15). Taken alone, these statements might be compatible with the interpretation that the mind can find in sensible data notions that are wider than the sensible, and see in sensible things an object, such as substance or being, that is more general than either the corporeal or the incorporeal. Such, in fact, is the impression given by Boethius' presentation of the first Aristotelian category. Substance is the highest genus, and is for Boethius divided into the corporeal and the incorporeal as its species.[1] In this sense the category was schematized in the Porphyrian tree and through the centuries has guided the first faltering steps of philosophy students in their initiation into Aristotelian logic. The impression is that just as one sees in man and ox a generic concept universal in regard to both, so in sensible things one sees a concept of substance that is generic in regard to both the corporeal and incorporeal, and accordingly more universal than either.

Is this sound Aristotelian doctrine? If it is, it will have important consequences in determining the object of metaphysics. It will allow the human mind to form, through an immediate inspection of sensible things, a concept that is wider than the sensible. It will require no mediating process of judging and reasoning to build a concept that is universal in regard to both the corporeal and incorporeal. Through simple apprehension alone it will furnish a notion capable of serving as an object for the study of what is beyond the sensible. In a word, it will permit the human mind to behold in sensible things a notion that is more universal than the sensible.

Is this situation possible in the Aristotelian noetic? An analysis of a much controverted text in the opening chapter of the *Physics* may throw considerable light upon the topic. The *Physics* begins with a rapid sketch of Aristotle's general concept of scientific knowledge. First, in any scientific discipline to know a thing is to know its principles or elements.[2] Secondly, the natural path of human knowledge is from things that are more knowable for men to things that are more knowable in themselves,[3] and this means proceeding from concretions to the distinct cognition of the principles and elements into which they may be analyzed. These two norms are regarded as applying to all scientific procedure. Here they are but outlined briefly as an introduction to the Aristotelian philosophy of nature.

Up to this point the chapter is recapitulating standard Aristotelianism in quite the expected way. In the Stagirite's general noetic, the origin of human knowledge lies inevitably in sensible things. Accordingly the present chapter of the *Physics* (I 1, 184a 21-25) is able to state succinctly that sensible composites are the more apparent objects of human cognition, and that from knowledge of them knowledge of their principles is derived. From knowledge of sensible composites, in consequence, all further human knowledge will be obtained in one way or another. The sensible things, however, are concretions. They are composites both in reality and from the viewpoint of the logician. In their own reality they are composites of form and matter (*Phys.* II 1, 192b 8-193b 18). From the logical viewpoint they are composites of genera and species and subject, or, in the special terminology of the *Categories* (2a 11-19), of secondary substance and primary substance. Their accidents may, for present purposes, be left out of consideration.

So far, then, everything is in order in these two initial assertions of the *Physics*. From the two premises, however, a rather surprising conclusion is drawn: διὸ ἐκ τῶν καθόλου ἐπὶ τὰ καθ' ἕκαστα δεῖ προϊέναι.[4] An unalerted reader would be inclined to understand this in English as: "Therefore one should proceed from the universals to the individuals." The meaning would in this perspective be that one knows the universal first, and from the universal proceeds to knowledge of individual sensible things. Such an understanding of the sentence, of course, strikes at once a jarring note. Elsewhere Aristotle's noetic regularly sees all human knowledge originating in the individual sensible things. The universal seems only a further and less definite way of considering things that are first known as individual.[5] In the *Posterior Analytics* (I 2, 72a 4-5) the universal is explicitly described as farthest from sensation, while, in direct contrast, the individuals are closest. Even within a Platonic setting Aristotle maintains that the proponents of the Ideas were actually going from "the things around us" (*Metaph.* A 9, 990b 1—Oxford tr.) to corresponding separate entities of the same name. In an Aristotelian context the notion of going from universals to singulars hardly makes sense. As Tannery noted in his discussion of this passage, towards the end of the nineteenth century, one would expect from all the analogous passages that Aristotle should say just the opposite.[6] The Stagirite should find his point of departure in the particular that is immediately attained in sensation, and proceed to the general or the universal as his goal. The particular things are first unknown, and in them and through them the universal is reached. One would expect to read: "Therefore we must advance from the particulars to the general." Yet the text clearly states the opposite. It asserts that one should start with the general or universal and proceed to the particulars.

The direction the procedure is to take, accordingly, appears with unmistakable clarity in the text. It is from the universal to the particulars. But what exactly is meant by "universal" and "particulars" in the present setting? Whatever is meant by them respectively, the statement as a whole cannot very well imply against an Aristotelian background that human knowledge starts with non-sensible objects. Procedure from universals, as intellectual abstractions, to concrete sensible things would not be any more acceptable to Aristotle than to Whitehead.[7] The first step in the investigation of the passage, therefore, will be to determine exactly what is meant by "universal" and by "particulars" in its context.

II

To what, then, does "universal" refer in the present passage? In English translations it may appear variously as "generalities" (Oxford tr.), "general character of a thing" (Wheelwright), or "the concrete whole" (Wicksteed). Among the ancient Greek commentators, Philoponus[8] had distinguished its meaning here from the primary sense of "universal," and given it the signification of an indeterminate particular concretion. Among the moderns, Bonitz (*Ind. Arist.,* 357a 16) classed its use in this passage as *alio sensu,* as a meaning other than its ordinary one. But he did not specify the sense or give other instances of the unusual meaning. Ross (*Aristotle's Physics,* p. 457) asserts that in the present passage the term "is not used in its usual Aristotelian meaning." He explains: "The reference must be not to a universal conceived quite clearly in its true nature, but to that stage in knowledge in which an object is known by perception to possess some general characteristic (e.g., to be an animal) before it is known what its specific characteristic is (e.g., whether it is a horse or a cow)." This would mean that the true nature of the universal is specific, while a genus is universal in another and not usual sense of the term.

But in Aristotle does *to katholou* have in fact a number of different significations? It does not seem to be characterized by him anywhere in this way, at least explicitly. It is not listed in Book Δ of the *Metaphysics* among the notions that vary in meaning. It is mentioned there as one of the divergent senses of "whole," namely as containing "many things by being predicted of each, and by all of them . . . being severally one single thing" (Oxford tr. of ὡς πολλὰ περιέχον τῷ κατηγορεῖσθαι καθ ἑκάστου καὶ ἓν ἅπαντα εἶναι ὡς ἕκαστον—Δ 26, 1023b 30-31). It seems, given the status of one of the definite senses of "whole," as though it itself had only one meaning. The meaning is that of something predicated of a number of instances, something that retains its own self-identity while existing in a number of different things. From a logical viewpoint the universal is regularly described by this capacity to be predicated of subjects. For instance, by "universal" is meant "that which is of such a nature as to be predicated of many subjects, by 'individual' that which is not so predicated" (*Int.*7, 17a 39-40; Oxford tr.). Examples are given: "Thus 'man' is a universal, 'Callias' an individual" (ibid). From a metaphysical standpoint the presence of the universal in a plurality of things remains its distinguishing mark. The universal is "that which is of such a nature as to belong to a number of things" ἣ πλείοσιν ὑπάρχειν πέφυκεν—*Metaph.* Z 13,1038b 11-12). Throughout the Aristotelian corpus the term bears consistently this one meaning. It does not seem to express a notion with many senses. Though it may apply with varying degrees of rigor in physical, mathematical, metaphysical, and ethical contexts respectively, the notion itself seems to remain the same in all its instances.

In particular,the view of John Philoponus that the universal in its primary sense means a determined and articulated nature, for instance man or animal, does not seem to express the notion of the universal that emerges from Aristotle's *Metaphysics*. In Book M (10, 1087a 16-23) the universal, clearly meant in its regular sense, is characterized as indeterminate—τοῦ καθόλου καὶ ἀορίστου. In Book Z (13, 1038b 6-1039a 14) the universal is denied the actuality that would be required to make in something definite in itself. A primary and secondary sense along these lines does not appear in the text of Aristotle. A further meaning of "universal" recognized by the Greek commentators[9] was in regard to a cause upon which other things depended, in the sense that if the cause were done away with, all its effects would thereby vanish. This conception was used to explain how the science of the separate substances was universally the science of all beings. It obtains support from the way Aristotle equates cause with universal in the opening chapters of the *Metaphysics*. But it is hardly applicable in the present context. *To katholou* in the text from the first chapter of the *Physics* is not regarded as functioning in any role of cause, but rather as an effect, as something whose causes or principles or elements are being sought.

Nor does it seem helpful to distinguish from the usual sense of the universal "the other and less frequent sense of 'concrete whole.'"[10] The universal, as first known in the sensible things from which human cognition takes its origin, is always a concrete whole. It is "something composed of this particular formula and this particular matter treated as universal" (*Metaph.*Z 10, 1035b 29-30; Oxford tr.), "the compound of both taken universally" (11, 1037a 6-7). All the universals that are predicated of sensible things will be composites or compounds of that type. In its regularly used sense, accordingly, the universal is a "concrete whole."

Finally, what about Ross's suggestion that "universal" in the present context means a generic nature, instead of the "true nature" of the universal that appears in the specific constitution of things?[11] At one place in the *Metaphysics* (H 1,1042a 13-15) "universal" is in fact contrasted with genus. There it seems quite clearly taken in the sense of the specific nature in its relation to singulars. But does this imply at all that the generic universals are not universals in the true sense? If the universals were principles, Aristotle (*Metaph.* B 3, 998b 17-19) argues, the highest genera would fill this role. In Mure's translation of the *Posterior Analytics* (II, 19, 100a 16-b 3), accordingly, the specific nature "man" is a "rudimentary universal," while the widest of the generic natures are the "true universals." The translation runs: "for though the act of sense-perception is of the particular, its content is universal—is man, for example, not the man Callias. A fresh stand is made among these rudimentary universals, and the process does not cease until the indivisible concepts, the true universals, are established: e.g., such and such a species of animal is a step towards a further generalization." In a note to the translation Mure states that the highest genera, the categories, are *"par excellence* universal" (n. 2).

Both these translators are sufficiently familiar with the varying moods of the Aristotelian text, so both should be right even when writing verbally opposite statements. Actually, both are right, as far as the positive side of their views enters into question. In the Greek text, the specific and the generic traits are alike called "universal."[12] No adjective is added in either case to distinguish what would be a "rudimentary" universal from a "true" universal. Species and genera both seem regarded as universal in the full sense of the term. In the above text from the *Posterior Analytics*, the specific nature that is perceived in the individual man is the starting point of the process. The next step is the establishing of the genus "animal," and so on in ascending scale until the highest genus is reached. According to this way of regarding the process of cognition, the object is first known in its specific nature and then gradually in its more generic traits. On the other hand, the Greek commentators[13] were inclined to interpret in the opposite direction the process signalized in the opening chapter of the *Physics*. The confused object initially known appeared in its more generic traits, as an object at a distance will first appear as a body, then as something alive, and then as a man. In either case, however, the notion of universality seems to be fully satisfied. Both the generic and the specific natures are predicated of subjects and belong in these subjects as identical with each of them.

What, then, is the exact sense of "universal" in the opening passage of the *Physics*? The context describes it as a "whole," a whole that contains a number of things as its parts. In it the parts are confused (συγκεχυμένα). What are these parts? Whatever they are, they will function as the καθ ἕκαστα towards which the process of knowledge advances. What is meant by parts in this context, accordingly, should provide the key to the meaning of "universal" as it is used in the present passage.

III

The usual meaning of καθ' ἕκαστον and ἕκαστα throughout the Aristotelian corpus is the singular sensible thing, or the particular event. In the *Categories* (2a 34-b 5) it is the logically primary substance, the individual that is predicted of nothing else while all the rest are predicated of it. In the *Metaphysics* (A 1,981a 15-24) it is the singular thing that one encounters in sensible experience, the particular compound that is brought into being or destroyed in the visible and tangible world. In the *Nicomachean Ethics* (VI 8-9, 1142a 14-1143b 5) it is the variable fact about which one may deliberate and with which moral life is concerned. This regular use of the term in logical, metaphysical, and ethical contexts is too familiar to readers of the Aristotelian treatises to require the citation of any more detailed instances.

The term, however, is also used at times to signify the different species of which a generic nature is predicated. In the *Posterior Analytics* (I. 5,

74a 25-30) it means the equilateral, scalene, and isosceles types that exhibit the general nature of a triangle. In a word, it stands for the different species of triangle.[14] It expresses something that is universal as a species, and not just a singular thing. It is meant in this sense when Aristotle (*An. Post.* II. 13, 97b 28) says that the καθ' ἕκαστον is more easily defined than the universal. In the meaning of an individual sensible thing it would not be definable at all (*Metaph.* Z 10, 1036a 2-5). The conclusion drawn is that one should proceed from the particulars to the universal.[15] In wording, this is just the opposite of the sentence in the opening chapter of the *Physics*. But the "particulars" from which the procedure here commences are clearly enough the lowest species. From them one goes on to the genera.

This use of the term shows that it may mean something universal. The term is therefore not restricted to the singular individual. In the opening chapter of the *Physics*, accordingly, there need be no absolute requirement for it to mean the particular sensible things. With this inhibition removed, one may approach the illustrations brought forward by Aristotle to clarify its meaning in the present context. The illustrations used (*Phys.* I. 1, 184b 10-14) are two. The first is that of a word compared with a definition. The word "circle," for instance, signifies an undifferentiated whole. The definition, on the other hand, divides the whole into its particular components (διαιπεῖ εἰς τὰ καθ' ἕκαστα—b 12). The second illustration is that children first call all men fathers and women mothers, but later distinguish the one from the other.

What does the first of these illustrations establish? The particular components into which the definition expressly divides its objects are clearly enough the genus and the specific differentia. In the case of a circle these would be "plane figure" and "with every point on its circumference equidistant from a given point."[16] The genus and the differentia are the καθ' ἕκαστα that the definition distinguishes separately in the whole signified by the word "circle."[17] The two aspects are fused together in the object expressed by the single word. They are divided from each other and expressed in separate notions by the definition. They are both contained in a confused manner in the one notion "circle," as expressed by the single word. The notion "circle" is immediately accessible to people in general.[18] It can serve as a starting point. The mathematical definition of a circle is not immediately known. But it can be reached through a study of what is known under the notion "circle." In this way one proceeds from what is meant by the word to the components that are expressed in distinct fashion by the definition.

Does the illustation, interpreted in what seems its obvious meaning, serve the purpose for which it was introduced? The overall purpose is to explain that natural philosophy, like any other science, has to proceed from what is more knowable in respect of human cognition to principles and causes and elements that are more knowable in themselves but are not immediately knowable to men. In natural philosophy these are found to be the entirely formless matter and the first form received by it. The matter and the form are contained in the sensible things that human cognition first attains. They are fused together physically in the sensible thing, just as in the logical order genus and differentia are fused together in the definition. From a study of the originally known concrete whole they are reached and expressed in separate notions through the procedure of natural philosophy. Just as the form is the actuation of the matter, moreover, so is the differentia the actuation of the genus (*Metaph.* H 6, 1045a 23-35). The analysis of definition into genus and differentia is the fact used in the *Metaphysics* (Z 12, 1037b 8-1038a 35) as an approach to the study of the composition of matter and form in sensible substances, and the problem dealt with in their regard is characterized (b 9-10) as helpful for the inquiries about substance. In the meaning of a concrete whole analyzed into its logical elements, therefore, the illustration of the word and the definition is quite what should be expected in Aristotle as an approach to the analysis of a physical whole into elements or principles or causes.

When a parallel passage has been found that seems to settle the question, however, it may still have to face objections from leading authorities. Ross (*Aristotle's Physics,* pp. 457-58), in fact, states that the present interpretation "seems impossible." Ross (p. 457), as already noted, identifies the "universal" in this context as generic knowledge, for instance the knowledge of something as an "animal."- The procedure, then, would be from the general characteristic as the starting point to the specific traits as the principles or elements, for example, from "animal" to "horse" or "cow." In this understanding of the procedure, the genus cannot be one of the elements reached by the scientific inquiry. As the starting point, it would be expressly contrasted with the elements that are reached as a goal. Hence, from Ross's viewpoint, it seems impossible for the elements in the illustration to be the genus and the differentia that make up the definition.

What alternative does Ross offer? He acknowledges (ibid) that the analysis of a genus into its species will not do here. But, he claims, the distinguishing of the various senses of an ambiguous term will serve the present purpose, and will provide the only interpretation able "to illustrate, even remotely, what it is put forward as illustrating, viz., the transition from the recognition of the generic nature of an object to the recognition of its specific nature" (p. 458). "Circle" in Aristotle is in fact an ambiguous term. Besides a geometrical circle it is also used for an epic cycle (*An. Post.* I. 12, 77b 33), and had still other meanings in everyday speech. Tannery's (*art. cit.,* p. 471, n. 5) suggestion that the καθ' ἔκαστα distinguished by the definition are the circumference of the circle and surface limited by the cirumference, both referred to indifferently in Greek mathematics by the word "circle," seems to be in essentials the same as that of Ross.

No one need question the admission that this interpretation is indeed remote. But does any immediate problem about the ambiguous use of terms really enter the consideration here? Where such a problem has an essential bearing up on his theme, Aristotle is usually not slow in bringing it to the fore. That he should use definition to illustrate his point, and without any warning understand by it solely the definition of ambiguous terms, does seem farfetched. It is not paralleled in Aristotle's use of the analysis of definition in the *Metaphysics* (Z 12) as an approach to the analysis of sensible things into matter and form. Moreover, the definition of an ambiguous term, insofar as it can have a definition, does not in fact distinguish its various senses, any more than the definition of a genus distinguishes its various species. A definition of "healthy," or "medical," or "good," would merely provide a vague description that could extend to all the various senses. It would not distinguish the meaning that "healthy" has when applied to food from the meaning it has when applied to color. One may reject, correctly, the possibility of interpreting the illustration in the sense of the division of a genus into its species; but by the same token a division into the various meanings of an ambiguous term becomes inapplicable.

The second illustration is that children at first call all men fathers and all women mothers, and only later distinguish other men from their fathers and other women from their mothers. The relation between these respective people parallels the relation between the components of a definition in the first illustration. "Man" and "woman" are more general, "father" and "mother" are more specific. Does the illustration mean, however, that a child commences with a specific knowledge of his father as father, and wrongly applies that knowledge in its fullness to men in general? Fourth-century Greek children may have been precocious. But to endow their first impressions with full specific knowledge of what it means to be a father, is rather overdoing things. Does the illustration mean, then, that they first have the general impression "man" and express this incorrectly by the word "father," getting only later the specific notion to which the word "father" is restricted?

In the rout simile at the end of the *Posterior Analytics* (II. 19, 100b1-3), the procedure of human knowledge is clearly taken to be from the specific nature "man" through the generic nature "animal" to the still higher genera, until the highest genus of all, the category, is reached. In one of a number of indiscriminate singulars that appear before human sensation the notion "man" is grasped, and then the other singulars are aligned with it one after another until the species is sufficiently established in one's cognition. In a further step men are viewed in a panorama with horses, cows, dogs, cats, and so on, and in a corresponding way the genus "animal" is reached. Animals are viewed along with plants in a still wider picture, and the notion "something living" is attained as a broader generic nature. The process continues until the highest genus, "substance," is isolated. This is the way the Porphyrian tree has been climbed by generations of students of Aristotelian logic from Boethius on. On the other hand, the familiar illustration used by the Greek commentators[19] went in the opposite direction. In seeing a distant object, one recognized it first as a body. Then on getting closer to it one saw that it was something alive. On still greater proximity one realized that it was a man, and finally that it was the individual Socrates or Alcibiades. The direction was from genera to species and singulars.

Each of the two ways of proceeding seems to have its legitimate place. From the logician's viewpoint, the singulars are first grouped into species, and then the species into genera, until the highest genus is reached. Epistemologically, however, a thing seems known first under the vaguest general notion of "something," and then its distinguishing traits are gradually seen as in the case of the object first perceived at a distance. Which of the two viewpoints is applicable here? Or are both on the same footing, as far as the present illustration is concerned?

The text reads as though "the one and the other" or "each of the two" (ἑκάτερον) into which the originally known confused whole is distinguished must be "men and fathers" or "women and mothers." Neither the more specific notion "fathers" nor the more generic notion "men" seems to be the concrete whole that is first known. They seem represented as concepts distinct from each other, the καθ᾽ ἕκαστα that emerge from a differentiating knowledge of the objects initially grasped through sensation. The starting point is neither the one nor the other as distinct notions, but rather a vague object in which both are fused and neither is differentiated. Whether the child first becomes accustomed to call the vaguely known object "Dad" or "man" or any other name, is beside the point. It is known first as a confused whole, and only later are the concepts of it as "father" and as "man" differentiated.

Interpreted in this way, the second illustration continues to press home the point made by the first. The καθ' ἕκαστα are the distinct generic and specific notions that were not differentiated in the initially known whole. καθ' ἕκαστα here cannot mean singular sensible things, but universal notions that set up the species and genera. The confusedly known object that serves as the starting point is, however, universal in regard to them all. It contains them by being predicable of each, for each of the components is a "known object" or "something," or whatever one wishes to call the initially grasped whole in all its vagueness. With each of them it is identical, one by one, while remaining a unitary notion in itself. In this way it fully and univocally satisfies the Aristotelian requirements for universality, namely as containing "many things by being predicated of each, and by all of them . . . being severely one single thing" (*Metaph.*, Δ 26, 1023b 30-31). The starting point, accordingly, is neither the lowest species nor the highest genus, but an as yet undifferentiated object that is universal to both. It may therefore be referred to simply as "the universal," while the genera, differentiae, and species contained under it may be called without hesitation its καθ' ἕκαστα.

IV

What Aristotle has been saying, then, is that the confused object initially known in sensation is universal in regard to its parts or components, and that from it one proceeds to the distinct knowledge of the components. That is what he says. But what does it mean, philosophically, in the present context? Sometimes one can determine satisfactorily enough what a Greek thinker is saying, and still encounter difficulty in assessing its correct philosophical meaning. In the opening chapter of the *Physics*, what is the exact bearing of the statement that one must proceed from the universals to their distinct components? It is brought forward as an introduction to a natural philosophy that proceeds from concrete sensible things to the matter and form that are principles or causes or elements of these things. Is it merely a comparison? Does it just mean that as in the case of a universal you analyze a whole into its parts, so in natural philosophy you analyze the initially known sensible concretion into its distinct components?

This may possibly be all the text asserts. The view, however, offers difficulties, plausible as it may appear at first sight. The notion of proceeding from the universal to its components is not introduced as a comparison, but as a consequence. It is introduced by διό—wherefore. *Because* we first know concretions, we have to proceed from universals. Such is the sequence of thought. It seems to mean that the concretions from which the reasoning of natural philosophy commences will somehow remain universal in regard to their principles and elements. Hence would arise the necessity of the elaborate explanation through the examples of the name and the definition, the fathers and mothers and the men and women.

Secondly, the principles reached by the procedure in natural philosophy have to be themselves more knowable than the concretions from which the procedure started. This requirement is stated expressly in the opening chapter of the *Physics*. The principles reached by the procedure are formless matter and its first form. But in itself the matter is unknowable (*Metaph.* Z 10, 1036a 8-9). As a principle for scientific knowledge of sensible things it will have to appear in a way that renders it more knowable than the observable things themselves. This cannot be the way in which it is present in the singular thing, where, taken apart from the form, it manifests no actuality or determination whatsoever.[20] Yet it is knowable by analogy (*Phys.* I. 7, 191a 7-12). As the bronze is to the statue and the wood to the bed, so is it to the substantial actuality of any body. What does this mean? It means that the basic concept upon which the concept of formless matter is elaborated, is the concept of a body, of the concretion originally known in sensation. It is the universal and vague concept of something corporeal. In this way the subject that receives the substantial form is represented as a corporeal substrate with the added negation that it lacks all the determinations given by the categories. The notion is formed by taking the universal concept of "substrate" as seen in things like a bed or a statue, and by adding to that basic concept the privation of any formal characteristic. In this way it remains basically the concept of a body, the concept of the concretion that was first known in sensation. In regard to it the concept of the concretion remains universal. The basic substrate of bodies is conceived as something corporeal. But it itself, as one of the καθ' έκαστα that come under this universal, is likewise represented in the status of a universal. As universal it can serve as a principle for scientific knowledge. It can be used universally as a principle for understanding all bodies. From this viewpoint it is more knowable in itself than the bodies it serves to explain, even though those bodies are more knowable to us.

The same considerations hold correspondingly for the formal principle of sensible things. It cannot be represented just in itself. Even though it is contrasted with matter, it has to be represented as something material. As the shape of the statue is related to the bronze and the shape of a bed to the wood, so the intelligible content of a substance is represented in relation to the formless matter that multiplies it in the many individuals of a species. The concept is basically that of shaped or formed body, with the negation of all substrate added as its distinguishing feature. The concept of something corporeal remains basic to it. The notion of the object originally known in sensation functions as a universal in regard to the form as well as the matter, and from an epistemological viewpoint subsumes both under itself.

Viewed in this perspective, *both* the principles that are reached by the analysis of sensible things in natural philosophy come under the object initially known in sensation, as under a universal. Aristotle is saying that the procedure of natural philosophy is from bodies as known universally in ordinary sensation to principles that are conceived and known under further determinations of the original universal concept. One is proceeding from the first known universal to a distinct cognition of notions that come under it but are as yet undifferentiated in it, somewhat as the definition of a circle differentiates the notions signified confusedly by the word "circle" and as children afterwards distinguish the notions of "father" and "man" that were undifferentiated in their earlier concept. What Aristotle has in mind, if the present interpretation is correct, is that the confused object first grasped in sensation remains universal in regard to all further knowledge. The origin of all human knowledge in sensation would mean, then, that all other objects have to be known basically in terms of concrete sensible things, with the necessary refinements and negations added through judgments and the conclusions of reasoning processes. This would safeguard the Aristotelian conception of scientific knowledge from any atomism in the epistemological sense. The ultimate principles reached by the scientific procedure do not have to be given the status of individually known building blocks from which the universe is to be constructed. Rather, any "correspondence theory" of truth that one might wish to attribute to Aristotle[21] would have to refrain carefully from placing a photographic correspondence between the ultimate principles themselves and the concepts by which they are known. The concepts are not at all immediate replicas of them, but are elaborations of the confused object originally known in sensation and contained under it as under a universal.

V

This interpretation gives the "universal" in the opening passage of the *Physics* the regular and univocal meaning that it has elsewhere in Aristotle. It also finds considerable importance in the use of the notion for the explanation of philosophical procedure at the beginning of natural philosophy, an importance that justifies the space given it in the condensed summary of scientific method. As the most pertinent overall result, however, it shows why the mind cannot attain in simple apprehension any concept that is common to corporeal and incorporeal things. The first confused notion for human cognition is that of "something sensible." This functions as a universal in the Aristotelian noetic for all further cognition. It brings under its scope every other concept, including those of incorporeal objects. It is the all-pervading notion that is always basic, and that is elaborated and build upon in one way or another to construct the concepts of formless matter, of substantial form, of accidents, and of spiritual beings. It does not allow any notion that extends beyond the sensible to be seen immediately in the objects directly presented to human cognition. Rather, it requires a process of judgment and reasoning to arrive at concepts of immaterial substance and immaterial being, or at concepts that are common to both the material and immaterial orders. It will help to explain why so many able thinkers in course of Western thought have not been able to recognize any kind of being except the sensible, and why a subject for the science of metaphysics has proven a stumbling block to them throughout the centuries.

In the Aristotelian noetic, then, the subject of metaphysics is not something that is offered immediately to men's intellects. It is something that has to be reached by a difficult reasoning process. For Aristotle himself the reasoning was from sensibly observed motion to the entirely separate or supersensible movents. To take natures found in sensible things and hypostatize them as separate, appeared to him to be the fault of the Platonic procedure and to result in a useless duplication of sensible reality. But even where the subject of metaphysics is held to be common being, as in St. Thomas Aquinas, the universality of the sensible in the knowing process is by no means eliminated. Existence, by actuating a nature other than itself, constitutes common being, the subject of metaphysics. This existence is indeed known in every judgment, but not as something that transcends the sensible world. The subject that it constitutes for intellectual consideration does not appear immediately as transcendentally common being. Rather, the notion is of something sensible, and the difficult process of demonstrating a foundation for the judgment that separates substance and being from the sensible still lies ahead. There is here no immediately known concept that escapes the universality that sensible nature exercises in regard to human cognition.

It may seem a bit hazardous to draw these far-reaching conclusions from a lone text of Aristotle. Yet the text occurs in a passage that summarizes Aristotle's overall conception of scientific method. Accordingly it lends itself in full to interpretation through other texts scattered throughout the Aristotelian corpus, in line with Trendelenburg's well-known norm of *Aristoteles ex Aristotele*. The passage itself is not self-explanatory. It caused trouble for the Greek commentators, and has continued to puzzle modern writers. Simplicius, apparently none too satisfied, concluded his own discussion of it with the remark: "If anyone can give a more convincing account of it, let him please do so."[22] The challenge has remained open. If interpreted as above, in the light of the other relevant Aristotelian tenets, it gives a much sharper meaning to the origin of all human cognition in sensible things.

7. Aristotle—Cognition a Way of Being

I

Explanation of cognition as a special way of being appears in Aristotle without traceable ancestry. Earlier, in Parmenides (*Fr.* 16; DK, 28B) and in Empedocles (*Fr.* 108; DK, 31B), the notion that cognition is somehow equated with the physical constitution of the knower at any given moment had been put forward. But the now rather enigmatic fragments of those thinkers fail to show how this notion foreshadowed any new kind of being over and above the physical. In fact, would it not seem incongruous to use the term "being" for something proposed by them in terms of change?

In Aristotle, on the other hand, a truly remarkable tenet in this regard finds definite articulation. To perceive or to know means that the cognitive agent has become and is something other than what he is physically. The tenet is expressed succinctly in the quite terse statement: " . . . the soul is in a way all existing things; for existing things are either sensible or thinkable, and knowledge is in a way what is knowable, and sensation is in a way what is sensible."[1]

What does this imply? The assertion covers all cognition, both perception and thought. In either case, according to the description, the soul *is* the thing attained in the cognition. The things it can be through cognition are unlimited in number. The range is "all existing things." But a qualification is added. The soul is all things "in a way." What is that way? The way is immediately characterized in terms of potentiality: "Within the soul the faculties of knowledge and sensation are *potentially* these objects, the one what is knowable, the other what is sensible" (*De An.,* III 8, 431b26-28; Oxford trans.).

This is still none too enlightening, even though the general background is made possible by Aristotle's radically innovative conceptions of actuality and potentiality. The assertions here are expressly (431b20-21) intended to recapitulate what had already been established in the *De Anima* about the soul. But how is the term "soul" being used in this context? It is obviously standing as a shorthand expression for the cognitive or appetitive agent. Aristotle had noted that "it is doubtless better to avoid saying that the soul pities or learns or thinks, and rather to say that it is the man who does this with his soul."² Yet, while acknowledging the nuance, Aristotle continues in the easier way of using the term "soul" to designate the agent, even though he had defined soul very carefully as an actuality, the first actuality of a natural organic body.³ This status of soul as "first" actuality leaves open to it the role of potentiality to something further, to habitual as well as to actual cognition (*De An.*, II 1,412a19-413a3). The soul accordingly continues to actualize the body at times when one is not perceiving or thinking. In this way its basic being is physical and stable, allowing "soul" to stand in shorthand parlance for the abiding cognitive agent that functions throughout a lifetime of changing perception and thought.

Soul is in fact described in the opening chapter of the second book of the *De Anima* in the same terms used to explain the physical composite of matter and form in the *Physics* and in the central books of the *Metaphysics*. Basically, then, it is assigned a physical way of being that belongs in stable fashion to itself alone and that differs from the being of any other thing attained by it in cognition. When in cognition it becomes and is the thing it knows or perceives, it retains intact its basic physical being. Physically, it has not become anything else. In its physical being it remains itself only.

But how does the cognitive potentiality of the soul for being all things differ from the ordinary physical potentiality of a thing for becoming something else, for instance from the potentiality of wood for becoming ashes?

In the actuality of thought or perception, the cognitive agent is found by Aristotle to be identical with the object, even though not identical with it previous to the act of cognition. The agent was only able to be so:

> Actual knowledge is identical with its object: potential knowledge in the individual is in time prior to actual knowledge but in the universe it has no priority even in time; for all things that come into being arise from what actually is. In the case of sense clearly the sensitive faculty already was potentially what the object makes it to be actually; the faculty is not affected or altered. This therefore must be a different kind from movement; . . ."⁴

When "knowledge" or "the faculty" is regarded in this passage as being made identical with the object, the same type of shorthand as just noticed is in play. In the Aristotelian framework an accident such as a faculty or an action cannot exist in itself, or do or undergo anything as an independent subject. It is always the substance that exists and acts and undergoes in the way it is modified by the accident. Less even than the soul could the thought or the faculty, strictly speaking, become or be the object. Always the cognitive agent, in the sense of the man or animal, is really meant when this shorthand is used. In texts like the above the perceptive or knowing subject is envisaged as a composite of matter and form existing in a physical way before the act of cognition. The cognitive agent is not as yet in any actual way the object known. But in the actuality of cognition, through the causal influence of another agent acting upon him, as well as through his own activity, the cognitive agent becomes and is an object that is other than himself, without ceasing physically to be his own self. This is quite obviously the implication of the above text.

In being aware of the other thing, the cognitive agent is thereby aware also of himself (*De An.,* III 4,429b5-10; 430a2-3). This is not surprising, if the identity of agent and object in the actuality of cognition is taken seriously. The two have become and are identical. So to know the one is *ipso facto* to know the other. Yet an order is observed. Only through knowing something else is the cognitive agent able to become aware of himself, unless the agent is a form separate from matter.[5] In a man, who is a composite, the cognition will be directly of the object with which he becomes identified, and only concomitantly of himself on account of that identity.

II

Percipient and thing perceived, knower and thing known, are accordingly seen by Aristotle to be identical in the actuality of cognition, even though they need not be identical outside that actuality. The identity, in a word, is not physical. Yet it is brought about by an efficient cause. This tenet emerges with sufficient clarity from the Aristotelian texts. In the act of cognition the cognitive agent becomes and is a thing that is physically other than himself. But, with Aristotle, becoming something is the result of efficient causality. It arises from the activity of agent upon patient. Becoming something else in the actuality of cognition is not at all regarded as an exception. In the text quoted above (n. 4) the general principle was in fact applied: "all things that come into being arise from what actually is." Yet in this case the becoming is recognized as a kind different from the physical type, which takes place through movement. It does not consist in an alteration or a modification of the faculty. It is a different type of coming into being.

The different kind of becoming that is meant is easily recognized, no matter how difficult it may be to explain. When something is heated, an agent that is actually hot causes efficiently the accidental form of heat in the patient. The patient becomes hot. When a fence is painted green, the painter brings it into a new accidental form. It becomes green. When animals engender a new individual in their species, they actualize matter with the most basic kind of form, form in the category of substance. The matter becomes physically an animal. But when you see something green you do not become green in the way a fence does. When you look at an elephant or a rattlesnake, you are not classed as a member of either of their species. Quite understandably Aristotle can note that what is involved here is a kind of becoming different from physical change, different from movement.

But any kind of change or becoming, according to the overall Aristotelian conception of change, means that a subject is brought from one form to another (*Phys.*, I 7, 189b30-191a22). How does this apply to the special kind of becoming that is found in cognition? The explanation given somewhat cryptically in the *De Anima* is that here the reception of the form takes place "without the matter." In regard to perception the text states:

> But universally for every sense it is to be understood that the sense is the recipient of the sensible forms without the matter, just as the wax receives the design of the signet ring without the iron or the gold . . . . Also in similar fashion the perception of each thing is undergoing the causality of the thing that has color or flavor or sound, yet not in the way this is designated the individual thing in those classes, but insofar as it is of this quality and in the required proportion.[6]

The illustration here may be expected to limp considerably. It is an instance of causality in the ordinary physical way, in which the smooth surface of the wax is changed into the design of the signet ring. It occurs just the way any other change of shape or figure takes place, namely through movement. Yet it is meant to illustrate a kind of actualization different from movement, a type of change in which the recipient himself "is not affected or altered" (*supra,*n.4). The key to the understanding of the comparison seems to be the reception of form "without the matter." What can that mean? Could the matter intended merely be the matter present in the agent? In every physical change the agent retains its own matter. The agent brings about the new form in the patient without thereby transmitting the matter from its own constitution. The form of heat is effected in the thing being heated, but without reception of the agent's matter. In procreation the specific form present in the parents is brought about in the offspring without transmission of the physical matter actualized by it in themselves. Reception of a form without the matter of the agent is common to all change, and could not play the role of differentiating factor for this new type. The gold and the iron are indeed mentioned expressly as the matter without which the form is received. But does this not illustrate something much deeper, if it is to lead up to a type of cognition, while the material reception of it brings a stone into being in the physical world. The form in each case makes the recipient be respectively what it is.

In this regard, however, Aristotle is insistent that "it is not the stone which is present in the soul but its form" (*De An.*, III 8, 431b29-432a1; Oxford trans.). The presence in the soul meant here is material, as emerges from what immediately follows: ". . . the soul is analogous to the hand; for as the hand is a tool of tools, so the mind is the form of forms and the sense the form of sensible things.[9] The framework of this reasoning is that of efficient causality through the use of instruments. By means of a causal chain the distant sensible thing acts upon the percipient.[10] Today there should be little difficulty in understanding what is at issue in this type of causality. From a television camera the electronic signals are beamed to a satellite and bounced back to another continent. Panorama with color is found only at the source and on the screen, and not in the signals along the thousands of intervening miles. Yet the signals, when received by the television set, program it into reproducing by its own activity the original colored scene. The role exercised by the signals is instrumental. They are not seen themselves, but they determine the television apparatus to produce the picture on the screen. Correspondingly in Aristotle the role of the received forms as real instruments is to determine the cognitive agent to a particular type of activity, a type in which the agent becomes and is cognitively the thing from which the form was received. The reception of the form is not immediately observable. It is only inferred through philosophical reasoning. What is immediately perceived or known is the thing itself.

The illustration by the television example limps of course just as much as does Aristotle's simile of seal and wax. The picture on the television screen is but a replica, another instantiation, of the panorama. Cognitional activity is not a process of photographing or of recording. In it the same individual, and not a replica or a record, becomes one with the cognitive agent in the actuality of perceiving or knowing. The radical difference between physical reception and cognitive reception of form necessarily escapes both illustrations. But the television comparison does serve to emphasize the role of the received form as a "tool." The mind is a form that makes use of the received forms as instruments for cognition, and correspondingly the sense uses the forms of sensible things. In that way Aristotle is effectively protected against any future caricature of his views as though they meant that a colored image somehow jumps out of the distant sensible object and is transported holus-bolus across the intervening media. Rather, this aspect of the cognitive process is no more difficult to grasp than is the activity of any physical agent upon a distant object through the instrumentality of a causal chain. It evokes the physical action in which perception takes place.

It is true, of course, that the form received as an instrument provides all the perceptible and knowable content in the object attained in the cognition, since for Aristotle the matter is unknowable as such. Matter, as potentiality, lacks the actuality required for an object of cognition. But that formal content is directly perceived and known only insofar as it is actualizing the matter of the object, and not insofar as it is actualizing the cognitive agent. There is always a concomitant self-awareness on the part of the agent, and through the elaborate reasoning of the *De Anima* the conclusion is drawn that the form of the object is also actualizing cognitively the percipient or the knower. But the direct awareness is of the object itself. In this activity the cognitive agent becomes and is one thing after another, justifying thereby the succinct Aristotelian assertion that the soul is in a way all things.

III

Such is the Aristotelian notion of cognition, as far as can be gathered from the brief extant texts. What is to be thought of it? Certainly it is expressed in staccato fashion. It requires much filling in at every point. This may help to substantiate Jaeger's theory that the Aristotelian treatises are school *logoi* meant to provide starting points for development in lively oral discussion. That development has its risks when undertaken today, at the present distance of time and culture from the fourth century B.C. What has just been discussed is open to controversy all along the line. But on the opposite side of the ledger this situation has its advantages. It keeps one from regarding the Aristotelian texts as deposits of ready-made doctrine, and casts them rather in their authentic role of insights meant to inspire the hearer or reader to do his own thinking.

In this regard one may note that the whole Aristotelian reasoning about cognition is based upon the tenet of the unity of knower and known in the actuality of cognition. No reasoning or attempt at proof is offered for this tenet. It seems to be accepted on what is stronger than proof and is the source of proof, namely immediate intuition. If one can accept this insight as a primitive intuition, the Aristotelian reasoning that explains how the identity comes about is cogent in its own metaphysical setting. The reasoning allows the cognitive agent to be the same individually as the thing known, and not just specifically as in photography or recording or in the simile of the design on wax and signet ring. But the whole epistemological structure rests upon one's acceptance of the cognitional union of knower and known as an immediate indemonstrable intuition.

If accepted, this explanation of cognition in terms of being offers adequate protection against a dogma that has plagued western philosophy since the time of Descartes, namely that nothing can be more present to mind than mind itself and its own ideas. The Aristotelian conception of awareness means that what the mind is cognitionally, is first and foremost and directly the external (*De An.,* II 5,417b20-21) sensible object. Only concomitantly and in virtue of being the external thing cognitionally, can the mind, as far as cognition is concerned, be itself. Epistemologically the sensible thing, as a substance in itself, comes first.[11]

This conception needs much greater development if it is to play its role successfully. It received significant treatment in the middle ages, where from Avicenna on there was no hesitation in asserting that the sensible thing exists cognitionally in the mind. A new viewpoint of existence gave the epistemological insights new development. In Aquinas this development reached a high point through explanation of existence as the actuality of every nature yet different from the nature itself. The same nature could readily be seen as open to two different ways of existing, namely in itself and in the mind. Today the Aristotelian conception of awareness still offers interesting possibilities for further development.

8. Aristotelian Soul as Cognitive of Sensibles, Intelligibles, and Self

With requisite clarity the soul is located by Aristotle (*De An.*, II 1, 412a6-28) in the basic category of substance. Still more precisely it is explained by him as a physical body's primary form or perfection (*eidos, entelecheia*-- a10;cf. 2,414a14-28). In man it is in this way "that by which we primarily live, perceive and think" (414a12-13). The soul accordingly is for Aristotle a real physical form. Obviously in this context the term "physical" is taken in the sense it has in his pholosophy of nature (e.g.,*Ph.,*II 1,193a33; 2,193b32). The soul as he conceives it is in consequence something that belongs to a composite. It itself is not a body, but is something that belongs to a body (*De An.,*II 2,414a21-22).

The composite, of which the soul is the primary perfection, is of course able to receive secondary perfections such as waking and sleeping (2,412a23-26), organic structure (b1-16), health and habitual knowledge (414a8-12; cf.III 4,429b5-9; *EN*, II 1,1103a32-b23), along with modifications such as heat and cold (*De An.,*II 12,424a32-b1). All these secondary perfections actuate the soul in its real mobile life. Consequently they are to be assessed in accord with the constitution of things subject to generation and change, as carefully discussed in the *Physics* (I 7,191a3-12). The thing's matter can lose one form and take on another. The model is the reception of the statue's form by the bronze or of the form of a bed by the wood. For double assurance of clarity today, the latter example may easily be spelled out in currently familiar details. The wood had first received the form of rough, standard sized lumber. Under the skilful activity of the cabinetmaker, it loses the standard shape of boards and acquires the artistic contours of a bed.

The concern of the present study bears on the activities of perceiving and knowing. The soul, as noted above, is "that by which we primarily . . . perceive and think." In both operations there is awareness of other objects and of self. In each of them reception of form (*De An.,* II 12,424a18; III 4, 429a15-16) is involved. The reception of a sensible form, however , may take place in two ways each contrasted with the other from the view point of relation to matter.[1] In the non-cognitive reception of heat or cold the change is described by Aristotle, literally and awkwardly translated, as undergone "with the matter" (II 12,424b3). In any sensation, on the other hand, the form of the sensible object is received "without the matter' (a18-19)

Exactly what does the contrast in reception of forms *with* the matter and *without* the matter mean? In the context here the overall import of the contrast is clear beyond doubt. It carries the weight of the distinction between cognitional and non-cognitional reception of form. Heat in being received as a form not only accelerates the movements of the molecules and modifies the temperature but also is *felt* by the hand. The two actuations occur simultaneously. Yet there is a crucial difference between being warmed and feeling warm. The plant is just made warm. The hand, too, is made warm. But unlike the plant it feels the warmth besides. Though the feeling will always have the accelarated molecular motion as concomitant, the distinction between the two types of reception stays firm. In plants and inanimate things the heat is received without any evidence that it is being felt, and the same Celsius degree of temperature is felt with different intensity by the same person at different times in accord with subjective conditions. The one type of reception may be called merely physical, and the other cognitional. At least this terminology seems to express in preliminary fashion the functional contrast between the two ways of receiving form.

The overall bearing of the contrast, then, is sufficiently pointed. But how does the phrasing "with the matter" and "without the matter" express the distinction as intended in the Aristotelian text just cited (supra.n.1). Each of the words has its problems. What sense do the prepositions "with" and "without" carry in the phrases? Is the signification merely concomitance, or does it involve instrumentality? Is the definite article correctly included in the English translation, and if so, what referent does it indicate? Further, does "matter" here mean physical matter, or is the term being used in an extended sense such as in the Aristotelian notion of "intellectual matter" (*Metaph.*,Z 11, 1036b35; cf. 10,1036a9-12; H 6,1045a33-35). "Matter" is certainly used by Aristotle in transferred meanings (see Bonitz, *Ind.Arist.*, 787a12-26), though with sensible matter as its basic signification. There is no difficulty in understanding that sensible matter such as wood or flesh is meant when the term designates the recipient of the new form in the case of something that is merely being warmed. But how can sensible matter be excluded in the case of the hand feeling the heat? As already noted, the physical change is here concomitant with the cognitional reception of the form. The physical matter is present throughout the sensation. It is not utterly excluded. Moreover, how can a subject that receives a form, even cognitionally, avoid being regarded as the recipient and thereby the matter that acquires the new form? The exclusion of matter seems to run violently counter to the Aristotelian principles that may be expected to apply in any case of change or reception of form. If a new form is at all received, is it not received into a subject? Is not the subject therefore functioning as the matter in the process? Does not the form, then, enter into composition with the recipient, giving rise to a third something and making this third thing the object of the cognition.?

The above questions are of prime interest to anyone approaching the Aristotelian text with epistemological interests today. Unfortunately no explicit answers to them are found in the treatises. The general principles of Aristotelian natural philosophy call for matter in the subject itself function as the matter receiving it. But likewise those principles demand matter in the agent that causes the sensation, for instance in the fire or the boiling water. The composite that possesses the form is what causes the warming (*Ph.*,VIII 5,257b9-10). Even to say that the soul grieves or rejoices or takes courage or fears, or that one's mind thinks or loves or hates or recalls, is but an abbreviated way of stating that the man does these by means of his soul or mind (*De An.*,I 4,408b1-29). Matter seems involved in every cognitive act performed by a man, as well as by every sensible agent that imparts the form. Is it then the matter of the thing perceived that is referred to in saying that merely physical reception of forms takes place with the matter, while cognitional reception takes place without the matter? Or is it the matter of the percipient? Or is the reference to matter in general, common to both and without definite location on either side? Here the Aristotelian text (II 12,424a19-21) in giving the example of ring, device and wax, would seem to indicate the matter of the ring that does the impressing. It is the matter of the ring that is not received, according to the example. But commentators have not always understood the text in exactly that way. As it stands it is open to different interpretations. The first and most extensive task of the present study will be to examine these interpretations against the background of Aristotle's general philosophical principles, and endeavor to see what light they throw on the meaning of the text.

What, then, is meant in this passage by reception "without the matter"?

II

The passage in question was intended by Aristotle to generalize his notion of what sense or sensation is. It reads in English:

By a 'sense' is meant what has the power of receiving into itself the sensible forms of things without the matter. This must be conceived of as taking place in the way in which a piece of wax takes on the impress of a signet-ring without the iron or gold; we say that what produces the impression is a signet of bronze or gold, but its particular metallic constitution makes no difference (*De An.*, II 12, 424a17-21; Oxford trans.).

In this assertion Aristotle illustrates the notion of "receiving . . . . without the matter" by the reception on wax of the device from the signet ring without the ring's iron or gold or bronze. Clearly enough the iron or gold or bronze is the matter to which reference is made. The device is its form, a form in the accidental order. The device stays with the wax, the iron or gold or bronze does not. As an illustration of the reception of form without matter, it is at least prima facie referring solely to the matter of the percipient, nor matter that is common to both. The matter meant is definitely the iron or gold or bronze located solely in the signet ring. The device is received without the matter it informed in the agent. What could be clearer in this illustration?

Nevertheless there are second thoughts. If only the agent's matter were meant, how would its exclusion illustrate any difference between cognitive and non-cognitive reception of forms? In every type of efficient causality observable in the universe does not the matter of the agent remain in the agent? It is not received by the patient. The matter of the carpenter does not pass over into the house he builds, nor does the matter that sustains the human form in the parents enter into the offspring. Yet the expression "without the matter" has to bear here the full burden of the distinction between cognitive and non-cognitive reception. To illustrate the point it must imply something more than merely receiving a form from the agent without receiving the agent's matter. Granting that the basic reference is somehow to the matter in the agent, one has to suspect that much more is involved by the term "matter" in this context.

Further, there is a definite indication that "matter" is not being taken in the phrase in a jejunely physical sense. The "matter" seems to mean the fully determined specific nature of the agent, as distinguished from the merely generic nature of a solid body. The "matter" that is not received is the specific nature of iron or gold or bronze. The generic nature of a solid body always accompanies the notion of a device, since an accident is inconceivable apart from the substance in which it inheres(*Cat.*, 1,1a24-25) and the substance required by a stable device is a solid body, whether iron or gold or bronze or wax. In this case, then, the distinction between matter and form is the distinction between a body specifically determined, such as gold, and the notion of body in general as determined by a definite accident such as a device. Here the reception of the form is indifferent to what the specific nature of the agent is. The agent impresses the form on the patient as the form of a solid body, and not as the form specifically of iron or gold or bronze.

One is tempted, however, to ask if precision of this kind is congenial to Aristotle. The answer has to be yes. It is used in the *Metaphysics*: "Of matter some is intelligible, some perceptible, and in a formula there is always an element of matter as well as one of actuality" (H6,1045 a33-35; Oxford trans.). The generic aspect is regarded as the matter, the differentia as its actuation. The last differentia, moreover, contains everything in the definition (Z 12,1038a19-20). The form is accordingly considered from this viewpoint as the whole of the thing, expressed by the differentia. The genus is treated of as though it had corresponding status in the order of potentiality, the order of matter. Aristotle's effort in the context is directed towards showing that they are not in reality two different things but only one. The doctrine, it is true, is not given in Aristotle the highly developed medieval contours of the composition of a whole with a whole.[2] But the essentials are there with sufficient clarity. Two separate notions of the same thing can be related as matter and form.

In one way, of course, the situation in *De Anima*, II 12, may appear as the reverse of that in *Metaphysics*, Z-H. In the *De Anima* text the specific nature of the iron or gold, as determined by the ultimate differentia, is what is left behind. It is regarded as the matter. The form is received without it. Only the generic notion of corporeal substance required by the accidental nature of the device accompanies the form as received by the wax. But the illustration comes into focus when one considers that the substance as a whole, in this case the iron or the gold, is the subject of the accidents and in that sense the matter in which they inhere and which they actuate. From that viewpoint, required here, the fully specific nature has the aspect of matter. But the specific nature of the iron or gold or bronze does not accompany it when it is impressed upon the wax. It is received without the specific nature of the agent. That would refine considerably the sense intended in the expression "receiving . . . without the matter."

This understanding of sensation as involving reception "without the matter" might suggest that the expression in *De Anima* II 12, bears rather on the doctrine of proper and common sensibles, shortly to follow in *De Anima* III, than on cognition in general. Each sense gives awareness of the same sensible thing under common and proper aspects. In these ways each sense grasps the whole thing without attaining the specific nature of the substance that serves as matter for the respective characteristics under which the particular sensations take place. Examples may be easily supplied. It is one and the same thing that is perceived by the hunter as first an object moving in the woods, then as something living, then as a man, and finally as Socrates. The same thing that is perceived through sight as a spoonful of white grains is specified to salt or to sugar by taste. Even though in *De Anima* II 12, the difference between feeling warm and being warmed is made to rest on the distinction of reception "without the matter" from reception "with the matter," the question still remains whether the distinction is meant to explain cognition in general or just the way in which a sense grasps a thing under a particular or common aspect.

The context in the *De Anima*, then, indicates that the "matter" referred to in the above expressions is the matter in the agent, e.g., the iron or the gold or the bronze. But it allows the notion to be understood in a highly refined way. How has this been interpreted by the commentators? Do their explanations support the more flexible notion of matter, and do they develop further latent possibilities in the phrase?

III

Our commentaries on the passage in *De Anima*, II 12, go back as far as Alexander of Aphrodisias, writing at the end of the second century or early in the third century A.D. In his own *De Anima*, a personal work, Alexander interprets the Aristotelian text as meaning that a sense in general is a faculty of the soul that is "through certain organs receptive of and discerning of the sensible forms apart from the matter underlying them."[3] The sentence as it stands alone can be read to mean by "the matter" either the matter underlying the sensible forms as they are found in the things outside the percipient, or as they are found in the activities of the sense organs. It could also mean that the reception and cognition take place in general apart from the order of matter. The preposition used by Alexander is *chôris*. It may express merely accompaniment as in the case of *aneu*, the preposition in the Aristotelian text. But it carries overtones of "separately from" or "independently of."

Alexander (p.60.6-62.1) himself, in the immediately following lines, keeps his attention focused on the matter in the sense organ. He emphasizes that in cognition the sentient powers are forms of the bodily organ, and that the sensation is in the organ not insofar as the organ is a body but insofar as it has a power of that kind.[4] He is looking towards the way sensation discerns sweet from white, and how the same sense discerns black from white at the same time. The same matter cannot receive contraries such as black and white simultaneously. The sense organs accordingly do not receive the qualities of the sensible thing as though the senses were matter for the reception, since sight does not become black or white in seeing these qualities.[5]

What Alexander understands by the matter that is excluded in the definition of sensation is in consequence the matter in the sense organ. He means apparently that sensation takes place "apart from" or "independently of" that physical matter. This is at first sight rather surprising, since in the Aristotelian example the matter indicated is clearly the bronze or gold or iron of the signet ring. However, Alexander's commentary here is not in the form of literal exegesis of the Aristotelian text. It is meant to give his own personal understanding of the doctrine in the passage. Granting that he understood Aristotle's example to indicate immediately the matter in the agent, one can see quite easily how he could take this to mean that cognition is concerned with form "apart from" matter, and accordingly concentrate, in his own thought, upon the way the form is received in the sense organ. It is a way different from physical change, since the recipient does not function as matter. Through the perception of whiteness, for example, sight does not play the role of a matter made white.

"Apart from the matter," then, means for Alexander that sensation is not a material modification of the sense organ. What is received without the matter of the sensible thing is received apart from composition with the sense organ. It is received not insofar as the sense organ is a body, but insofar as the sentient power is a *form*. This sounds quite like the notion that in cognition form is received not into matter but into form. At first hearing it may seem unaristotelian for sensation, even though for Aristotle (*De An.*, III 4,429a27-28) there is approval of the view that the soul is a "place of forms" in intellection, and (430a3-4) that in things "without matter" intellect and intelligible object are the same. Is a parallel tenet possible for sensation? If so, it might do away with the objection that every recipient functions as matter for the form it takes on. True, there is no mention of form receiving form in the text. Yet the way lies open for Alexander's interpretation, insofar as the form of the sensible thing may be regarded as functioning in cognition "without" the matter it actuated in the real world, and the form of the sense organ may be looked upon as receiving the new form from an outside agent. With Alexander's own reasoning the reception is seen in that way to be "apart from" the matter of the recipient. In any case, Alexander's point is that sensation is not a material reception of form by the *organ*.

This line of interpretation can be seen explicitly followed out in Themistius, in the fourth century A.D. Repeating much of Alexander's reasoning and some of his phraseology, Themistius in his *Paraphrasis* explains the Aristotelian phrase "without the matter" as meaning that only the qualities of the signet ring come through to the senses, and not the matter or subject (p.77.28-34). But he sees in this a further thrust, formulated much more clearly than it had been in Alexander. Here, in contrast to non-psychic motion, only the *form* of the agent moves the sense organ. In cutting or burning, on the contrary, it is the *composite* of matter and form, i.e., the knife or the fire, that causes the effect. Like Alexander, Themistius (p.77.34-78.10) emphasizes that the senses do not become matter for the sensible forms. The two ways of undergoing the activity of the agent differ greatly from each other. No matter is able to discern the form that is brought into being in the patient, since matter is something that lacks intelligence and is undiscerning and insensible. Different from the non-psychic reception of form by matter, sensation means that form grasps or apprehends form.[6]

For Themistius, consequently, the matter referred to in the Aristotelian phrase is first of all the matter in the agent, the matter of the thing that is perceived. But for him this involves a more important consideration. It means that only the form of the sensible object, and not the composite of matter and form, produces the cognitive effect in the percipient. In corresponding fashion, the form is not received into any matter, but is grasped solely by form. In neither agent nor recipient is there any cognitional functioning of matter. The crucial difference between cognitive and non-cognitive reception of form is seen first of all in the action of the agent through form alone and not as composite of form and matter. But it is also seen, as with Alexander, in the exclusion of a role for matter on the part of the patient in the reception. In a word, the Aristotelian expression is interpreted as setting aside the functioning of matter in both agent and patient. That is given as the reason why the activity is cognitive. All goes as though here form receives form instead of matter receiving form, and as though this immateriality is the charcteristic of cognition. But no attempt is made to show how Aristotelian composites can act and undergo through form alone.

About the second quarter of the sixth century A.D., Philoponus also made the Aristotelian phrase bear first upon the matter in the agent. The form is received in sensation without the sensible thing's matter. But he observes that this holds for all non-generative efficient causality. No patient at all receives the matter of the agent, but only its form. Yet here the reception has to be cognitional, an impression of the pure *logoi* of the sensible thing. The sense becomes what the sensible thing is, not through generation, nor as mirrors and substances for molding receive impressions, but in a way that gives awareness and discernment. This is according to form alone, not by way of composite, and is caused by the form only of the sensible thing.[7]

Philoponus, accordingly, continues the stress on the lack of matter in the functioning of both agent and patient in sensation. In the accompanying process of being warmed and the like, the composite of matter and form is functioning both in the sensible thing and in the sense organ. But the distinguishing characteristic of sensation requires something further. It is not sufficient that the form be received as an image on a mirror or as an impression on a plastic material. Rather, the form has to be received cognitively (pp. 437.20-21; 438.13). This seems to be defining cognition merely by cognition, unless Philoponus is assuming that Aristotle has elsewhere established a general doctrine that form existing or functioning apart from matter is by that very fact cognitive. Themistius (*De An.*, p. 78.10-12) had already put forward the notion that reception of form without the matter brings about cognition, since matter is non-cognitive. At any rate, Philoponus describes the contrasted notion of reception "with the matter" as meaning "materially and bodily."[8] He notes that some have explained the phrase as referring to the matter of the recipient. He has no quarrel with this exegesis, since non-psychic recipients undergo the action of the composite, while in sensation the activity undergone is on the part of the form alone. The Aristotelian phrase did refer to the matter in the sensible object, but the meaning extends in this way to the matter in the recipient (*In de An.*, p. 440.27-35). In general, Philoponus continues the reasoning of Themistius in more developed and closely knit fashion. The tenet that the sense becomes what the object is instead of just being affected by it is brought into explicit play. Finally, the phraseology of receiving a form "materially and bodily" may be seen as opening the way for the contrasted notion of receiving a form immaterially, or immaterial reception, as the explanation of cognition.

Simplicius, a contemporary of Philoponus, like the commentators before him allows the nature of cognition to carry the burden of the distinction between the two types of reception. With his strong Neoplatonic background, he is interested in showing (*In de An.*, p. 166.1-34) that the sensible forms come from the outside while the intelligible forms come from within. In order to go into action, the sense has to presuppose simultaneous action upon itself by the sensible thing. To that extent its action has the aspect of passivity (.12-.13). In the context, actualizing is understood as contrasted with undergoing (.4-.5; .24-.25), not however as producing but as discerning. The Aristotelian doctrine that the actuality of the agent is in the patient is exploited (.19-.21) changes to explain how undergoing the action of agents in the order of form makes what is proper to them appear in the patient. In this way the sense expresses the sensible object and is aware of it in accord with the stable form, which is received "without matter" (.28-.32). The article is not used here before the term "matter," as though matter in general is meant without any particularization to the matter of either the agent or the patient. In accord with this stable type of reception sensation takes place. Not the matter, but just "what appears" (*emphasis*-- .19; .22; .27; .31) in the sensible thing, is received by the sense organ, in this way allowing the sensible thing itself to be perceived.[9]

With Simplicius, then, the tendency to make the nature of cognition account for the reception of form without matter, instead of vice versa, is maintained. The role of the sensible thing's "appearance" in giving the sense a stable form received "without matter" is emphasized, along with the way the sense is thereby made aware of the thing. Even though the Aristotelian text is read in a Neoplatonic framework, it is accorded a faithful exegisis in these respects.

Sophonias, writing as far as is known around the end of the thirteenth or the beginning of the fourteenth century A.D., pursued the topic in the language and reasoning of his predecessors, especially of Simplicius, though in his own particular manner of paraphrase and without noticeable Neoplatonic cast. But he gave definite expression to the tenet that the forms (*logoi*) of the sensible objects are impressed upon the sense "immaterially and cognitively" (*De An. Paraphr.*, p. 102.29). Reception in the order of form only bears the brunt of the distinction between the sentient undergoing and the merely corporeal undergoing of activity by sensible things (.30-.35). Yet more is required. Reception of forms that leaves the matter unaffected as in the case of substances for molding, or in the case of mirrors, does not suffice for cognition. The reception has to be vital and has to give concomitant awareness of what is taking place (.35-.37). The recipient in bodily change is affected in its own matter, not in the matter of the agent, and in general every agent transmits form, not matter, to the patient (p. 104.10-13).

Sophonias tries to face the question brought forward by Philoponus about the reception of images on mirrors and plastic material. He grants that these forms are received without affecting the matter of the recipient, but has only the same answer as Philoponus. The forms in this case are not received cognitively. The real reason for the difference is that in sensation the reception is cognitive. Cognition is still explained by cognition.[10] But the deficiency of Aristotle's example comes to the fore when it is required to explain awareness. As it stands it would apply, at least in Sophonias' understanding of it, to any non-cognitive reception of design by a plastic material. Moreover, the example indicates the matter in the agent. But that matter is not received by the patient even in merely physical change. The example, accordingly, fails to account for the really significant difference between cognitive and non-cognitive reception of form.

The tradition of the Greek commentators, then, ends in a hardly satisfactory explanation of the Aristotelian immaterial reception of form in cognition. It shows clearly enough how the Aristotelian example of wax and signet ring limps. It focuses rather upon the immateriality on the part of the recipient sense. The sense functions immaterially in sensation. This is a signal gain from the viewpoint of interpretation. But the type of immateriality is left unexplained. The type cannot be that of separate substance, for any soul is the form of a body. In sensation it cannot be the functioning of a sense power apart from its material organ, since to act separately it would have to have separate existence, as Aristotle (*De An.*, III 4,429a18-b22) reasons in demonstrating the separate status of mind. What is meant by the sense functioning solely in the order of form in cognition, and what is meant by form grasping form in sensation, is not dealt with satisfactorily. There is scarcely more than the affirmation that the sense does not function as matter informed by the sensible object, but only as form apprehending form.

A new basis for explaining the difference between material and immaterial reception of forms is brought forward in Averroes. It springs from the different ways in which a sensible thing can exist. The new viewpoint is accordingly that of existence. The background appears in Avicenna. For the Persian thinker the nature of a sensible thing, for instance equinity, was of itself neither singular nor universal. As existent in sensible things it was singular. As existent in the human soul it was universal.[11] This is a radically different approach from that of the Greeks. In Aristotle himself the viewpoint was from the side of the soul. The soul was all things potentially, and became the things of which it was aware. The Greek commentators kept their thought within that perspective. The new approach in medieval times was from the side of the things known or perceived. These existed first in themselves in the real world, and then in human cognition. In neither case was there question of the senses producing originally the objects of which they were aware. In this respect the cognitive faculties remained passive from both viewpoints. But the medieval perspective offered a new way of explaining immaterial reception. The immateriality consisted in a different way of existing. To exist in matter meant that the form was received materially. To exist in the soul meant that the form was received in a different way, a way that in contrast could be termed immaterial.

Against this new background Aquinas repeats the tenets that every patient whatsoever receives form without matter from the agent, and that an agent "acts through its form and not through its matter." But he goes on to locate the meaning of "without matter" in the different mode of existence had by the sensible thing in being perceived. In his terminology the sensible form has natural existence in the sensible thing, but intentional or spiritual existence in the sense.[13] Elsewhere, citing Averroes, he speaks of the forms being received immaterially, with the type of cognition depending upon the degree of immateriality.[14] The notion of immaterial union of subject and object as the explanation (*ratio*) of cognition was given serious attention in the tradition of the Thomistic commentators.[15] With the two ways of existing so sharply distinguished, the subject and the object were readily described as different in real or material existence but one and the same in cognitional or intentional existence. Their real distinction but cognitional identity was no longer a problem. In real existence the two remain really different.

Finally, to round out the picture, it might be well to note Zabarella's observation that the soul is the active cause of sensation because of its judging aspect, even though when dealing with the reception of the form Aristotle stresses the passive aspect. But the soul could not act in sensing unless the passive reception of the form had preceded.[16] This was implicit in the Greek commentators (supra, nn.3,5,6,7 and 9) through their added requirement that cognitive unlike non-cognitive reception of form had to be "discerning," and that while passively receiving the form the sense went into action (see Simplicius, 166.12-17; supra, n.9).

What leads may be gathered from this survey of the commentators? They show convincingly enough that reception "without the matter" cannot mean merely that the matter of the agent is not received by the patient, since that is common to all action and could not be the distinguishing mark of cognitive reception. The meaning, they make clear, has to be that cognitive reception takes place in an immaterial way, that is, without any matter being brought into a new form. This leaves the conclusion that only form receives further form in cognitive reception. For a Neoplatonist commentator that could hardly present difficulty. In the doctrine of Plotinus (*En.*,VI,5,6) all the forms can be in any one form and are one in many. Yet the Aristotelian tenet that sense and the thing sensed are one in the actuality of cognition seems fully open to the notion that their forms become one in a way different from the reception of form in matter, which is a union that results in a further thing, the

composite. What is perceived is not a composite made of object and percipient, but the object itself or the percipient itself. This aspect of cognition is not used by Aristotle to explain the present text, but it has to have
been in his mind if the text is to have pertinent force.[17] It is introduced
early in Book III of *De Anima*, and the use of the phrase "without matter" continues,[18] as though an integral part of that doctrine of cognition.
The two belong together as different facets of the same epistemological
doctrine.

Against the background of the interpretation developed in the Greek
commentators, the retention of the article in the English translation
"without the matter" may tend to be deceptive. The Greek article no
more particularizes the matter than it does the term "sense" in the same
sentence. In both instances the article serves to generalize. Reception
"without matter," or "immaterial reception," or "receiving a form immaterially," would carry the notion much more exactly.

But if the identity of sense with sensible object in the actuality of
cognition is the premise from which the immateriality of cognitional
reception is drawn, how can Aristotle fail to mention the premise at this
stage? When he states the premise elsewhere,[19] he offers no proof of it.
He proceeds as though a mere mention is necessary to recall the notion.
He seems in those places to take for granted that it is familiar to and accepted by his hearers. In the present text, he neglects even to mention it.
Nevertheless the notion does have to be presupposed in order to understand the assertion that the physical splitting of the wood and the sound in
the percipient are different kinds of effect produced by the one cause, the
thunderbolt (*De An.*, II 12,424b3-18). Laying aside the Cartesian
philosophical notion that material things are inert, and keeping in mind
the immense energy their nuclear structure contains as well as present
tendencies towards limited acceptance of abiogenesis, there seems
nothing too objectionable against the tenet that the energy emitted by a
material thing should bring about both a new physical form in the patient
and a cognitional form in the sense organ.

The difference between the two types of effect is immediately described in the text (424a26-32). Cognitional reception is located in a definite
mean, in contrast to the indefinite (b15) aspect of physical reception.
Physical movement can be had in any intensity, while sensation is always
definite. Elsewhere the difference is placed as that between the actuality
of something perfect, on the one hand, and the actuality of something
imperfect on the other. This is understood in a way that allows the actuality of what is perfect to be expressed by the present and perfect tenses
taken together. Sight and pleasure, for instance, are complete from the

start.[20] Hence they are always able to be expressed by the present tense. But they are continuous, and while they are taking place they are fully open to expression by the present. To be seeing, accordingly, means to have seen. To be knowing means to have known.[21] This has to mean that sensation is complete in its specific perfection from the moment of initial actuation. The contrast with movement is sharp. Movement, for example in the process of building, allows a distinction between the process that is going on and the form of the finished house. But cognition permits no such distinction. Here the present always involves the perfect. In a word, material reception of a form by a subject is a gradual process from imperfection towards perfection. Cognitional reception, on the contrary, does not consist in a process even though there is always concomitant physical motion when the cognition is sensible. The motion is the actuality of something imperfect, the cognition the actuality of something perfect.

There is a further significant point about the reception of a form. For Aristotle (*Metaph.*, Z 17,1041b7-28) a form causes a thing to be and to be what it is. In accord with this general tenet, the sensible form received without matter makes the percipient be the sensible thing immaterially.[22] The cognitional unity is expressed by Aristotle in the stand that the percipient is identical with the sensible thing in the actuality of cognition,[23] and that the soul is potentially all things.[24] The causality of form extends to the individuality of the thing. The same individual thing that exists materially in the sensible world is the thing that is perceived. It is the singular thing that the soul becomes immaterially. Otherwise not it, but something else would be what is attained in perception. What one is aware of would be a new and different thing.

To anyone accustomed to regard a form as universal, or as the source of universality only, this way of looking at the question will seem strange. Yet in the beginning of the book of the *De Anima* (II 1,412a8-9) in which the immaterial reception of form is introduced, the form is clearly regarded as the source of individuality. Matter in itself, according to that text, is not something individual. The form is what gives the individuality. The Hett translation of the text runs: "shape or form, in virtue of which individuality is directly attributed." This tenet, laid down at the beginning of Book II, has to continue in application to the form that is received in the cognitive agent. Just as the form makes Socrates be the individual that he is, when it is received materially in the real world, so that same form, received immaterially, causes the percipient to become the same individual Socrates cognitionally. The percipient thereby becomes aware of the individual in front of him.

Reception of form "without the matter" is in consequence an explanation of the cognition of sensible objects, as such. It is not just an introduction to the difference between common sensibles and proper sensibles, in the question raised at the end of the second section of the present paper. It is meant as an explanation of the nature of cognition itself, insofar as cognition and immateriality coincide. To be a thing immaterially is to be aware of it.

IV

The question how intelligible objects are known for Aristotle is to be approached in this altogether special context in which cognitive agent and sensible object are identical through and through in the actuality of cognition. For human cognition, the objects have to be contained within the sensibles (*De An.,* III 7,431a14-17). There is ordinarily no other way in which objects can be presented to it. But how is the cognitive agent capable of knowing intellectually the things perceived through the senses?

The answer, quite obviously, lies in the throughgoing cognitional identity of the sensible thing with the cognitive agent. The whole thing is identical with the percipient, and accordingly present to it with its substance and other characteristics that cannot be discerned by the senses. In this way the senses and imagination make the intelligible objects present to the cognitive agent. The question of global presence offers no difficulties, for already the sensible thing itself is identical through sensation with the agent that is able to know it.

The difficulty arises rather from another source. The sensible things through their action upon the senses brought the percipient immaterially into the new forms. But what is to bring the mind into the intelligible forms of those same objects? The sensible things are unable to act upon mind. That is the least that can be taken out of Aristotle's succinct assertion that the mind is impassive (*De An.,* III 4,429a15). Yet in accord with the pattern of human cognition already developed, the mind has to be "receptive of the form of an object, *i.e.*, must be potentially the same as its object, although not identical with it: as the sensitive is to the sensible, so must mind be to the thinkable" (*De An.,* III 4,429a15-18; trans. Hett). The intellectual capacity (*pathêtikos nous*) has to be actuated, just as does the sense or any potentiality, by the required form. But what can bring this capacity into actuality? What can make it receive forms immaterially? It has to be something of the same order, the order of mind and not the order of material agents. The obvious fact that we know things intellectually shows that there is such a mind at work. It has a mind that brings about all things in the potential mind, as light makes potential colors actual (*De An.*, III 5,430a10-17).

What does this mean? The nature and identity of the Aristotelian active intellect has puzzled commentators through the centuries. There is still no satisfactory explanation. There are difficulties in recognizing it as an efficient cause. Aristotle had stated shortly before (*De An.*, III 2,426a2-11) that the actuality (*energeia*) of the efficient cause is in the patient. He can hardly be expected now to attribute without reservation efficient causality to a fully actualized separate mind. He has to represent light as though by its mere presence it renders potential colors actual. Apparently in the presence of the separate intellect the things attained in phantasms become actually understood. Likewise from the side of the potential mind efficient causality, as Aristotle knew it from the sensible world, seems inadmissible. At least in this respect the mind is impassive even in receiving forms (4,429a15-16). Though entirely potential, it cannot be acted upon in the way matter undergoes change. In this respect it receives the forms immaterially. On its own level it becomes the thing known parallel to the way the percipient becomes the thing perceived. On both levels the one and the same thing is attained by the one and the same cognitive agent. Concomitant sensible and intellectual cognition is thereby accounted for, the potentially intelligible in the sensible object becoming actually intelligible.

V

Each of these two levels of cognition, namely sensation and intellection, is accompanied for Aristotle by a corresponding awareness of self. In the light of the foregoing considerations the reason is not hard to see. Since in the actuality of sensation the percipient *is* the thing perceived, there cannot be awareness of the one apart from the awareness of the other. The two are identical in the closest of all unions, that of cognition. Every sensation accordingly involves self-awareness (*De An.*, III 2,425b12-28). In strictly exact language this means that the percipient, that is, the man or the animal, is aware of himself in every act of sensation. Perceiving the object, he concomitantly perceives himself. It is always the man who perceives by means of the sense and is thereby aware of himself.

Correspondingly the mind that has been actuated by the forms of other things through the active intellect becomes those things intellectually. It is identical with them in cognition. In knowing them it thereby knows itself. Moreover, it remains habitually informed by them and in this way is habitually capable of self-knowledge: "But when the mind has become the several groups of its objects . . . the mind is then capable of thinking itself" (*De An.*, III 4,429b5-10; trans. Hett). This in fact is for Aristotle the condition on which the human mind can have knowledge of itself. Unless it knows other things it is not immediately able to know itself.[25] Unlike a Cartesian mind it does not have itself as an object independently of the cognition of sensible things. All human knowledge for Aristotle has accordingly its origins in the objects provided by sensation.

In both sensation and intellection, then, an object other than self has epistemological priority over self-awareness. This explains the assertion "But it appears that *knowledge* and sensation and opinion and *thought* are always of other objects, and only incidentally of themselves" (*Metaph.*, Λ 9, 1074b35-36; trans. Apostle).

VI

For the purposes of the present inquiry, then, the picture rounds out very roughly but sufficiently. All the intelligible objects are encountered originally in the things of the sensible world. They are made present to the mind through the union of identity achieved in sensation, in which the cognitive agent, the man, is identical with the thing itself that is perceived. The thing's intelligible aspects necessarily continue in the thing when it is perceived, and are there to be known through the operation of the mind, as cognitional identity with the thing is pursued on the higher plane. The separate and active intellect supplies for the efficient causality of the sensible thing, which could act upon the sense organ but not upon the mind. In this way the parallelism of the immaterial reception of forms runs through the Aristotelian doctrine of cognition on both the sensible and the intelligible levels.

Though definite enough in its broad outlines, the doctrine inevitably stirs up a hornet's nest of trouble. The separate intellect has to be "something" (*De An.*, III 5.430a10-12) of the soul's nature. Certainly it is a required factor for intellection. How then can it remain separate? It cannot function as an efficient cause in the full sense, yet it has to bring a potentiality into actuality. It has the aspect of a *hexis* (430a15), suggesting that it already has the intelligible forms as it were in a relatively habitual state and accordingly is able to bring them into actuality when the sense images are present to the cognitive agents. Yet in its separate status it is its own self only (a22-23). These difficulties are not answered in the text of Aristotle. They are loose ends left dangling. But each conclusion is reasoned to carefully and cogently. Together they provide globally an insight into human intellection that would be difficult to match in any other philosophy. They are themes that still reward careful and patient study, even though modern philosophy has not as yet chosen to follow them out in depth. The philosophical principles they involve are unmatched in the explanation of our immediate awareness of the sensible world, of which, as even Locke (*Essay*, IV, 11, 3) observed, nobody seriously doubts. With that immediate certainty, things external to ourselves and existing independently of us can serve as the objective and common measure of truth.

9. A Note on Aristotle, De Anima 3.4,429b9

I

The conclusion drawn by Aristotle at *De Anima* 3.4,429b9-10 has been understood traditionally to bear in one way or another upon the knowledge the human intellect has of itself. The manuscript text, handed down without significant variants, allows only that meaning.[1] This text reads: καὶ αὐτὸς δὲ αὐτὸν τότε δύναται νοεῖν. It is rendered in the Oxford translation "the mind too is then able to think *itself*" (J. A. Smith), in the Loeb "moreover the mind is then capable of thinking itself" (W. S. Hett), and in similar ways in other English versions—Wallace (1882), Hammond (1902), Hicks (1907), Foster-Humphries (1951)—before Hamlyn's translation (1968).

Likewise self-knowledge of the intellect was what the Greek commentators undertook to explain when dealing with the Aristotelian text at this point. Though radically divided in their understanding of the manner in which the human intellect knows itself, they regularly focussed their attention on the problem of self-knowledge for discussion here. That way of accepting the text can be documented as far back as Alexander of Aphrodisias in the late second and early third centuries of our era.[2] In orthodox Aristotelian fashion Alexander (p. 86.14-29) accounted for the self-knowledge in terms of the cognitional identity of knower with what is known, for in this identity the one could not be grasped cognitionally without awareness of the other. He referred to the Aristotelian parallel of the tenet with what had been shown to take place in sensation. But he also explained that just as the intellect when exercising its cognition is identical with the form known, so on the habitual level it is already *able* to know itself once it possesses that form. It has the habitual knowledge directly and *per se* of the known form. But coincidentally[3] it is able to know itself because it *happens* to have become that which it knows. There can be no doubt that Alexander is understanding the line in the sense that the intellect is able to know itself, and is able to do so because it has been actualized by the habitual possession of the form or forms of something else.

In the fourth century, Themistius (p. 95.19-32) gave the same general explanation of the passage as Alexander. The intellect is able to know itself, he emphasized, when it has habitual knowledge of things lying beyond it, since it is nothing other than the things known. He understood in the same way as his predecessor the respective opposition and identity of knower and known.

In the first half of the sixth century the passage was approached against a deep Neoplatonic background, but the problem was still definitely self-knowledge. For Simplicius (p. 230.12-29) the crucial concern in regard to the Aristotelian assertion was to show that contrary to Alexander the intellect knows itself not coincidentally (cf. above, note 3) but directly, in Neoplatonic fashion. The expressions used here by Simplicius are reminiscent of the way the intellect is fecundated in Plotinus (*En.* 5.2.1.10-21). Once fecundated the intellect for Simplicius (line 27) knows both itself and the forms within it, while the passivity implied by the fecundation does not involve any change. In the same epoch Philoponus (pp. 527.37-528.9) discussed problems arising from 429b10-12. He was concerned with upholding the impassivity and the self-actualization of intellection when the object is a material thing and other than the intellection itself. His conclusion was that insofar as the intellect is intellect it knows itself. The explanation is thrown (p. 528.25-26) into a strong Neoplatonic setting, with express reference to Plotinus. What continued to be the relevant theme in the discussion of the Aristotelian text at this point was self-knowledge.

In the same Neoplatonic setting Sophonias (13th-14th century) stated at this section of the text that in intellection the soul "finds the objects by gazing upon itself as possessing them" (p. 125.14). The intelligible object is not outside but inside the intellection, he reminds his Neoplatonic readers, nor is it wholly other than the intellection. No bodily change takes place. The only resemblance to passivity is fecundation as from something else, though this differs from passivity to the extent that the perfecting of intelligence is from itself (p. 125.8-13; cf. Aristotle *De Anima* 1.4,408b29-31). In this way Sophonias kept up the Neoplatonic assertion of direct self-knowledge instead of accidental dependance upon external causes.

The unvarying tradition of the Greek commentators, accordingly, understood the text at 429b9-10 as concerned with the intellect's self-knowledge. This should support convincingly enough the only reading that is given in the extant manuscripts. Whether the self-knowledge was explained as concomitant, or in Neoplatonic fashion as direct, the topic at issue was taken by all to be the intellect's knowledge of itself. This understanding of the Aristotelian text continued through the Latin mid-

dle ages, as in Aquinas (*etiam tunc potest intelligere seipsum—In III de
An.*, lect. 8, Pirotta no. 704), and the Renaissance, as in Zabarella (*intelligit se secundario, quia non per speciem propriam, sed per
alienam—In III. Aristot. Libros de Anima*, 3 text. 8, col. 783AB). The
text continued to be read in this sense of self-knowledge through the first
three quarters of the nineteenth century, as may be seen for instance in
Trendelenburg (1833) and Torstrik (1862). Right up into modern times,
then, the tradition of reading the text in the meaning of the intellect's
knowledge of itself seems unbroken.

II

In the year 1885, however, Ingram Bywater claimed that the question
of self-knowledge does not belong to this stage of Aristotle's discussion at
all. Rather, the proper place for that topic would be "in the section at the
end of the Ch., when Aristotle comes to deal with . . . the question
whether νοῦς is νοητός." The point of the text at 429b9, a point "too important to be ignored," is that when actuated by the forms of other things
the intellect has the "characteristic of free and self-determined 'energy' "
that puts it in a position to exercise at will its power of thinking. For
Bywater this was "the required sense." It was obtained by changing the δε
αὑτόν at 429b9 to δί αὑτοῦ. By means of this very slight change, he maintained, "we not only get a clause that we want, but also rid ourselves of
the one that we do not want." He translated it "of himself," in the sense
of "at will" (417a27).[4]

Bywater's case for the proposed emendation of the text was immediate-
ly endorsed by Susemihl as "convincing."[5] But it was not mentioned by
Biehl in the revision of his text in 1896, and was expressly rejected by
Rodier (1900) in favor of the traditional interpretation established since
Alexander. It was mentioned in the critical apparatus by Hicks (1907),
Apelt (1911), Förester (1912—with note on page 174 that it was probably
right), Siwek (1965—with unqualified approval on account of the context[6]) and Jannone (1966), though none of these editors admit it into the
text. With Ross (1961), though, it entered into the text itself. Because
"there would be no point in a reference here to self-knowledge," Ross
(292) found Bywater's emendation "clearly right," and saw support for it
in the δί αὑτοῦ at 429b7 (as did also Siwek, *loc. cit.*) and in the ἀφ ἑαυτοῦ of
Sophonias on p. 125.13. Hamlyn (58) translates the emended text as "and
then it can think by itself," without comment and without alerting the
English reader to the different meaning accepted in the unbroken Greek
tradition.

A survey of the history of the emendation, then, shows that the text at *De Anima* 429b9 was given a new reading without any manuscript authority at all. The change has been introduced admittedly for doctrinal reasons—to get "the required sense" (cf. above, note 4). A textual emendation is of course permissible when warranted by serious considerations of the meaning that is involved. Copyists do make mistakes. But extremely sensitive care is demanded where there is the possibility of trying to make the text conform to one's own understanding of the doctrine. Especially where a long tradition of commentaries has discussed the text in its accepted wording and found no occasion to challenge it, should one be on the alert in regard to doctrinal reasons for its rejection. In the present case the discussions centered around a radical issue in the interpretation of the Aristotelian conception of intellectual self-knowledge. The question was whether this knowledge was direct, or merely concomitant with the knowledge of something else.[7] The issue was crucial, but the Neoplatonic commentators did not attempt to evade the adverse bearing of the traditional text by any claim that it was not meant to express the notion of self-knowledge. They considered it carefully, and were satisfied that it referred to self-knowledge, even though in the Neoplatonic setting it posed serious problems. The attitude of these commentators in accepting a text even though its prima facie meaning did not accord with their doctrinal approach, suggests care in emending the text for doctrinal reasons today. Consideration in depth seems called for, to make sure that the reasons are sufficient to justify the change when both unanimous manuscript tradition and pertinent discussion by the commentators are against it.

But from the philosophical viewpoint has the question involved in the text at 429b9-10 enough genuine interest to merit a close investigation? Bywater, in calling for the emendation of the text, maintained that the point he was trying to make "is too important to be ignored" (*loc. cit.*). The point is that in contrast to sensation the actuation of the intellect by the forms of other things permits thought about them even when they are not physically present. Possessing the forms habitually, the intellect can think about the things at will.[8] Without doubt that point has its philosophical importance. Its status and bearing in the general structure of the passage deserve scrutiny. One may well ask whether in actual context the tenet excludes reference to self-knowledge, or whether it leads up to it as to a conclusion. Bywater's stand is that the reference to self-knowledge "has no place here," and Ross's similarly is that there would be no point to it here. In itself the problem of the intellect's self-knowledge is vital to Aristotelian epistemology. The origin of all human knowledge in sensation has to be safeguarded, and the intelligible objects are to be located in the sensible forms (*De An.* 3.8,432a3-14). The intellect's knowledge of itself can be no exception in the Aristotelian noetic. The way intellectual self-knowledge is explained seems to make the radical difference between Aristotle and Neoplatonism. But also in the much wider arena outside the intramural discussions of the Greek commentators the issue is of perennial importance. If Aristotle has a worthwhile contribution to make on the way things outside the intellect become known, it is surely to be found in his tenet that only knowledge of those external things makes possible the intellect's knowledge of itself.

There is no question, then, of the importance of the problem of intellectual self-knowledge in Aristotle. The one point at issue is whether the clause at 429b9-10 is the appropriate place at which the epistemologically important conclusion expressed in the traditional text should follow from the Aristotelian premises.

III

To answer this question, the structure of the Aristotelian reasoning in the passage as a whole requires examination. The passage, with the traditional text retained at 429b9, reads:

> Once the mind has become each set of its possible objects, as a man of science has, when this phrase is used of one who is actually a man of science (this happens when he is able to exercise the power on his own initiative), its condition is still one of potentiality, but in a different sense from the potentiality which preceded the acquisition of knowledge by learning or discovery; the mind too is then able to think *itself* (*De An.* 3.4, 429b5-10; Oxford trans.).

The general structure of this long sentence is apparent enough. First, the state of habitual knowledge is described. The intellect has become its objects one by one, in the way of a man who actually knows the things but is not thinking of them. This state is indicated by the ability to go into the activity corresponding to the habitual knowledge at will, or just alone. That is the basis for the two assertions that follow about the intellect in the remainder of the sentence. The first assertion is that the intellect is still in a state of potentiality, though of a different type from before. The second is that it can then know itself, if the traditional text is followed, or, in Bywater's emendation, that it can then think on its own initiative. Zabarella (col. 779F) expresses this outline very clearly. The subject of the proposition is the intellect in the habitual state, and of it

Aristotle asserts two predicates, one that it is still in a potential condition, the other (col. 781C) that it can then know itself.

One may quite securely go a step further and analyze the structure into a ground and two conclusions that follow with equal immediacy upon that ground. The ground is the intellect habitually actuated by the forms of things it has become in cognition, as shown by ability to think about the things at will. In this way the basis for the reasoning is established, since if that ground is present the two other assertions hold good of the intellect. They have accordingly the status of conclusions. The Greek particles μὲν . . . δέ in introducing the two conclusions suggest equally immediate sequence from the one ground. There is no indication that the second is meant to follow through the first.

In the emended text, the second conclusion is that the intellect is then able to think by itself. There is no doubt about the truth of this assertion for Aristotle, nor about its importance. Equipped with the forms of other things, the intellect is not dependent upon the external causes to provide it with the forms required for thinking. It can now think by itself.[9] But this ability to think by itself had already been laid down in the first part of the sentence (429b7). Ability to think by itself was the indication used to show that the intellect possessed the forms habitually. It established the basis for the reasoning. Reasserted in the conclusion it would be at best a useless repetition, and at worst a *petitio principii*. Its only possible but unlikely justification would be that at 429b7 the text stated generically that the intellect could go into activity by itself, and at 429b9 specified the activity as that of thinking.

On the other hand the assertion that "it is then able to know itself" follows cogently as a second conclusion from the basis laid down in the first part of the sentence. When actuated by the habitual possession of the forms, the intellect is (a) still in potentiality towards actually thinking about the things, and (b) rendered capable of thinking about itself. The text of the *De Anima* (429a21-24) had just explained that the soul's intellect has no other nature than potentiality. Now it is regarded as having received the forms of other things, and made actual in the way form actualizes potentiality.[10] Yet in this state it is (a) still in potentiality towards actual thinking, and (b) able to know itself. Possession of the forms of other things, in a word, equips the human intellect to think about itself as well as about the things. This follows cogently enough from the opening statement (429b5-6) that the intellect has become the other things. Accordingly it could not know them without thereby being aware of itself, on account of the cognitional identity. Through knowing other things the human intellect is made capable of knowing itself. The assertion is philosophically important, for it means that the human intellect has to know other things in order to be aware of itself, and it follows naturally and cogently as a second conclusion in the way required by the structure of the sentence.

But is this the appropriate place for introducing the topic of intellectual self-knowledge? Bywater's contention (cf. above, note 4) was that the proper place for it would be towards the end of the chapter in the course of the discussion about "a wholly different matter," namely whether the intellect itself is knowable. Yet, in the sequence of thought found in the *De Anima*, is self-awareness "a wholly different matter" from the cognitional reception of forms?[11] Book 2 of the *De Anima* had ended with the explanation of sensible cognition through the reception of the forms of the perceptible things (12,424a17-b18). After a discussion of the common sensibles in the first chapter of Book 3, the second chapter went on immediately to show that every sensation involves self-awareness. The reason is that the actuality of the sensible object and that of the sensitive faculty are one and the same (2,426a9-19). This epistemology means that the object could not be perceived without self-awareness on the part of the percipient, since the two are identical in the actuality of cognition. To be aware of the one is to be aware of the other. The fourth chapter reaches the problem of intellection, and in parallel fashion shows that here too the form of the object is received by the knower (4,429a15-18). Different from an external sense, however, the mind retains habitual possession of the forms, and is thereby equipped both to think of other things at will and, according to the traditional text, to know itself. The latter conclusion seems required to round out the parallelism with sensation, in which the cognitional reception of the form results in identical actuality of percipient and perceived and thereby in self-awareness. Contrary to Bywater's view, then, the problem of the intellect's knowledge of itself is not "a wholly different matter" from its habitual possession of forms.

The *De Anima* goes on to treat of knowledge of form in contrast to knowledge of composites, and then concludes the chapter by raising and discussing two aporiae. One of these is about the common aspect in acting and being acted upon. The second, really a particular application of that topic, is whether the intellect itself is knowable. Aristotle's answer is that the intellect is potentially the things known, and this potential identity itself provides the common aspect without requiring admixture with anything further (b23-31). It is here that Bywater would like to see the first introduction of the intellect's self-knowledge. But does not the aporematic setting presuppose rather that the self-knowledge has already been established? The double aporia is that if the intellect is simple and accordingly has no composition with anything common, how can it have the passivity necessary for knowledge and how can it have the common aspect expressed in the two notions of knower and known? The solution proceeds not by explaining how the intellect knows itself but by showing that it does have a common aspect with its objects. The solution regards the intellect's self-knowledge as already accepted, and undertakes to defend this self-knowledge against an objection.

The context, accordingly, requires that the conclusion about intellectual self-knowledge be drawn earlier than in the sections indicated by Bywater. The traditional reading at 429b9 draws the conclusion from its appropriate basis. This would seem to be the proper place, then, for showing how the intellect becomes able to know itself. It is rendered capable of doing so by the habitual possession of the same forms that enable it to think of other things. Far from "no point in a reference here to self-knowledge" (Ross 292), the habitual possession of the forms of other things is what makes *possible* the intellect's knowledge of itself, in the sense of possibility now under consideration. In the sequence of Aristotle's thought, this is exactly the place for the conclusion about intellectual self-knowledge. Siwek's assertion that the context by all means demands Bywater's emendation is not borne out by close analysis of the Aristotelian procedure.

What about the supporting considerations from the text and from Sophonias? Ross (292) advances the δι'αὐτοῦ at b7, two lines earlier, as an indication that the same phrase should be expected at b9. From the philosophical viewpoint, however, this repetition of the phrase causes the difficulties seen above. It would mean a useless restatement of what had already been said, or, if the procedure is regarded as reasoning, it would involve a *petitio principii*. But even from the viewpoint of textual transmission is it any support for the emendation?

Paleographically, the presence of δὲ αὐτοῦ at b7 could help explain a corruption of δὲ αὐτόν into δι' αὐτου. Fresh in the mind of the copyist, the latter phrase might have been inadvertently substituted for δὲ αὐτόν two lines later. But the alleged corruption here is just the opposite. One has to explain how δι' αὐτόν, the supposed original, became δὲ αὐτόν. As the corruption had to have become established before the time of Alexander, it cannot be accounted for in terms of apostrophe, breathing mark, or accent. It would have to be explained through the substitution of an *E* for an *I*. This in itself is quite possible. But it can hardly appeal to the occurrence of δι'αὐτοῦ at b7 as a support. Rather, the occurrence of the phrase there would tend in the direction of perpetuating the alleged original reading.

Ross's other indication of support, approved by Siwek, is the use of αφ' εαυτοῦ by Sophonias, p. 125.13. Sophonias' literal use of the wording of the *De Anima* seems to end with the mention of the separate intellect at 429b5. (Sophonias, p. 125.5-6), just before the passage with which the present discussion is concerned, and commences again only with the beginning of the following chapter (*De An.* 3.5—Sophonias, p. 125.15). The intervening lines of Sophonias are a digression from the Aristotelian text in order to give a Neoplatonic account of the intellect's ability to know its objects. The intellect is fecundated by something else (υφ'ἑτέρου–p. 125.10), but the thinking (*ibid.*), i.e., the perfection of the intellect (p. 125.13), is from the intellect itself (αφ' ἑαυτοῦ). The notion suggested by the preposition ἀπό in this setting is that of origin rather than of the instrumentality that would have been implied in Aristotle's alleged use of διά here (see *De An.* 3.8,432a1-3). Sophonias is insisting that the mind originates its own knowledge of its objects. He is not regarding it as an instrument for knowing them. It finds them rather in gazing at itself, as possessing them.

In this context, even with the best of will, can Sophonias' repeated use of the phrase ἀφ' ἑαυτοῦ be seen as reflecting a second occurrence of δι' αὐτοῦ in his text of *De Anima* 3.4,429b7-9? He is not, it is true, specially concerned with a further conclusion that the intellect actuated by the forms is able to think of itself. For him this self-knowledge is already presupposed by the intellect's knowledge of the forms, since it finds them in knowing itself. What seems reflected is rather the ὑφ' ἑαυτοῦ of Philoponus (p. 527.39; p. 528.1 and 3) and Simplicius (p. 230.21) in the sense that the knowing is done by the intellect itself as the agent. Philoponus on facing the aporia why being known did not make the thing an intellect, explained that to be an intellect the object had to be known "by itself," as agent. Simplicius, in giving his explanation of *De Anima* 429b9-10, meant that the intellect in being known "by itself" as agent remains unchanged, and unaffected by anything exterior. The latter seems to be the immediate background against which Sophonias is thinking, for he is facing the same problems. In this Neoplatonic tradition his meaning was that the intellect in its own way originates its knowledge of other things. That meaning bears no immediate resemblance to the assertion that once the intellect is equipped with the forms of other things it is able to think at will. Yet that is the meaning the expression expression ἀΦ ἑαυτοῦ would have to have if it had been intended by reflect the reading at *De Anima* 429b9 as conjectured in Bywater's emendation. In the context it reflects the Neoplatonic stand that the intellect *qua* intellect knows itself (Philoponus, p. 528.9), rather than any new capability given the intellect by the habitual possession of the forms of other things.

V

What is called for in the Aristotelian noetic is a cogent presentation of the tenet that in man the intellect when actuated by the forms of other things acquires the habitual capacity to know itself. In the *Metaphysics* (Λ 9,1074b35-1075a5) Aristotle assumes in an aporia that prima facie the intellect seems to know itself only concomitantly in and through the knowing of something else, and in opposition to the universal extension of that view to all intellects he justifies his tenet of direct self-knowledge in separate substance. In the same book of the *Metaphysics* (1074 b24-26), as well as in the *De Anima* (3.4,430a2-6; 5,430a22), he distinguishes the uninterrupted thinking in separate substance from the interrupted type of which men are conscious in themselves.[12] These are but occasional references, passing statements prompted by the confrontation of separate intellect, which is actuality only, with the soul's (*De An*. 3.4.429a22) intellect. What is required is an explicit assertion that this latter intellect, which of its own nature is potential, becomes actually *able* to know itself as soon as it possesses the forms of other things. In the traditional text, is not that conclusion found just where it is to be expected, in close parallel with the preceding explanation of self-awareness in sensation? The assertion is brief and concise. But, like numerous other important statements in Aristotle, is it not presented in a manner quite in accord with that of a school *logos*? It is sharply etched, and definitive enough to serve as adequate basis for oral discussion. It allowed Aristotle (429b30-430a2) without further ado to proceed with the tenet that the intellect is actually none of its knowable objects prior to an act of cognition, like a writing tablet on which nothing has been written.

In general epistemology the traditional text at 429b9 offers an important contribution. If accepted, its doctrine justifies philosophically the knowledge of things existent outside cognition, since only through cognitional identity with external things can the intellect know its own self. The problem how to get outside the intellect does not arise. But that would be a much longer story.

10. Aristotle's Definition of Soul

I

On account of both its worth and its accuracy, Aristotle at the beginning of the *De Anima* (1 1. 402a1-7) ranks knowledge of soul among the topics that enjoy the highest priorities. He regards it as making great contribution towards the acquisition of truth in general, and in particular towards the philosophy of nature. Against this background he may be expected to show keen interest in working out a correct and penetrating definition of soul. According to the norms of his own logic, the nature of a thing as expressed in its definition is the starting point of every demonstration in scientific procedure;[1] and where, as in the present case, the subject is introduced as offering an especially high degree of accuracy, the enticement to spend sufficient time on the basic definition involved could hardly help but make itself felt.

The definition that Aristotle (1. 1. 402a7-b26; 403a25-b13) requires, then, is clearly one that will make manifest the substantial nature of soul. This type of definition is contrasted with a mathematical definition and a metaphysical definition (403b14-16). Yet its function is thought out on the lines of the basic mathematical notions that make geometrical reasoning possible (402b16-25), even though the contribution made by prior knowledge of the attributes is cautiously emphasized and the possibility of encountering metaphysical considerations is suggested. Further, Aristotle sounds a warning, necessary in his own day as well as in ours, against restricting the inquiry to "the human soul,"[2] since the scope of the investigation is much wider.

In accord with this project, the first book of the *De Anima* surveys the rich literature of preceding Greek thought about the nature of soul. It discusses the philosophical notions at considerable length, with mention (5. 410b28-30) of the Orphic religious traditions. The overall tendency of Greek tradition is found to interpret soul in terms of movement and sensation and knowledge, as though soul were somehow the source of these activities (2.403b25-404b30). In that setting the following book in its two opening chapters (2. 1-2. 412a3 ff.) undertakes directly to elaborate a satisfactory definition. The aim expressly is "to give a precise answer to the question, What is soul? i.e. to formulate the most general possible definition of it."[3]

Returning to grass-roots considerations after the discussion of the preceding philosophical views, Aristotle notes (412a13-15) that of natural bodies some have life and some do not, and that by "life" people mean self-sustenance together with growth and wasting away. Explaining this in terms of his own philosophical notions, he shows that a living body is to be located in the category of substance as a composite of matter and form. Form is entelechy, and this has two senses, illustrated by the relation to each other of knowledge and thinking.[4] The first conclusion drawn is that such a composite living body cannot be soul. The reason is that a body is not an attribute, but functions rather as subject and matter. The second conclusion follows immediately. The soul has to be substance in the sense of the form of a natural body that potentially has life (412a16-21). In this way the first formulation of the definition of soul is reached. The notion "natural body" is later (412b11-17; cf. *Ph.* 2. I. 193b3-12) contrasted with artifact, and not with geometrical solid, in this context. Since form is entelechy, the second version of the definition presents soul as the "entelechy of the kind of body just described" (412a21-22).

What is to be thought of this reasoning? The attributes in question are apparently those of "living" and "non-living," as they bring about the basic distinction just mentioned between the two kinds of bodies. "Life" seems regarded as the distinguishing attribute that has to be explained, and, in the light of the philosophic discussions already surveyed, it has to be explained by soul. Soul, then, will not be the body, since body can also be characterized by the attribute of "non-living," and accordingly can exist without the requirement of soul. Rather, soul will have to be the feature that characterizes a living body in the category of substance.[5] This will make it formal in nature, and locate it in the category as form in contrast to matter. Aristotle's reasoning, though elliptic, is cogent enough. The obvious objection is that it uses logical distinctions to attain the real distinction between form and matter. "Body" is already a genus with its own identifiable characteristics, unlike matter that in itself has no distinguishable traits.[6] The further differentiae "living" and "non-living" cannot be regarded as really distinct from "body" in the way form is distinct from matter. Yet here Aristotle passes lightly from the order of logic to the order of reality. He seems to feel no inconvenience in this process. In the *Metaphysics*[7] the ultimate differentia is what best expresses the form in a definition. Here the differentia is "life." If "life" is the feature that entails soul in the bodily substance, why should it not be used in the foregoing way to show that soul has to be the formal element in the living substantial composite?

In Aristotelian procedure, then, there seems to be no strenuous objection to this way of passing from the differentia "life " to the real soul. It does, however, require further explanation of the relation between soul and life, and Aristotle at once obliges. Since entelechy or perfection has two senses, comparable respectively to knowledge and thinking, he explains that soul is entelechy in the way in which knowledge is a perfection even when no thinking is done. The reason is that soul is present in both sleeping and waking. Accordingly the waking state may be compared to thinking, while sleep is like having knowledge without actualizing[8] it. In the same individual the process is from knowledge that is first there, and then exercised. This prior status of knowledge from the viewpoint of process results in a further amelioration of the definition. The third formulation is that soul is the first entelechy of a natural body potentially having life (412a22-28).

The only addition made has been the insertion of "first" before "entelechy." The explanation is clear enough if the illustration is kept within its Aristotelian setting. The difference between sleeping and waking in regard to the possession and exercise of knowledge shows how one can have a perfection without actually exercising it. So one can have the perfection that constitutes a living body without actually performing the vital operations for which one is thereby equipped. Since from this viewpoint having is prior to actualizing, soul has to be defined as the first entelechy. In the illustration two dangers are to be avoided. One would be to press the illustration of "sleep" to the point where it would have to mean no activity at all. This would be impossible, since sleep is a vital activity in its very nature. The analogy resides merely in the role of sleep as impeding the exercise of thought, in contrast to the actualizing of thought that takes place in the waking state. For Aristotle anyone who has knowledge exercises it in actual thinking, unless something is impeding this exercise.[9] Similarly, the second danger would be to regard the activity as a really distinct actuality superadded in the manner of a Scholastic "second actuality."[10] The latter expression is not used by Aristotle. His use of "first" in this respect is explained solely in terms of the priority of having to exercising in a knowing process that takes place in the one and the same individual.

Finally, the kind of body that potentially has life is shown to be organic body. The fourth version of the definition, consequently, is that every soul is the first entelechy of a natural organic body (412b1-6).

A few concluding and enlightening observations are added. The composition of matter with form is such that the unity is found dominantly in the form in a way that renders superfluous any question about the composite's unity.[11] Accordingly a body apart from soul does not qualify as a potentially living body. A dead body is not the subject of which Aristotle has been speaking. He has been speaking throughout of a living body, and distinguishing in it the first entelechy that plays a role analogous to sleep in respect of waking state. Yet the possibility that parts of the soul, on the other hand, may have separate existence looms large.[12] Even the question of a relation of soul to body in the manner of sailor to ship is raised in this context.[13] But in regard to the notion of "potentially living body" or "organic body," the text leaves no doubt that it means a composite already endowed with form as first entelechy, yet considered on the generic level on which "body" does not express the differentiae of "living" and "non-living." The addition of the differentia "non-living," as in "dead body," would disqualify the body from having a place in the definition of soul.[14]

The chapter ends by offering the formula now reached as "sketching a rough model"[15] for the further and exact elaboration of the soul's definition.

II

In what way is the elaboration of the definition to take place? Not only the fact (τὸ ὅτι) but also the cause (τὴν αἰτίαν), Aristotle suggests at the beginning of the second chapter (*De An.* 2. 2. 413a13-16), should be present and manifest in the definition. A mathematical instance is used to illustrate the point. The squaring of a rectangle could be defined as the construction of an equilateral triangle equal in space to the oblong figure.[16] That would state the conclusion of the geometrical process. Or it could be defined as the finding of the mean proportional that is the line upon which the square is to be constructed. In that case the definition exhibits the cause (τὸ αἴτιον) of the object in question (413a16-20).

What logical framework is being invoked here? It seems unmistakably that of the *Posterior Analytics* (1. 13. 78a22 ff.). There the distinction is established between an intellectual process that establishes a fact (τὸ ὅτι) and one that makes apparent the immediate cause of the fact (τὸ διότι). For scientific knowledge and demonstration a conclusion can be established in different ways. One way is through the thing's immediate cause, the cause that may be called the *first* cause in the sense of the immediately proximate cause. In this case there is no intermediate factor whose absence could prevent the issuing of the effect from the cause. Effect and cause are here reciprocal. To posit the one is to posit the other. What is given is therefore *the* reason why, in the sense in which the Oxford translation finds itself obliged to insert an adjective and render "*the* cause" (τὸ αἴτιον - 78b15) as "the strict cause."[17] The illustrations given are nearness as the reason why the planets do not twinkle, and spherical figure as the reason why the moon waxes (78a40-b7). In those context *the* cause in the *De Anima* (2. 2. 413a20; cf. a15) text, used in explicit contrast to the *fact* (τὸ ὅτι), can hardly mean anything else than what the Oxford translation renders as "the strict cause" (*An. Post.* 1. 13. 78b15) in the sense of *the* reason why (τὸ διότι) of the *Analytics*.

As regards the contrasted knowledge of the fact, the *Analytics* gives two ways in which such knowledge may be had. A conclusion may be demonstrated on the strength of an effect. For instance, planets may be shown to be near because they do not twinkle, and the moon to be spherical because it waxes. Though the effect and the cause reciprocally involve each other, as in these examples, the demonstration now is through the effect, not through the cause. Here the effect is better known to *us*, and can therefore serve as a starting point for the reasoning process.[18] Once one knows on other grounds (78a33-35) that great distance from the observer causes the phenomenon of twinkling, the failure to twinkle gives *a* reason why the planets must be close. It is *a* reason for the conclusion, but not the full-fledged reason in the sense of providing the exactly fitting cause for the relative nearness of the planets. Unlike the first type, namely through "the strict cause," this second method of demonstrating is not restricted to cases where cause and effect are reciprocal (78b11-13). Any effect indicates in some way its cause, one may add to complete the picture, and the occurence of an effect may well imply a number of remote causes besides the immediate cause.

The other way in which knowledge of the fact may be had is by demonstration through a remote cause (78b29). The example given is that a wall does not breathe because it is not an animal, with illustration by the claim that the Scythians have no flute-players because they have no vines. This way demonstates a negative conclusion cogently enough. It gives *a* reason, and a convincing reason. But it does not give *the* reason, in the sense of "the strict cause." To be an animal does not immediately require ability to breathe. To be an animal and to breathe do not reciprocally entail each other, in the way "the strict cause" reciprocally entails its effect. A kind of cause (78b23-24; b28) is given, but not the "strict" or exactly fitting cause that would unavoidably give rise to the effect.

What bearing do these directives from the *Analytics* have upon the problem faced by the *De Anima* in elaborating the definition of soul?

"Potentially living body," or "organic body" would be the effect of which soul is the formal cause. Further, form in general would have the role only of a remote cause, since it is a cause of both living and non-living bodies, and not immediately determined to either. What is required to make it *the* cause of a living body, in the sense of "the strict cause," is a differentia that would restrict it to living bodies. The differentia is not to be explained merely by relating the general notion of form to "living body," for in that case the explanation would be through the effect, and not genuinely in terms of cause. Just as the notion of form in general comes directly from the intelligible content met with in things, so a notion of "vital form," as differentiated from non-vital form, will have to be isolated as something immediately intelligible in the data that confront human cognition. Nothing less will satisfy the norms of "the strict cause" indicated by the background of the *Analytics* to which the reference here seems unavoidable.

In the mathematical illustration, the construction of the square would be the effect or conclusion. "Line" in general would be a remote cause for the construction, while the line that is the mean proportional would as a parameter be the "strict" or exactly fitting cause. The parallel is exact, and there is no doubt that the procedure works in the mathematical realm. But can it do so in the case of the soul? At least, the attempt can be made.

III

The formulation reached in the first chapter of *De Anima* 2 (412b5-6), then, will have to be elaborated in a way that will change it from a definition given in terms of the fact to one given in terms of "the strict cause." How is this to be accomplished? The wording "first entelechy of a natural organic body" gives a remote cause, "entelechy," that can exercise the role of formal cause in regard to both living and non-living bodies. To restrict it to the notion of "soul," the effect "organic body" is inserted into the definition. The definition, accordingly, makes plain the fact without giving the immediate cause. In order to formulate the definition in terms of immediate cause, the formal aspect that differentiates the form of an organic body from the form of a inorganic body will have to be brought to light. In a word, the differentia of organic body has to be isolated solely in terms of formal aspect, and not in terms of the composite living body that is its characteristic effect.

The procedure indicated, consequently, is a closer look at the notion of "living," to see if just in itself it makes manifest a formal differentia.

A return to the starting point recalls that what has soul is distinguished from what has not by the characteristic of living. Living, however, is spread through various senses, in mind, sensation, local movement and rest, and in the nutritional processes and growth and wasting away. Nutrition is obviously basic for all these instances of life. Sensation characterizes animal life, with touch the fundamental sense. Where local motion follows, there will be imagination, appetite, pleasure, and pain (413a20-b24).

When intellection is scrutinized, however, it gives rise to a difficulty that at first sight seems to keep bothering Aristotle unduly.[19] Intellection conjures up the problem of its own separate existence (413b13-16; b26-27), a problem that Aristotle had in mind at the end of the preceding chapter (1. 413a6-7). Intellectual activity seems to indicate "a widely different kind of soul, differing as what is eternal from what is perishable."[20] At least, it would imply a part (2. 413b13-14; b27-28) of the soul that has this characteristic. Nevertheless the unity of the soul is not for a moment called into question. As the form of the living body the soul is the origin (ἀρχή) of all the vital activities just mentioned (b11-13), fully in accord with the tenet of the *Physics* (2. 1. 192b13-193b5) that the form is the active principle (ἀρχή) of motion in all natural bodies. Further, these "parts" or capacities of soul are distinguished from one another on the basis of the differences between their immediately known activities.[21] This general principle is of prime importance for the interpretation of the whole chapter.

Life, the survey shows, is at its minimum the vegetative. Upon the vegetative follows the sensitive, and then the intellective. With "life" in its minimum sense used to denote the vegetative activity, the distinguishing characteristic of soul may now, on the basis of vital operations immediately known, be expressed as "that whereby we live and perceive" (414a4) and also as "that whereby we know" (a5). All reference to the effect, namely the living body or organic body, has been eliminated from this formulation. The characterization is given solely in terms of reflexively or internally known activities. In the source whose specific character is reached through knowledge of these activities, Aristotle's concern for the moment is to distinguish two grades. Just as "that whereby we know" may mean either knowledge (a quality) or soul, so "that whereby we live and perceive" may have the two corresponding senses. As a parallel, "that by which we are healthy" is health on the one hand and body on the other. Knowledge and health are viewed in this respect as form and, as it were, actuality of the two different recipients, a recipient capable of knowing and a recipient capable of being healthy.[22]

Since soul, then, is that "by or with which primarily we live, perceive, and think" (414a12-13; Oxford tr.) the conclusion is that it has to be form, and not matter or subject (414a14).

But is this conclusion justified by its immediate premises? And what is the exact force of the emphatically placed "primarily" in the context? True, the conclusion that soul is form coincides with its function as primary entelechy in the preceding chapter (1. 412a19-21). Moreover, the passage goes on (414a16-27) to show that soul requires a body specifically adapted to it, an appropriate kind of matter. [23] The burden of the discussion, then, tends towards explaining the kind of body in terms of the formal element, rather than explaining soul in terms of the composite effect, the living body. If this is what has been accomplished, will not the new elaboration of the definition of soul meet the requirement of exhibiting "the strict cause," as envisaged at the beginning of the present chapter? [24] To this extent the conclusion would seem to fit neatly enough into the overall framework of the chapter. Yet if in the immediate parallel the recipient is body, and the form received is health, should not soul as the recipient [25] of knowledge and in general of life appear rather in the role of a quasi-matter on the strength of this reasoning, as Sir David Ross suggests? [26] Should not soul function as the subject that receives the qualities of knowledge and life? Yet from the premises Aristotle draws the opposite conclusion. The soul, by which we *primarily* live and perceive and know is not matter or subject, but form. In this respect it would seem to have the same function as that of first entelechy in the preceding chapter.

Certainly there is a difficulty here. To illustrate the notion of first entelechy in the opening chapter, Aristotle had contrasted knowledge with thinking, and in that framework had explained soul as first entelechy after the model of knowledge (1. 412a22-28). Now, however, knowledge is contrasted with soul (2.414a5-6) as form with recipient. But is there anything impossible in this shift in the role of knowledge for the two different illustrations? As a learner a man can be in potentiality to knowledge, and after he has learned, he can still be in potentiality to thinking, as the *Physics* (8. 4. 255a33-35) asserts. May not knowledge, accordingly, be used on the two different occasions respectively to illustrate the soul's relation to its activities and to elucidate the formal element and the knowing subject? Can it not first, in the opening chapter, illustrate the function of soul as basic entelechy in contrast to subsequent vital operations? From that viewpoint soul as primary entelechy informs matter within the category of substance. Secondly, may not knowledge in its role of a qualitative form received by the knowing subject aptly clarify the more basic but less known formal principle of the substance in which it inheres? In this way knowledge as an illustration focuses attention on the function of soul as the basic *formal* capacity for living, perceiving, and knowing - a formal character that can be grasped through the regular way of object, activity, and faculty. In the present perspective is not knowledge as a qualitative form geared to explain the formal side of its recipient substance, and consequently to establish soul as a form, and not as matter or subject in the first of the categories?

How, in fact, could this other substantial principle, matter, be ranged for Aristotle under "that by which we know," since for him matter is unknowable in itself and an impediment to cognition? Rather, just as knowing requires knowledge as a formal principle on the qualitative level, so on the substantial level it requires a corresponding formal principle, a principle that has to be contrasted with matter. The conclusion indicated by the framework, then, is that in accord with the illustration, soul is the *form* by which basically we live and perceive and think, and not the matter or ultimate subject. As in the opening chapter, soul still appears as the primary entelechy, the entelechy in the category of substance. The backward reference ("as we said," 414a15) in giving the reason why soul is form throws the discussion squarely into the context of the preceding chapter where form in a twofold sense of entelechy was contrasted with matter (1. 412a6-11). The result, accordingly, is that while knowledge as a form and, as it were, an actuality is received in the knowing subject, the soul even as a component of the recipient is similarly an object with intelligible content (*logos,* 414a9) and a form.

Is not that precisely the conclusion one would expect from the illustration through knowledge in the two contexts? The abrupt change from one role of knowledge (potentiality for thinking, as at *Ph.* 8. 4. 255a34) to the other (entelechy of a recipient) is confusing, but is it not possible enough against the background of Aristotle's double relation of knowledge, in the one case to thinking, in the other to the knowing substance? Even though Aristotle in the preceding chapter ranged knowledge with having and not actualizing (1. 412a22-26), he seems to balance this out now (2. 414a9-10) by recalling in a parenthesis that knowledge is "as it were an actuality," since the actuality of an efficient cause is in the passum. Learning and health, in fact, are elsewhere (*Ph.* 3. 1. 201a18; 3. 202a32-b22; *Metaph.* θ 7. 1049a3-8; K 9. 1065b19) viewed as actualities produced by efficient causes. The subsequent actuality that is the activity of thinking takes place therefore through knowledge and through soul, both of which are forms. Correspondingly, we perform the other vital operations through the informing qualities and soul. Does not the situation itself, then, call for the stated result clause: "it follows that soul must be a ratio or formulable essence, not a matter or subject"?[27]

The reason why soul cannot be matter or subject is immediately introduced with the conjunction γάϱ (414a14). As an entelechy the soul has been already established as formal, and therefore can be neither matter nor body. In this way it is something of the body, in the sense of the form of a body. But as the basic form it cannot be fitted to an already constituted body. Rather, it itself determines the appropriate kind of body or matter.[28] From all this, Aristotle asserts, it is *clear* that soul is an entelechy of that which has the potentiality to be of this kind (414b14-28). "Of this kind" seems to mean the special type of body that is specified by soul, as at a22, in the context in which the kind of body is determined by the form, here the soul. But the differentia that makes manifest the specific type of form has now been explained on the basis of the formal notions of life, sensation, and knowledge.[29] The specification is given entirely in formal terms, and no longer in terms of the relation of form in general to an already constituted living body.

If this is admitted, the structure of the second chapter of *De Anima* 2 becomes intelligible. A definition through "the strict cause," as outlined in the *Analytics*, is envisaged and allegedly reached. The burden of the chapter is to show that as a special kind of body, "living body" is determined by its first entelechy and is not made "living" by the insertion of a soul into the already constituted body. The notions of life, as made known through nutrition and growth, and of sensation and intellection, are therefore the determining notes of the definition. But these notions more obviously belong to the categories of quality or action and passion. They have to be read back into the category of substance. Hence arises the use of the illustration of soul in contrast to knowledge and body in contrast to health, with the preoccupation of throwing the considerations into the category of substance (414a15) as described earlier (1. 412a6-21) in working out the initial definition of soul as first entelechy. This preoccupation would amply justify the use of "primarily" in the emphatic position in the formulation "with which primarily we live, perceive, and think" (414a12-13).

A suggestion that the "primarily" refers to the order in which the two alternatives are mentioned seems entirely untenable. In the twofold sense of entelechy illustrated in the first chapter (412a10; a22), the soul does come under the first-mentioned sense. But in the illustration in the second chapter, soul is expressly contrasted with the first-mentioned sense of vital principle, now illustrated by knowledge (414a5-6); and the contrast seems continued by the repetition of the same particles μέν with knowledge and δέ with soul at lines a8 and a12. Here soul is unmistakably kept in the second-mentioned of the two senses.

Another suggestion is that the "primarily" means "prior from the point of view of definitional precision,"[30] in the sense that life and sensation and knowledge are the formal characteristics of which soul is the strictly appropriate recipient. This suggestion is attractive. It focuses sharply on the requirement of defining soul in terms of the exactly fitting differentia. But it seems hard to accommodate with the immediately following explanation (a14-28) that the soul is form in the sense of one of the elements in the category of substance. For the same reason it is difficult to understand the "primarily" as implying "the first cause" in the sense of the immediate or "strict" cause in the *Posterior Analytics* (1. 13. 78a25), even though this might be suggested by the aims of the present article. Aristotle does not use this characteristic of "first" in outlining the framework of "the fact" and "the cause" at the beginning of *De Anima* 2. 2. A reference to it as used in the *Analytics* would seem farfetched. A reference to the "first entelechy" of *De Anima* 2. 1, on the other hand, seems entirely normal.

IV

But with this overall interpretation of the chapter granted, does Aristotle's reasoning actually achieve a definition in terms of "the strict cause" of the *Analytics?* An obvious objection, that receives no satisfactory answer in the Aristotelian setting, is that the formal notion used is too wide. The formal notion is life in its various senses (*De An.* 2. 2. 413a22-25). That notion extends to separate forms, to substances that are not forms of bodies. This tenet is abundantly clear in the *Metaphysics*, and keeps bothering Aristotle in the present discussion in the *De Anima* (1. 413a6-7; 2. 413b24-27). But a soul has to be the form of a body, of matter (414a20-21). Life, accordingly, is a notion that ranges wider than soul, just as "animal" in the *Analytics* (1. 13. 78b15-31) is too wide to entail the conclusion that something breathes. A remote cause is given, but not "the strict cause." Definition of soul with "life" as the specific differentia does not meet the terms of the requirement set up at the beginning of *De Anima* 2. 2.

What has been happening? Aristotle, in full accord with the spirit of Greek intellectual optimism, seems to have had no doubt about the power of the human mind to penetrate the specific differentiae of natural things.[31] In the present instance he is encountering a privileged case. One is aware of one's own vegetative life, sensation, and intellection in an intimate way quite other than the quantitative and qualitative observation by which one knows external things. One is aware of the waving of one's own hand in a markedly different way from the perception of the waving of a friend's hand as the train pulls out. One experiences, moreover, the differences between the grades of vegetative, sentient, and intellectual life, and the hierarchical orientation (see *Pol.* 1. 8. 1256b15-22) of one to the other. But does this reflexive awareness provide the type of insight that can be communicated in definition?

There is, of course, no question of leveling a charge of subjectivism against Aristotle. His conception of specific form as the basis of universality[32] involves a specific unity of human experience in all individual men. What one man experiences in regard to life, sensation, and intellection will be specifically the same as the corresponding experiences in other men as made known through conversation and writing. The specific unity of human nature provides a solid basis for objective communication. The present difficulty does not lie there. Rather, the difficulty is located in the failure of human intellection to penetrate this awareness of life, sensation, and intellection in a way that would allow reasoning from a "strict cause" to effects. The notions of life, sensation, and intellection, no matter how certainly they are experienced through internal awareness, do not give the clarity and penetration that would allow a science of the soul to be developed in the way a science of geometry is built up from the geometrical differentiae.[33] One may be conscious of the graded hierarchy in life, sensation, and intellection, conscious of it with unshakable certainty. But one does not penetrate this knowledge in a way that yields specific premises for scientific conclusions. The privileged knowledge establishes the *fact* of specific difference between the living and non-living, and between the sentient and the intellective. But it does not make manifest the differentia in the way required for functioning as "the strict cause" in the definition. The trouble does not stem from a failure in objective communication. Not the medium but the message is at fault.

Aristotle is unhesitant in maintaining the fundamental unity of the human agent,[34] and in seeing in soul a unifying principle "with which primarily we live, perceive, and think." He realizes that our privileged awareness of life as specifically differentiated is on the operational level, and has to be read back into its qualitative and its substantial source. In this twofold source, the substantial as the more basic may be called "primary." Hence Aristotle insists on the notion "primary" in the definition of soul. He drives his effort as far as possible in the direction of defining soul in purely formal terms, instead of through reference to its matter, the organic body. But does he not meet frustration in the failure of the internally experienced differentia to make manifest the "strict cause" of the vital effects? The differentia does not explain, for instance, how intellection can be separately existent and yet be an activity of the one agent that grows and perceives. Nor in general does it give knowledge from which the specific properties can be deduced.

Aristotle's insights are too keen to be victimized by any temptation towards facile systematization. But the penalty is that key issues have to remain in a state of *aporia*.[35] Among these is the substantial nature that the definition of soul tries to express. A definition that will "enable us to discover the derived properties" (text *supra*, n. 1), in accord with the geometrical model of a demonstrative premise, has not been reached. Nor, insofar as soul is an object of human cognition, is a definition of this type available. Psychology as a special science requires development through the experimental methods of modern research, while knowledge of the spiritual falls within the scope of metaphysics. To sum up, the nature of soul cannot be grasped in a way that would furnish a satisfactory definition within an Aristotelian philosophy of nature.

The direction taken by the work on the definition of soul in the first two chapters of *De Anima 2*, however, seems clear enough. The first chapter describes soul in terms of the general notion of form in relation to a special effect, the living body. Against the background of the *Analytics*, the second chapter strives to elaborate the definition in terms of soul as "strict cause" of the living body. It reaches its notion of soul through the features of life more readily known first on the operational and then on the qualitative levels, reading them back to the substantial level, and showing that the type of form so reached requires a living body as its appropriate matter. The procedure is from immediate cause to effect, and not from effect to cause as in the preceding chapter. But success eludes its grasp.

11. The Aristotelian Argument for the Material Principle of Bodies

I

Even a perfunctory acquaintance with the first two books of Aristotle's *Physics* will indicate clearly enough that his argument for an ultimate material principle is based on the generation of natural bodies. The argument, moreover, is summed up in the form of an analogy with artifacts. Knowledge "by an analogy" is in fact the explicit designation given to this grasp of the ultimate material principle. The starting point of the reasoning is the observable change wrought in bronze or wood by art and craftsmanship. The point of the observation is then extended to anything whatsoever that may be considered in a status prior to the reception of a designated form. Finally, the conclusion focuses on a substrate that has this relation to the existent individual substance. The text that sums up the argument reads: "The underlying nature is an object of scientific knowledge, by an analogy. For as the bronze is to the statue, the wood to the bed, or the matter and the formless bronze before receiving form to anything which has form, so is the underlying nature to substance, i. e. the 'this' or existent."[1]

Misgivings may arise when this succinct and well-known passage is viewed against the general background of Aristotelian philosophy. The philosophy of nature is regarded by Aristotle as a crucially important science. If there were no separate substances, it would indeed be the first, the highest of the sciences.[2] Its first principles, one would accordingly expect, should be established with the certitude proper to science in the strictest sense. These first principles, the procedure of *Physics* I makes clear, are matter and form. Each of these is called "nature" by Aristotle. Together they constitute the composite known as a natural thing (*Phys.* II 1, 193 a 28 - b 6). But if one of the principles, the matter, is known only by analogy, does not the genuinely scientific status of natural philosophy seem at first sight to be jeopardized? If analogy is understood in anything like its currently accepted meaning, how can it serve as the process by which a basic principle for a philosophic science may be established?

Further, if the only fact on which the argument itself is based is generation in the sense of the change of one natural body into another, how conclusive can its reasoning be? Is not the change of one substance into another easy to question or to deny, and extremely difficult to defend? Was it not denied almost unanimously by the Presocratics? Did it not continue to be rejected in the Atomistic tradition that blossomed into Epicureanism so shortly after Aristotle's own time? How, then, can this alleged fact be expected to bear the whole weight of the argument for establishing one of the two first principles of Aristotelian natural philosophy? Yet what further reasons are to be found in Aristotle's treatises? Are any other reasons given at all?

The pertinent questions emerging from a consideration of the above passage, then, are sufficiently clear and pointed. First, what kind of knowledge is meant by analogy in this context? Does analogy here mean just probable reasoning, unable to terminate in the certitude required for scientific knowledge? Or can analogy be for Aristotle a type of cognition that establishes in apodictical fashion the first principle for a genuine science? Secondly, is the fact of generation, in the sense of change that takes place within the Aristotelian category of substance, sufficiently certain to ground an argument for setting up a first principle in the philosophy of nature? Thirdly, in the event of a negative or unsatisfactory answer, does Aristotle provide any alternate way to reach entirely formless[3] matter as a first principle for this science?

II

The solution of the problem that arises from the use of the notion 'analogy' may depend entirely on the removal of historical misunderstandings. The term has come to mean a sort of vague resemblance or likeness. In the context of the *Poetics* (21, 1457 b 6-25), it is true, analogy is associated by Aristotle with metaphor. Along with species and genus, it is able to serve as a foundation for metaphorical expression. But it itself is not regarded as a figure of speech. Rather, like generic and specific knowledge, it is accepted as something certainly present in a literal sense. It does not imply mere probability. For instance, the metaphor of old age as the evening of life (b 24) is grounded on the analogy "As old age (D) is to life (C), so is evening (B) to day (A)" (b 22-23). This analogy is obviously regarded as something certain. It is an instance in which the general definition "the second (B) is to the first (A), as the fourth (D) to the third (C)" (b 17-18) is exemplified. There is no introduction of probable reasoning. The comparison does not at all mean that old age *probably* comes at the end of life since evening comes at the end of day. On the contrary, the analogy is a definite and certainly known ground upon which the metaphor can be built. The function of analogy in grounding metaphor in no way means that what is analogical is necessarily metaphorical. Even in this context, then, analogy does not signify a type of probable reasoning.

In general, as the above association with genus and species suggests, analogy implies for Aristotle a kind of unity that is wider than the specific and the generic.[4] It involves a sameness that has greater range than generic sameness. What follows from this conception of analogy as a type of unity and sameness? The unity of species, as a foundation for universal predication, requires that what is necessarily included in a specific notion be predicable of every singular in the species. The predicate bears upon the species as a whole—καϑόλου[5]—and not on just some of its members. Likewise the unity of a genus requires that everything necessarily implied in the generic notion be predicable of each species in the genus. Correspondingly, in the still wider unity of analogy, everything that belongs within the commonly analogous notion itself will be present in all its analogates. One need only prove that a certain condition is required by the very notion at issue. Then one is able to conclude with all due rigor that the condition is to be found in this or that instance of it.

In the present case, the analogous notion is that of change. Under its unifying coverage are included all things that are changeable. The notion of change necessarily involves a substrate that loses one form and acquires another. Necessarily, therefore, any changeable thing will be composed of subject and form. Were it not so composed it would not be able to undergo change. It would not be a changeable thing. Natural substances, however, are changeable.[6] Therefore in natural substances there has to be a substrate that is able to lose one form and acquire another.

Does this have any appearance of probable reasoning? Hardly. It seems entirely apodictical in character. It is quite evidently based on the notion of change itself. It draws a necessary consequence from the very notion of change, wherever change is found. Accordingly, once natural substances are accepted on other grounds as changeable, they come under its all-embracing scope. As a result, the presence of a substrate within the Aristotelian category of substance seems to have been demonstrated by the test of the *Physics* in apodictical fashion.

The gradation in the test itself helps bear out this interpretation. The observable instances of bronze becoming a statue and wood a bed are first noted. The reception of form directly observed in these instances is then universalized to everything that first lacks a certain form and afterwards receives it. So universalized, the notion is applied to change within the category of substance. The procedure is accordingly standard Aristotelianism. The universal object is first seen through a scrutiny of singular after singular (*An. Post.* II 19, 100 a 12 - b 5), and once it is established to the mind's satisfaction it is applicable χαθόλου. It is applicable to every instance known to come under its scope, and consequently is able to serve as a middle term for rigorous syllogistic discourse.[7]

Likewise the general development of the reasoning throughout the first book of the *Physics* points to an interpretation along the above lines. As usual in Aristotle's treatises, the book commences with a dialectical survey of the topic in his predecessors. After some opening remarks (*Phys.* I 1) on method, it finds that preceding philosophy had required contraries as the principles of change. Concentrating on the result so reached, the treatise proceeds to establish the conclusion by strict reasoning: "But we must see how this can be arrived at as a reasoned result, as well as in the way just indicated" (I 5, 188 a 30-31). Aristotle's own reasoning follows. The principles of change are shown to be contraries, plus a subject that loses one contrary and acquires the other. This allows the contraries to be identified as a form and the corresponding privation of form (I 5-7). The reasoning takes place in the most general framework of the topic: "We will now give our own account, approaching the question first with reference to becoming in its widest sense: for we shall be following the natural order of inquiry if we speak first of common characteristics, and then investigate the characteristics of special cases" (I 7, 189 b 30-32). Among the special cases that of substance is paramount: "Only substances are said to 'come to be' in the unqualified sense" (7, 190 a 32-33). In all other cases, however, the need for a substrate is obvious: "For we know that when a thing comes to be of such a quantity or quality or in such a relation, time, or place, a subject is always presupposed . . . But that substances too, and anything else that can be said 'to be' without qualification, come to be from some substratum, will appear on examination" (a 34 - b 3). The illustration used is that seed is required for the generation of animals and plants, suggesting a common substrate for the process of change to a different form. The conclusion is then drawn that "everything comes to be from both subject and form" (b 20). Towards the end of this chapter the reasoning is summed up in the passage in which scientific knowledge of the material principle in substances is described as analogous.

The overall procedure of *Physics* I, therefore, shows clearly enough that Aristotle establishes a general notion of change from an investigation of its observable instances. The general notion, required wherever change is found, is that a subject passes from the privation of a form to the possession of the form. In all the categories except substance the substrate is observable. Since change everywhere requires a substrate, a corresponding subject within the category of substance is necessary to make possible the change of one substance into another. Though not directly observable, this substrate within the category of substance is scientifically knowable as a subject that stands in relation to substance as substance itself stands in relation to accidental composites.

No tincture of probability weakens this reasoning of Aristotle in the overall procedure of *Physics* I. How, then, does the reluctance to accept it as apodictical arise? Already in ancient times, on the topic of word formation, Quintilian (I 6, 12-16) had noted that analogy could not be everywhere applied, that it was based not upon reasoning but upon example, and that it was not a law of speech but the result of custom. Where it did apply, however, he regarded it as a means of using what was certain to probe what was uncertain. With Quintilian as his background for the notion, Butler, in his widely read treatise *The Analogy of Religion* presented analogy as a means of probable reasoning, in contrast to strict demonstration. Zoology, biology, psychology, and linguistics joined in this acceptation of the term. Accordingly analogy became catalogued in logic as a merely probably argument by which "we conclude because A resembles B in one or more properties, that it does so in a certain other property."[8] Need one be surprised, therefore, that this commonly accepted modern notion of analogy throws such a smoke screen over the Aristotelian argument in *Physics* I?

In Aristotle's own language, in fact, it is hard to see how this currently accepted notion of analogy, if proposed as a demonstration, would not come under the fallacy of accident. It reasons from one accidentally connected predicate to something else that is accidentally connected: "It is, however, not always true, e. g. suppose that A and B are 'the same' as C *per accidens*; for both 'snow' and the 'swan' are the same as something 'white' " (*Soph. El.* 6, 168 b 33-35). The sameness in which snow and swan coincide here is merely accidental. The notion in which artificial change and change within substance coincide in the argument of the *Physics*, however, is required by the nature of change wherever it occurs. It is not something accidental to the various instances of change. It is essential to each of them. If it were lacking, the instance would no longer be one of change.

The contrast of the fallacy of accident with reasoning by analogy in Aristotle brings out sharply the ground for present-day hesitation in accepting as demonstrative any argument labeled 'analogy'. To contemporary ears, analogy is either tentative or presumptive reasoning with no other basis than the unjustified assumption that if things resemble each other in some attributes they should do so in others. One does not have to go further than the *Oxford English Dictionary* (s. v.) to see that analogy is understood as "probability from a parallel case," something that "warrants the conjecture," that "is not proof, but illustration." A logician may accordingly warn the public against its evils, and require as the only safeguard for countering them a correct insight into its logical nature.[9] With this popular image built up against the demonstrative force of reasoning by analogy, need one be surprised at the spontaneous reaction in face of an argument that presents itself explicitly as analogous in character? Need there be wonder at the difficulty in seeing how for Aristotle, in accord with its mathematical model of a four-term proportion, it meant that knowledge of three of the terms enabled one to reason apodictically to the fourth?

The analogous way of knowing the material principle has its bearing on one's general understanding of Aristotelian natural philosophy. The method proposed (*Phys.* I 1, 184 a 16-25) for the science starts from composites more knowable to us, and proceeds to principles that, while less knowable to us, are more knowable absolutely. The principles sought throughout the first book of the *Physics* are the principles of change in natural things. One of these principles, the matter, is unknowable in itself.[10] Yet to serve as a principle for explaining sensible bodies it has to be more knowable than they. How? Obviously, in the Aristotelian way of knowing it, it is universalized under the analogous notion of substrate. The notion is taken from observable subjects of change, and is extended universally by analogy. The necessary precisions, of course, have to be made to apply it within the category of substance.[11] Yet by means of analogy one has a universal notion that it more intelligible in itself than the sensible composites it is meant to explain.[12] Analogy as rigorously scientific reasoning makes possible the knowledge of matter as a principle for natural philosophy.

Here, of course, one has to be careful about another popular conception that may be found attributed to Aristotle, that of a 'correspondence theory' of truth.[13] In regard to the ultimate material principle known by analogy, there evidently cannot be any photographic resemblance between the principle itself and the concept by which it is grasped. In itself the principle has no intelligiblity at all. As grasped under the analogous notion of substrate, it is more knowable than the concrete sensible things. The concept, accordingly, is not an immediate replica of the principle itself. Rather, the concept is the result of intellectual elaboration that remains true to the original data while representing separately two principles that cannot have separate status in reality, namely the matter and the form of sensible substances.

III

Although the Aristotelian conception of analogy permits apodictical reasoning from sensible things to their ultimate material principle, it cannot be any more certain of its conclusion than of its premises. One of the premises for this reasoning is that changes do occur within the category of substance. Aristotle GC II 1, 329a24 - b 1; 4, 331a7 - 332a 2) has no hesitation in accepting the changes of earth, water, air and fire into one another as changes of substance. Was it really evident that air was one substance and fire was another? Not only was it not evident—it was wrong. Today, one is still conscious of one's self as a different thing from the food one is about to consume. On that model one considers every other man, every clearly designated animal or plant, and perhaps every molecule in inorganic objects, as a distinct thing, a distinct substance. Accordingly the elements and compounds into which a man or an animal or a plant dissolves after dying appear to be different things, different substances. Yet it was possible in Greek times, and it is still possible today in view of common spectra and equality of weights, to conceive these things as basically mere rearrangements of particles that do not change internally in themselves. Basically, then, the same things would remain after the change has taken place.

Against the acceptance of this view, of course, stands the disconcerting fact that the same things could be in a combination that acts like a man or a dog, on the one hand, and on the other in a combination that behaves like a solid block of marble, without any greater difference than rearrangement of internally undisturbed particles. This is difficult to accept—just as difficult, perhaps, today as it was in Aristotle's time. The profound differences in the specific character of the activities seem to indicate radically different agents. Some thirty-two elementary particles may explain things satisfactorily on the level of experimental physics. Yet viewed from another level of thought, the things of the cosmos seem to require something deeper than the polarity of subatomic particles to account for the statistical regularity of the quanta and to explain the radically new kind of activity after certain types of change.

The truth, therefore, seems to be that the evidence for or against the fact of substantial change is neither more nor less, in any really relevant manner, than it was in Aristotle's day. There is no more reason at present for rejecting the fact of generation, understood as change within the category of substance, than there was in the fourth century B. C. Earth, air, and fire can no longer be accepted as substances. But this only means that the question becomes focused on about a hundred chemical elements and countless inorganic and organic compounds. On the other hand, there is no more reason now than then for accepting the fact of generation in the Aristotelian sense. The facts of nutrition and death are the dominant considerations. Food is changed into animal body, an animal decays into other substances. In these occurrences there seems to be a change of one thing, in its most basic nature, into another. But the human intellect has no intuition of this change. The nature of the change has to be reasoned to from observable activites and qualities that do not permit an incontrovertible conclusion. To the extent, accordingly, to which the fact of generation was acceptable in Aristotle's time, it remains so today. To the extent to which there was then reason to question it, it may still be questioned today, though of course in almost infinitely greater detail.

What occasions the lack of definite knowledge in this area? Is it irremediable? Or is there some hope of obtaining further insight? For Aristotle, as the long opening chapter of the *Parts of Animals* clearly shows, knowledge of a sensible thing's form could be obtained from a study of the thing's functioning or purpose, since final cause and formal cause were identical. Just as through the artist's design one may learn the details of the artifact, so through knowledge of the form one may acquire detailed knowledge of natural phenomena.[14] Centuries of chemical and physical research have thoroughly discounted this contention. The detailed knowledge of nature that has resulted from modern science is not attained from any knowledge the human intellect has of substantial forms. The specific traits of bodies can be attained only qualitatively and quantitatively. It is by putting a measure on them that they have been probed in depth by scientific investigation. Knowledge of form within the category of substance has not helped at all in this tremendous expansion of scientific vistas.

What do these considerations indicate regarding the penetration of human insight into the substantial forms of bodies? Do they not imply convincingly enough that one's insight into corporeal form does not go beyond the generic grade of corporeity? But in that generic grade all bodies coincide. On its level no means is provided for distinguishing bodies specifically, for intuiting the specific difference of one substance from another. Through it one cannot reason to a change from one kind

of substance to a different kind. It is knowledge of substance that suffices for reasoning in Aristotelian fashion to a material principle, once
the fact of generation in the Aristotelian sense has been granted. But it
cannot establish that fact.

The possibility of knowing substantial forms specifically, which in the
atmosphere of ancient Greek optimism still seemed open to Aristotle, is
therefore for practical purposes closed today. True, the evidence is
negative in character. No insight into a substantial form beyond the
grade of corporeity has yet been obtained. But if after so many centuries
of intensive investigation no intuitive knowledge of any specific differentia in the natural world has been attained, the working presumption is
that no such insight will ever be reached by the human intellect. The
hope, then, of establishing substantial change as a starting point with a
certitude comparable to the certitude in the starting points of mathematical or metaphysical demonstrations, has to be given up. One may accept
the fact of generation with the same assurance with which one counts
one's self a different being from the earth on which one walks and the
food of which one partakes. But the insight that would enable one to
answer philosophic objections against the specific distinction of these
bodies and the generation of one from the other, is entirely lacking.

Does Aristotle, then, offer any other argument to reach the material
principle of bodies? On a couple of occasions he mentions that things in
the one species are the same in form, but different in matter. Does this
mean that multiplication of singulars in a species requires a material
principle? If so, does it not constitute a separate argument, independently of substantial change, for the presence of entirely formless matter in
bodies? The form, from its own standpoint of form, has to remain
the same in all the singulars. Any formal difference, any addition or
subtraction in formal characteristics, would mean a new species (*Met.
Eta* 3, 1043 b 32 - 1044 a 11). Here the species remain identical as the
singulars multiply. Does not this observable plurality of singulars, then,
enable one to reason to the requirement of absolutly formless matter? Is
it not the case that for Aristotle a separate substance, because it lacks a
material principle, cannot be pluralized (*Lambda* 8, 1074 a 31-37).
Multiplication of singulars in the same species, therefore, would suggest
an argument for a material principle that has no formal characteristic at
all.

Does Aristotle himself ever use this argument? In one of the relevant
texts speaking of things like plants and animals that are propagated in a
species, he notes that generation is caused by "another member of the
same natural species having the same form (thus, men generate men).

This is the way things are generated naturally."[15] Yet he does not use the sameness of form in a plurality of singulars as an argument to show the presence of matter. Rather, he had shown it in the immediately preceding lines by the argument from generation: " . . . all things produced either by nature or by art have matter; for each of them is capable both of being and of not being, and this capacity is the matter in each."[16] The multiplication of singulars in the same species, accordingly, is not used here by Aristotle as a means of arriving at the material principle. It is merely mentioned after the principle has been considered established on the basis of the argument from generation and perishing.

The other pertinent text, dealing with singulars like Callias and Socrates reads: " . . . they are different in virtue of their matter (for that is different) but the same in form; for their form is indivisible" (*Met. Zeta* 8, 1034 a 7-8). The form that is contrasted with matter in these lines is clearly enough the physical form that is achieved by the agent in generating a new individual. But in this chapter also the observation presupposes that the material principle is already known through the argument from generation: "Since everything which is produced is produced . . . from something (and let this be taken to be not the privation, but the matter; for the meaning we attach to this has already been explained) . . . In some cases indeed it is even obvious that the begetter is of the same kind as the begotten (not, however, the *same* nor one in number but in form), i. e. in the case of natural products (for man begets man)" (ibid. 1033 a 24 - b 32). Again the multiplicity of singulars in a species is not used as a new argument for a material principle in bodies.

Not only in the *Physics* but also in these texts from the *Metaphysics*, then, no further argument from specific sameness in individuals is brought forward to supplement the one from generation. As a separate argument it would be immune to the objection that arises from the lack of insight into the specific natures of bodies. Multiplication of instances in spatial distinction from one another would be all that is required for its cogency. For that, an understanding of bodies just as corporeal in nature would suffice. Yet not even in the case of the heavenly bodies, where for Aristotle the argument from generation would not apply, is it offered by him as a supplementary proof.

The feature upon which the cogency of the above argument is based, however, suggests another approach that would be independent not only of knowledge of the distinction between species, but also of knowledge of the distinction between individuals. If multiplication of the form without any formal addition requires the presence of a material principle, by the same token the extension of a nature through parts outside parts, without any addition from the side of form, will likewise require that principle. In a word, sensible nature, in contradistinction from supersensible being, must have a material besides a formal principle.[17]

Does Aristotle ever argue in this way? He does insist that every sensible thing has matter, as potency within the category of substance: ". . . sensible substances all have matter. The substratum is substance, and this is in one sense the matter (and by matter I mean that which, not being a 'this' actually, is potentially a 'this')" (*Met. Eta* 1,1042 a 25-28). But what proof does he advance for this assertion? It is the regular argument from change: ". . . for in all the opposite changes that occur there is something which underlies the changes, . . . and similarly in respect of substance there is something that is now being generated and again being destroyed, and now underlies the process as a 'this' and again underlies it in respect of a privation of positive character" (a 32-b3).

Even when mentioning that singulars are different by reason of their matter, and that all sensible substances have matter, then, Aristotle has recourse to the one argument from generation to show the presence of the material principle. He uses only one of the arguments, and not either of the latter two. A further question, however, is whether these three arguments are basically different, or from the plurality of singulars in a species and the argument from spatial extension seem readily enough to coincide in the one demonstrative ground. Both find their probative force in the requirement of a non-formal principle to explain the presence of the same form, without any addition from its own formal standpoint, in new individuals and in parts outside parts. But how does this reason compare with operative feature in the argument from the perishing and generation of substances? Aristotle himself, as the passages just cited show, seems to see the same reasoning at work throughout all these considerations.

The proof from generation rests on the apparent capability of one sensible substance to become another. The basic potentiality required for this change turns out to be the material principle in the substance.[18] Does the starting point here coincide, as far as the argument's operative feature is concerned, with the manifest capacity of a sensible nature to be instantiated in different individuals and to be extended in parts outside parts? In each of these cases the starting point is a capability in sensible things that is not able to be explained by entirely formal characteristics. That is the common feature that becomes operative in the reasoning in each case. The manifest potentiality in each of the three cases, accordingly, requires the entirely non-formal principle in the substance. Does not this requirement suffice to merge the manifest potentiality in the three cases into a common basis for argument? Is there not apparent, in each of the three ways of commencing the demonstration, a common aspect of potentiality that leads to the same completely non-formal principle in the substance itself, whether seen as the capability of the one substance to become another, or of the same nature to be extended through parts and mutiplied in singular instances? The common aspect, in a word, is potentiality that does not coincide with the sensible thing's formal characteristics.

In contradistinction, separate substance is completely self-contained in its form. It cannot even know anything outside itself.[19] Lacking all admixture of potentiality it cannot be multiplied in a species, it cannot be extended spatially, it is not subject to generation and perishing. The same feature seems to account for these three ways in which supersensible substance stands so opposed to sensible substance. In contrast, potentiality is highlighted as the common ground for the three contrary characteristics in sublunar bodies. Needless to remark, the anomalies arising from the supposedly ingenerate nature of the heavens, so disturbing to medieval commentators, do not cause any difficulty today.

The two arguments that have been added by later thinkers, to supplement the one Aristotelian argument from generation, do not then seem to exhibit any radical difference from the proof originally developed by Aristotle. Sensible substances manifest characteristics of potentiality, thereby allowing one to reason to a material principle in their natures. Whether the manifestation that forms the starting point of the argument is seen in generation or in individuation or in extension, the nature of the reasoning seems quite obviously to stay the same, at least in its general lines.

IV

From an overall study, consequently, Aristotle's argument for a material principle in bodies emerges as reasoning that is meant to be demonstrative in a strict sense. Though expressly called analogy, it is not the argument from analogy in the modern acceptation of that phrase. It does not infer from the way natural bodies resemble artifacts in one respect, namely in undergoing change, that they also resemble them in another respect, namely in having a substrate. If it did, it would thereby be open to the Aristotelian notion of fallacy of accident, and could hardly be expected to function in the critically important task of establishing a first principle for natural philosophy.

Rather, the argument reasons apodictically from the very notion of change itself, a notion grasped in universal fashion through sufficient concentration on observable instances, as any universal is grasped for Aristotle. Of its own nature change requires a substrate. Knowing in two different instances of change the two composites and only the one substrate, the intellect can accordingly reason to the presence and corresponding nature of the second substrate. It can reason here with apodictical assurance proportionate to its certainty that the number five replaces the variable in "Eight is to four as ten is to x." Though analogy grounds metaphor, it itself is not metaphorical. The association cannot in the Aristotelian argument from analogy be used to infer conclusions from traits in the metaphor that are only accidentally connected with the analogical feature, as are the resemblances on which the modern notion of analogy is based. The Aristotelian analogy of old age with evening, for instance, would not even suggest that old age might occur periodically every twenty-four hours, or that evening be a subject for geriatrics.

Further, a global view makes the operative force of the Aristotelian argument of the material principle in bodies rest upon the aspect of potentiality that is manifest in sensible things. One way in which the potentiality is seen appears in the capacity of these things to be changed into one another. On that manifestation Aristotle focuses attention for the starting point of his demonstration. It is the only starting point used by the argument in the *Physics*. The first major step (*Phys.* I, 2-6) in the dialectical approach had been to justify the fact of change, in confrontation with the Eleatics and the later Presocratics. As a result of the polemic Aristotle regarded as established to his own satisfaction the change of one substance into another. Change did exist and in a stronger sense than alteration from one quality to another or local rearrangement of particles.[20] Against that background the indicated procedure was obviously to argue from the fact of substantial change. The matrix for the discussion was formed naturally in the hearers from their absorption in Presocratic problems and in those of the *Timaeus*. The mediaeval controversies on the principle of individuation and the later concern with the conditions of extended substance did not enter into the ferment.

Aristotle accordingly shows no awareness of need to seek a more incontrovertible manifestation of potentiality in natural substances, in the sense of potentiality within their own category. That he was so wrong in some of his basic instances of this change, as in the cases of earth, air, and fire, and so mistaken in his conception of the unchangeableness in celestial substances, has understandably given pause in face of the argument in *Physics* I. Burnt children fear the fire. People who have striven to perpetuate the Aristotelian tradition have quite naturally turned to other arguments that would be independent of the starting point found in change within the category of substance. Yet may one not still be convinced that soil is something basically different from the trees growing out of it, that oats are different bodies from the horse feeding upon them, that a living human organism is a radically different thing from the sum total of elements and compounds into which it disintegrates after death? In these instances may not the manifestation of potentiality from which the Aristotelian reasoning commences maintain its pristine vigor.

However, since lack of insight into specific natures deprives one of the knowledge necessary to answer with complete satisfaction the objections that may be brought forward against substantial change, the supplementary manifestations of the potentiality, namely in the spatial extension of sensible substance and its multiplication in singulars, have in point of fact been developed in later tradition. They give rise to fundamentally the same argument. Accordingly they fit into the same framework of Aristotelian analogy. Just as the image of President Kennedy is plurified in the striking of each new fifty cent coin on each additional piece of silver amalgam, so in the multiplication of instances in a substantial nature must a corresponding substrate be present. Just as the same image is without formal difference extended over a larger quantity of metal in a wall plaque of Kennedy, so through growth the same animal form vivifies more material in the cat than it did in the kitten. The notions of individuation and of extension function in the analogy in correspondingly the same way as the notion of change.

The consideration of these supplementary arguments, therefore, need not at all suggest a desire to save the principles of Aristolelian natural philosophy at all costs. Rather, it evinces an effort to understand these principles in thier full and global implications. But, for the record, the fact should be clearly pointed out that Aristotle himself used only the reasoning from change, and not the two further arguments[21].

12. The Teleology of Nature in Aristotle*

I

An approach to the question of teleology in nature for Aristotle requires first of all a sufficiently clear understanding of the terms involved. In regard to the notion of teleology itself, there can hardly be any pertinent difficulty. The term is a modern one, and is quite definitely fixed in meaning by contemporary use. It seems to have been coined in eighteenth-century philosophical Latin to denote the study of final causes in nature.[1] It became readily accepted in modern philosophical vocabulary. Against this historical background it is commonly understood today to focus on "purposive or goal-directed activity."[2] In application to nature it assumes that purposive activity is present and asks how the activity is to be identified and described. The initial problem, accordingly, will lie not with the notion of teleology but rather with the other term, 'nature'.

What is 'nature' for Aristotle? As is well enough known, the Stagirite had no hesitation in recognizing a number of different meanings for the term 'nature'.[3] In his formal division of the sciences, however, he restricted it technically, as an object of philosophical study, to mobile things.[4] These are the things of the visible and tangible universe, things permeated through and through by motion as though by "a sort of life."[5] This Aristotelian restriction of the term 'nature' may have been somewhat arbitrary, but it was in full accord with the current use of the Greek verb φύομαι to denote growth or development. It meant in practice that 'nature' in strict philosophical use was limited to things that undergo sensibly perceptible motion.

According to the Aristotelian analysis of motion, a mobile thing requires two components. These are form and matter. Form is the intelligible or knowable content of the thing. It is the thing's actuality. Matter, on the other hand, is unknowable just as matter.[6] It is knowable only in relation to form. It is a potential principle that can lose one form and acquire another, thereby rendering change possible. On the level of natural

---

*This paper was read at the meeting of the Metaphysical Society of America held at the University of Southern California on March 16, 1968.

philosophy the observed face of change requires explanation through these two components. Each of them for Aristotle is 'nature', and the composites to which they give rise are accordingly "things constituted by nature."[7]

These considerations set out in a fairly clearcut picture what 'nature' comprises for the Stagirite. Nature will include in its scope all the things of the visible and tangible universe. To that extent it coincides satisfactorily enough with the ordinary conception of nature today. The world of nature is readily understood to be the world we see and hear and feel around us. It is in ceaseless motion, from the gyrations of the fundamental particles to the tremendous outsurge of the receding galaxies. Roughly, the two conceptions of nature—the Aristotelian and the modern—coincide in scope. In regard to man, there may be some partial discrepancy. To what extent, then, is man included under nature in the Aristotelian framework?

For Aristotle, a man is composed of matter and form, just as is anything corporeal. As with all living things, moreover, the form here is called a soul. Soul is accordingly nature for Aristotle, even in the case of man.[8] Further, in man one part of the soul is intellect.[9] But intellect is twofold. There is passive intellect and there is agent intellect. Passive intellect is perishable.[10] This is sufficient to bring it under mobile being. There need be little hesitation, then, in regarding the Aristotelian passive intellect as pertaining to nature in the sense in which nature is the subject of natural philosophy. The other kind of intellect, however, is separate and imperishable.[11] Consequently it does not come under the Aristotelian philosophy of nature. It seems to function as an agent in a way that receives no satisfactory explanation in the Aristotelian text. But there is enough in the text to justify the conclusion that it does not operate as an agent composed of matter and form. It may accordingly be regarded as outside the scope of nature in the sense now under consideration.

To sum up, nature for Aristotle comprises all visible and tangible things, living as well as nonliving. It includes human nature as regards both soul and passive intellect, but not active intellect. Hardly necessary to remark, a danger signal is already flashing. If mobility is the distinguishing characteristic of nature, if motion runs through all nature as "a sort of life," the teleology of the motion may reasonably be expected to show the teleology of nature itself. But the study of motion in the Aristotelian *Physics* leads to the eternal rotary movement of the spheres as the efficient cause of all sublunar movement, and in the *Metaphysics* this perpetual motion is shown to have separate substance as its final cause. The overall conception would seem to require that the whole teleology of nature be directed towards separate substance. But if separate substance is outside nature, and unable to be connected with nature by any satisfactory explanation, does not trouble lie ahead?[12]

II

Subject to this general warning, however, one may proceed stepwise to the different levels that are progressively involved in the Aristotelian teleology of nature. Within the individual thing constituted by the principles of nature, the form coincides with the final cause. The form *is* the final cause.[13] In the context, there does not seem to be any particular initial difficulty about that approach. It means that in each individual natural thing there is an all-pervading intelligible aspect to which everything else in the thing is subordinate. Form in its structural role is the intelligible content of the thing, and in its primary or basic occurrence in the thing it serves as the focal point towards which all else is directed. This teleology, present throughout all natural things, is most readily observable in the case of living organisms, in which the functions of the various parts aptly converge towards the welfare of the whole. Aristotle writes:

> For Nature, like mind, always does whatever it does for the sake of something, which something is its end. To that something corresponds in the case of animals the soul and in this it follows the order of nature; all natural bodies are organs of the soul. This is true of those that enter into the constitution of plants as well as of those which enter into that of animals. This shows that that for the sake of which they are is soul.[14]

In this passage, the functioning of mind is the model used to illustrate the workings of nature. Mind in directing activity proposes a certain purpose or goal, and then adapts the rest to that end. In another work, Aristotle makes this general meaning clear in the example of house building:

> For elsewhere, as for instance in house building, this is the true sequence. The plan of the house, or the house, has this and that form; and because it has this and that form, therefore is its construction carried out in this or that manner.[15]

To the basic form, then, everything else in the natural thing is adapted. In this respect nature works in a way analogous to mind. In the case of animals and plants, the basic form is the soul, the primary principle of life. All other things in the animal or plant are instruments or organs of the soul. They are meant for the soul. They are directed, in their functioning, towards the continuance of the soul as the vital principle of the matter involved. In a word, they have the soul as their purpose, or goal, or end.

This is the clear meaning of the text from the *De Anima*. It is borne out by ordinary observation of the way in which the various parts of an organism strive to secure and maintain the life of the whole. It is affirmed by Aristotle just as clearly in the chapter from which the above passage of the *De Partibus Animalium* is taken:

> Thus we should say, because man is an animal with such and such characters, therefore is the process of his development necessarily such as it is; and therefore it is accomplished in such and such an order, this part being formed first, that next, and so on in succession; and after a like fashion should we explain the evolution of all other works of nature.[16]

The teleological direction of everything in the individual towards the basic form is accordingly seen in man as an animal and in like fashion in "all other works of nature." Nature is projected as bringing all the details to bear upon a definite goal, just as mind does. But how? For Aristotle there can be no Platonic demiûrge, that would control things in the manner of an external efficient cause.[17] The reason has evidently to be sought in nature itself, and in this case in the form. The form is the knowable content, the principle of intelligibility in the individual thing. It seems regarded without further ado by Aristotle as functioning in an intelligible manner, and therefore after the fashion of mind. As the basic actuality of the thing, it appears understood to actualize everything in the individual in an intelligible mode, and accordingly to direct everything to itself in an all-pervading teleological way. But no explicit account is given in the Aristotelian text. Probably if he were pressed for an answer, Aristotle would have replied as on another occasion[18] that such is the way natural things are, and that they have to be accepted as they manifest themselves to human cognition.

This general viewpoint may seem innocent enough, and hardly rising above a common sense outlook. The tragedy latent in it, however, becomes set when Aristotle makes use of this conception for determining the methods of scientifically investigating nature. If the final cause of a thing coincides with its form, to know its final cause is to know its form, since the one is the other. By finding out the purpose of a thing, then, one has attained knowledge from which all the natural properties of a thing may be deduced, just as the essential notion of a triangle provides the ground for reasoning to its geometrical properties. It is as though one had insight into the forms of natural things in the way one can read the blueprint of a house, and reason from the plan to the details in actual reality.

In Aristotle's own application of this method, the results prove discouraging enough. For instance, because the heart appears as the starting point of the arteries and veins and the productive source of the blood, it will have to be made of the same kind of materials as they:

> And as to the heart, the very starting-point of the vessels, and the actual seat of the force by which the blood is first fabricated, it is but what one would naturally expect, that out of the selfsame nutriment of which it is the recipient its own proper substance shall be formed.[19]

From an intuitive understanding of the heart as the organ from which the blood vessels make their start, one is supposed to be able to reason to the kind of materials out of which it has to be made.

Similarly the observed circular motion of the heavenly bodies, on account of its unchanging character that has been recorded for ages, requires a corporeal substance different from any of the four sublunar elements. Because of this purpose of functioning as substrate for perpetual rotary motion, the required type of body can be shown to be ingenerate and imperishable, unalterable and neither light nor heavy, and the inexhaustible origin of movement in the sublunar world.[20] Likewise fire, on the basis of its appearances, is accepted as a distinct substance existent in itself.

The disastrous consequences of this conception of method in natural science is only too well known. The plain fact is, that despite Greek optimism, the human mind does not have any intuitive grasp of specific substantial forms in natural things.[21] To know that the eye is meant for seeing does not provide the means of zeroing in on specific knowledge of the organ's basic form. It does not in fact give the premises for reasoning to all the details of the organ's structure and functioning, in the way the nature of a triangle furnishes the ground for reasoning to all the triangle's geometrical properties. The stupendous success of the qualitative and quantitative procedures in the natural sciences since the sixteenth-century stands out in vivid contrast to the sterility of a method that sought first the final cause, identified it with the formal cause, and then tried to use the form as a blueprint for understanding the details of natural things.

III

Today, then, it is easy enough to set off explosives in the midst of the Aristotelian teleology of nature, and to take for granted that nobody will be even interested enough to pick up the pieces. Yet Aristotle remains so deeply involved in the development of European thought that one finds difficulty in believing that this can be the whole story, even in the comparatively restricted domain of teleology. Is it just possible that one may be missing the woods for the trees? Does the Aristotelian wisdom in regard to nature function on a different level from that of the experimental sciences? May one readily grant that Aristotelian natural philosophy has no means of entering into any part of the field of experimental science, and nevertheless maintain that it still has much to say about the teleology of nature? Aristotle himself recognized separate status for sciences like astronomy, optics, harmonics, and mechanics.[22] He did not bring them under his natural philosophy. He placed them on another level, on which the norms of quantity and not those of substance played the formal role.[23] In principle, why should not this viewpoint be extended to all the natural sciences that have been developed each in its own right since Aristotle's day? Theoretically, there seems to be no reason to the contrary. This would mean, then, that in principle the experimental sciences of today do not at all encroach upon the characteristic field of Aristotle's natural philosophy. Room should be left, accordingly, for an investigation of teleology that will be distinctively Aristotelian in outlook and will pertain to the Aristotelian philosophy of nature.

But when one penetrates beyond the qualitative and the quantitative determinations from which the experimental sciences take their start, is any intelligibility left in natural things? Granted, as already seen,[24] that the specific differentiae of natural things are impenetrable to human intelligence, does their generic nature as bodies nevertheless remain open to intellectual analysis? Here the answer, in the Aristotelian context, is affirmative. At the generic grade of body the things of nature may be analyzed in terms of the two substantial principles, matter and form, and in this way become the subject of a distinct philosophical study, the philosophy of nature. Further, through reflexive consciousness the differences between the grades of vegetative, sensitive, and intellectual life are experienced with a clarity sufficient to provide a basis for philosophical investigation.[25] Does Aristotle find any natural teleology between these grades, and in what direction does the teleology in general tend?

The general direction is expressed definitely enough in regard to living things. For each of them "the most natural act is the production of another like itself, an animal producing an animal, a plant a plant, in order that, as far as its nature allows, it may partake in the eternal and divine. That is the goal towards which all things strive, that for the sake of which they do whatsoever their nature renders possible."[26] The overall purpose of the activities in plants and animals, this passage asserts, is to achieve as far as is possible for them the character of the eternal and divine. This character, as may be gathered from Aristotle's metaphysical views, is to be found primarily in the immobile and purely actual separate substances, and in all other things in secondary and graded ways, through imitation.[27] In animals and plants the appropriate grade of permanence is achieved through the perpetuation of the species: "Since then no living thing is able to partake in what is eternal and divine by uninterrupted continuance (for nothing perishable can for ever remain one and the same), it tries to achieve that end in the only way possible to it, and success is possible in varying degrees; so it remains not indeed as the self-same individual but continues its existence in something *like* itself—not numerically but specifically one."[28]

Though it is not made explicit in regard to nonliving bodies, where the vivid illustration of permanence through progeny is lacking, the overall teleology is apparent in the way they imitate circular motion by changing into one another until they complete the circle.[29] So: "Imperishable things are imitated by those that are involved in change, e.g. earth and fire. For these also are ever active; for they have their movement of themselves and in themselves."[30] The activities of perishable things accordingly strive to imitate the eternal and unchanging motion of the heavenly bodies, that keep going around and around in perpetual orbit for ever and ever. But before adding the 'amen', one should take further cognizance of Aristotle's metaphysical views. The purely actual separate substances move the spheres through being loved and desired. This presupposes that the spheres are besouled, a doctrine stated expressly elsewhere.[31] All the activities of nature, one would conclude, have as their supreme purpose the task of providing a substrate for intellectual contemplation by the sphere souls. It is as though the more regular and more permanent the motion, the less is the possibility of distraction from this contemplation, much as in the case of man the security and amenities of civilized life are laid down by Aristotle as necessary prerequisites for the supreme human goal of contemplating separate substance. In any case, whatever particular explanation may be given for it, the overall teleology of natural things is towards the permanent actuality found in the separate forms. The ultimate explanation is metaphysical, insofar as the good for which all things strive consists principally in separate entity.[32] Even with man left out of the picture for the moment, the general teleology of nature is towards something above and outside itself.

In the context of the assertion that all things aim at the good, Aristotle is accordingly able to emphasize, aporematically, that the naturally good goes beyond the individual itself: "But perhaps even in inferior creatures there is some natural good stronger than themselves which aims at their proper good."[33] This theme is exploited in the *Politics* through a graded teleology of plants in regard to animals and animals in regard to men: " . . . we may infer that, after the birth of animals, plants exist for their sake, and that the other animals exist for the sake of man, the tame for use and food, the wild, if not all, at least the greater part of them, for food, and for the provision of clothing and various instruments."[34] The specific purpose of plant life, according to this view, is to provide for animal needs. Animal life, in its turn, is meant to provide for the needs of human life. The teleology of plant nature, consequently, requires that the tendency towards this specific purpose be stronger than the plant itself, and that the plant is meant by nature to give up its own existence for the welfare of the animal kingdom. Correspondingly, the brute animals are destined by nature to give up their existence in providing food and clothing and tools for men.

This teleology establishes a clearly etched hierarchy of the rational, animal, and vegetative orders. The specific good or purpose of the lower order brings it into complete subordination to the one immediately above it. Needless to add, the same reasoning would make the inanimate kingdom correspondingly subordinate to the plant world, even though this is not mentioned by Aristotle and mention of it could hardly be required for anything more than textbook systematization. Substances like salt and water provide for vegetative life just as obviously as plants serve animal life. But what happens in Aristotle when the Teilhardian ascent leaves the biosphere and enters into the noosphere with man?

IV

The passage just quoted from the *Politics* immediately applies the results of its reasoning to man:

Now if nature makes nothing incomplete, and nothing in vain, the inference must be that she has made all animals for the sake of man. And so, in one point of view, the art of war is a natural art of acquisition, for the art of acquisition includes hunting, an art which we ought to practise against wild beasts, and against men who, though intended by nature to be governed, will not submit; for war of such a kind is naturally just.[35]

Because in this teleology nature has made all things for the sake of men, the hunting and slaying of animals is an occupation intended by nature. So far the reasoning causes no surprise. But the norm is not directed solely against brute animals. It is at once applied to a certain class of men. This class consists of those who are intended by nature itself to be governed by other men, but who will not submit to the quasi-animal status in which nature has placed them. By nature, accordingly, war against them is just.

Who are these men intended by nature to have the status of mere property of their masters?[36] In the *Politics* Aristotle had laid down as elementary the principle that nature adapts some men to be masters and others to be slaves: "For that which can foresee by the exercise of mind is by nature intended to be lord and master, and that which can with its body give effect to such foresight is a subject, and by nature a slave."[37] In solidarity with the aristocratic Greek tradition, he explains in this sense the poet's conception of Greek superiority over the barbarians: "Wherefore the poets say,—'It is meet that Hellenes should rule over barbarians'; as if they thought that the barbarian and the slave were by nature one."[38] He takes account of an opposite opinion that "the distinction between slave and freeman exists by law only, and not by nature."[39] But he experiences no difficulty in giving his own clearcut answer, that "from the hour of their birth, some are marked out for subjection, others for rule," and concludes "It is clear, then, that some men are by nature free, and others slaves, and that for these latter slavery is both expedient and right."[40] The slavery is explained in the sense that a human being is here a piece of property that belongs wholly to the master, a possession that has the status of an instrument for use.[41]

The fact of being a man, consequently, does not for Aristotle raise an individual above the natural teleology that makes all material things subservient to those who are endowed with intellectual gifts. There is nothing sacred about man, in the sense of natural inviolability. Accordingly deformed children are to be abandoned to death by exposure,[42] suicide is wrong only because of its disadvantage to the state,[43] and friendship, though it makes the friend's good one's own good, does so ultimately for one's own sake, in order to enable oneself to carry on the life of individual contemplation.[44] Everything seems directed by nature towards providing the gifted few with the opportunity for intellectual contemplation, through which they attain perfect happiness in a godlike life, during the years of their maturity on this earth. As with the sphere souls, the whole teleology of nature seems meant to make the contemplation possible.

V

There are, of course, a number of lacunae in this teleology of nature, from a philosophical viewpoint. Aristotle constantly regards nature as acting like mind for a purpose. Yet for him nature as such is not endowed with intelligence, nor is there any outside demiurge or world soul or creator to do the directing. The all-pervading direction of natural activities towards a purposive goal seems accepted merely as a fact, on the ground of immediate observation and deduction. The internal teleology of the parts of an organism towards the well-being of the whole structure may be open to exploration on qualitative and quantitative lines, we are well aware today, but hardly on the basis of an intuitive insight into the specific substantial natures of observable things. The teleology that extends outside the individual agent, and destines the individual to be sacrificed for a higher good, has a somewhat more accessible foundation in substantial nature. Reflective experience provides awareness of the natural tendency of parents to sacrifice themselves for their progeny, and of the gradated way in which the vegetative and sensitive orders are oriented towards the intellectual. On the basis of this internal experience the externally observed facts can be readily interpreted, as the biosphere is seen to converge upon the noosphere. Correspondingly for Aristotle the whole teleology of nature is found to be directed towards the whole individual, individuals towards the species or towards regular cyclic continuance of generation in inanimate things, the vegetative towards the sensitive, and finally towards man and separate substance—all to provide a comparatively few men and the sphere souls with a suitably enduring framework for pure contemplation.

The crucial impasse here lies in the difficulty of putting the Aristotelian man together. As a besouled body, he is meant only for earthly life. Yet he can think. This calls for mind as one of the parts[45] of his constitution. But mind should make him a separate, not a besouled, substance. This dilemma receives no satisfactory solution in Aristotle. It has caused endless trouble to his commentators. It was sharply criticized by Plotinus as the forced insertion of another soul or intellect, over and above the soul that animates the body.[46] Likewise in regard to the sphere souls, there is no explanation of the way in which they bring the separate substances within their intellectual grasp, and the difficulties are correspondingly the same as in the case of man.

The result is that the Aristotelian teleology of nature, in spite of its many penetrating and still useful insights, lacks the completion that might give it overall appeal today. Though humanistic to the extent that it directs all other terrestial things to man's service, it leaves man himself far too much a thing of nature. Only in the gifted few destined by nature for the contemplation that is beyond nature, does anything approaching what we have later learned to call the order of spirit appear. Man just as man does not call for respect. Unless he has the required intellectual gifts, a man is destined by nature to be the property of another in the bonds of slavery.

To the extent that this attitude reflects the accepted viewpoints of ancient Greek culture, too much theoretical or rigid consistency need not be required. In that sphere, for Aristotle as well as for Plato, general philosophical views hold only roughly and for the most part. We have advanced a long distance in respect for the human person, it is true, from the mentality that allowed the harsh punishments of the *Laws* to seem normal in the thought of a highly cultured philosopher like Plato. At the same time, the innate respect for the dignity of the human person and human life could not help but make itself felt among the Greeks, as for instance in the general approbation accorded to Xenophon's anger at the prospect of an unconscious but still living soldier being buried to avoid the inconvenience of waiting for the death that soon was bound to come.[47] So Aristotle acknowledges the presence of the view that slavery is against nature. Rather than the abandoning of healthy children to death by exposure in order to avoid excess population, he recommends abortion "before sense and life have begun; what may or may not be lawfully done in these cases depends on the question of life and sensation,"[48] as though fetal life in humans demanded a certain respect. Further, he allows full rights of freedom and citizenship to those who practice the virtues aside from contemplation, on the ground that this activity is a secondary degree of the good life and befits human estate.[49]

Views such as these may hang rather loosely together with the consequences of a natural teleology that orientates towards contemplation all material composites, including man as a besouled body. Yet they are not set aside by Aristotle in the interests of doctrinal systematization. His insights are keen, and his attitudes are those of his culture. His own development of the insights does not give the final answers. One can learn from his mistakes. In his wake the project of calling on an internal teleology directed towards substantial form, in order to explain the specific traits and functions of natural things, was tried long enough through the centuries, and without success. It should serve as a sufficient warning against expecting philosophy to do any of the work of the experimental sciences. In the ethical sphere the bland acceptance of slavery and of exposing deformed infants to death is intolerable to moral sense at our present stage of social development. It would be radically incompatible, for instance, with the rationale of our care for retarded children and of our dedication to many other such humanitarian undertakings.

But is there not more here than just learning from mistakes? As Teilhard de Chardin's noosphere may be deemed eminently worthy of salvage after a blockbuster has demolished his general procedure,[50] so with still greater appropriateness may not the Aristotelian hierarchical teleology of nature be explored for fruitful consequences? May not the respective orientation of the inanimate and vegetative kingdoms towards the animal order, and the animal towards the intellectual, still be important for both epistemological and ethical considerations? The hierarchical subordination is grasped through internal experience of the way in which in ourselves vegetative life is found naturally contributing to sensitive life and sensitive to intellectual. This internal grasp is again too global and too unrevealing to allow philosophy to do any of the work of psychology or cultural anthropology. Yet it is certain enough and convincing enough to serve as antidote against an overall mechanistic interpretation of nature. It provides a solid philosophical basis for rejecting views that would place all the things of nature on a uniform level, for example the Cartesian tenet that plants and animals are mere automata and the human body a machine.[51] It lays open, or at least leads to, profound philosophical reasons for the instinctive shying away from an outright mechanistic interpretation of the natural world— an instinctive attitude that is experienced by many of us, and perhaps by all who have not been sophisticated to the thoroughgoing mechanistic approach.

Finally, though the link with the intellectual remains an impasse in Aristotle himself, it offers a challenge to explore the topic further for grounds that will extend the dignity of spirit to all human beings without exception. Here especially, as the history of the commentators shows, does the Stagirite's thought remain an open philosophy, a deep penetration into the issues, and a cordial invitation to continue to do our own thinking upon them.

13. The Grounds of Ethical Universality in Aristotle

What is the full import of Aristotle's tenet that choice is the basic factor in moral actions? Can the tenet allow sufficient universality for human conduct to function as the subject matter in a genuine science of ethics? Does it give consistency to Aristotle's varied and allegedly contradictory statements on the role of choice in regard to means and in regard to ends and in regard to moral weakness?

The tenet is asserted in the *Metaphysics* in a context in which the radical difference in location for the starting points of the things treated respectively in the three basic kinds of Aristotelian sciences is being described. Natural philosophy, which deals with things that have in their own substance the starting point of their motion and rest, is neither productive nor practical but theoretical (*E* 1, 1025b18-27). It is not a productive science nor a practical science: "For the starting point of things produced is in the producer, either mind or art or some capability; while that of things done is in the agent, choice—for what is done and what is chosen are the same" (b22-24).

Choice (*proairesis*) is accordingly seen as the starting point or first principle of things done, in the sense in which "doing" means acting in a specifically human way that is not shared by brute animals or by children.[1] The tenet is taken up again in the *Nicomachean Ethics* (VI 2,1139a31): "The starting point of action, then, is choice." But its fundamental role in the structure of a distinctively human action becomes apparent in the epistemological context in the *Metaphysics*. There the contrast is clearly between starting points or principles that are found in the substance of natural things, and starting points that do not lie in the things but in the human producer or agent. A further contrast then takes place between the determined contours of intellectual intuition or art or some human faculty, and the open or antecedently undetermined starting point that is set up in choice.

Are these distinctions definite enough, and able to be understood in a modern setting? The location of the principles for the things with which theoretical science deals seems sufficiently intelligible. With "theoretical" understood in the Aristotelian sense of that which can be contemplated or studied in a thing regardless of any basic contribution made by one's own handling of it, the starting points are sought entirely in the objective reality that confronts the mind (e.g., *EN* VI 5, 1140b13-16). They are not found in the activity of the knower. This procedure seems common enough in the disciplines that are popularly called sciences today. The attitude of the scientist is objective. His own subjective dispositions or preferences are not supposed to intrude themselves into his research. The starting points for his reasoning, whether in regard to mathematics or to nature or to conduct, are regarded as present in the materials with which he is dealing, and not as originating in his own spontaneity. In this way he is able to claim public status for his conclusions - any other scientist or competent reader will be able to walk the path that he has broken. Even where he has a choice of paths, for instance between Euclidean and non-Euclidean geometries, the starting points for each are already set up in the nature of abstract quantity or in the multifaceted workings of the real universe or in the observed vagaries of human behavior. The starting points do not depend on the way he wills them to be. He prides himself rather on following the objective evidence faithfully in spite of any personal feelings for or against. Similarly in the Aristotelian example, the first principles of real bodies are matter and form and are located in the corporeal substance itself. The starting points here do not basically depend upon the way the knower sets them up, but are present in the real world antecedently to his activity. In contrast, the choice made in the agent is for Aristotle the basic constituent in the structure of things done, and from this viewpoint functions in a way comparable to the role played by form and matter in the intrinsic constitution of physical bodies. Morally good actions are done from choice (12, 1144a19), and accordingly receive their basic characterization from their efficient (2, 1139a31-32) cause. They are things chosen.

Epistemologically, of course, a number of qualifications have to be made according to the varied modern viewpoints from which the topic is approached. But in broad outline the distinction between principles or starting points that may be regarded as present in an object before one starts to manipulate it, and those that are set up according to the wishes of the knower, seems clear enough. The novelist can construct his world as he wishes, the physicist has to interpret his as he finds it. In construction work the starting point is a blueprint drawn up by the mind of an architect, in geology the starting points are the data found already in the rocks by the scientist. The difference between science, as it is commonly understood today, and art is sufficiently clear. It illustrates trenchantly enough the meaning of a starting point that already exists in the nature of things, on the one hand, and on the other a starting point that comes into being only through the wish of a knower. This seems sufficient to establish the radical distinction between the Aristotelian theoretical science on the one side, with its starting points present independently in the nature of things, and the other two types of science, types that find their starting points in the knower and not in the thing.

But the further distinction between the starting points of things produced and those of things done may be somewhat more surprising. That the process of building a skyscraper starts from the blueprint designed by the architect, that the novel grows out of the plot conceived by the writer, that the speech develops from the plan thought up by the orator, can hardly be questioned from the viewpoint of intelligibility. But what does it mean to say that choice in the agent is the starting point of things done? Choice is understood clearly enough by Aristotle as taking one thing instead of another after a process of reasoning and understanding and deliberation (*EN* III 2, 1112a15-17). It is thereby seen to be something more than mere "taking" (*hairesis—EE* II 10, 1226b6-8). The observed fact of choice so understood in human conduct is accepted as sufficient for the purposes of practical science. No metaphysical discussion of its possibility or its causes is given. Indeed, this theoretical problem could hardly find place outside an existential setting, such as that for example in which Christian philosophy developed. In Greek philosophy, on the other hand, the basic presence of choice in the moral order could be accepted as an acknowledged fact in the wake of the criteria of praise and blame, and of the use of reward and punishment in both government and education. Even a rigid atomism did not exclude choice from the ethics of Democritus (e.g., *Frs.* 96, 207 DK). The fact of choice was there in human conduct for anyone to observe. It did not coincide, specifically at least, with wishing something. It was a distinct act in regard to alternatives over which a man had control. For Aristotle (*EN* III 2, 1111b19-1112a15) it came generically under voluntary action but with its own characteristic differentia. It not only wanted its object, but adopted that one object in rejecting others that also had their own desirability. It presupposed that the power of selecting one alternative instead of the others lay with the agent.[2] The selection of the alternative, and consequently the origin of a distinctly new course of action, resided in this power. The starting point of anything done, accordingly, was the choice made in the mental activity of the agent.

This conclusion becomes startling. Does it not mean, at least prima facie, that every deliberatly undertaken course of human conduct has an utterly new beginning, a beginning not determined in anything that anteceded it in the universe? Does it not imply that every act of choice is an absolutely new start, springing from itself only and from nothing that has gone before? Is it not setting up on each occasion a totally unheralded starting point that crashes rudely from without into an otherwise orderly universe? Will it not be making the very notion of science impossible in the practical order?

II

These questions merit separate answers. Does the prima facie impression of an absolutely new and previously undetermined beginning, first of all, find any confirmation in Aristotle's overall procedure in the practical sphere? The mention of choice as the starting point in book *E* of the *Metaphysics* is not duplicated in the corresponding instances. The parallel passage in book *K* does not include it, nor do the other passages in which Aristotle gives the division of the sciences.[3] Yet the passage in book *E* is the most extensive and detailed of all, and the most highly developed. It can safely be taken as giving Aristotle's mature conception of the sciences. It has much greater authority than the presumably earlier and comparatively tentative formulation of book *K*, and the rather fragmentary sketches in the other passages. Its inclusion of choice in the description is formal. The inclusion is not just a chance entry or an aside. It is an essential part of a carefully balanced contrast between the substance of the thing known, the artistic intuition or plan or capability, and choice. The sequence of thought requires that these be viewed respectively as the starting points of the subject matter dealt with by the three types of science. The first two are obviously enough and understandably enough meant to be taken in the fullest formal sense. How then can the third be exempted or interpreted in any diluted way? The balanced structure of the reasoning seems to require that all three members stand on an equally well laid footing and enjoy equally serious status in their function of sciences that proceed from carefully distinguished types of starting points or principles.

Further, Aristotle pauses long enough on the occasion to give the reason why choice appears as the starting point of things done. The reason is that a thing done is the same as a thing chosen. A thing done, in the Greek philosophical sense of doing in contradistinction to making or producing, meant a thing that proceeded in an altogether special way from the agent. It was a way in which the control over the performing of the action remained with the agent. It was accordingly something chosen, in the sense in which doing was not shared by animals or children, as has been seen.[4] The mention of choice as the starting point, then, is quite apparently the result of a carefully thought out tenet regarding the deliberation in virtue of which characteristically human conduct makes a determination. It does not at all seem like a casual aside that happens to be noted here but which would have no essential bearing on Aristotle's conception of practical science.

The omission of the concept of choice in the shorter passages on the division of the sciences finds a ready enough explanation in the concern of Aristotle on those occasions in stressing the bearing of theoretical science on knowledge only, while practical and productive sciences bear on something over and above mere knowledge.[5] But the omission in book *K* of the *Metaphysics* requires more consideration. There he mentions explicitly art or some other capability as the starting point for productive science (*K* 7, 1064a13). The starting point of practical science, on the other hand, is not specified. In neither *E* or *K*, however, is the starting point for the philosophy of nature specified, though it can be ascertained definitely enough to be form and matter from the first two books of the *Physics*. The omission in book *K* of definite specification of the starting point for things done need not, then, be regarded as an insuperable objection to the fully formal role of choice in the description given in book *E*. Book *K* can be content with the generic conception "motion" (1064a15) in the doer for the starting point of a thing done, just as both *B* and *K* do not go further than the generic concept of the starting point of motion in the thing itself for natural philosophy. Even though the specification is an essential factor and not an aside in the starting points themselves, it does not require mention if a generic description is sufficient to bring out the lines along which the sciences are divided. Motion, however, is generic in respect to conduct (*EE* II 6, 1222b29).

Accordingly the *Nicomachean Ethics* (VI 2, 1139a31; cf. a19-20) can without further ado assert that choice is the starting point of conduct. However, enough hesitation is engendered to prompt one to look at Aristotle's actual procedure in his development of moral science. Does he in fact seek the starting points for his ethical discussions in the choices made by the individual doer?

The starting points of moral science, he states[6], are grasped through appropriate habituation. What is the habituation? It consists in the moral virtues.[7] But the moral virtues are habits of choosing, of choosing in the way a man of prudence would determine.[8] They either consist in choice or do not have being apart from choice (*EN* II 5, 1106a3-4). From either viewpoint they will function by choosing. Starting points grasped through them will accordingly arise from choice. The starting points will be embraced immediately by the one who has been brought up in the virtues, without need for the reason to be given (I 4, 1095b4-8). The most important starting point, the supreme goal, is chosen (5,1095b20; *EE* I 2, 1214b7) by different types of men in different ways. The three most prominent types choose pleasure, or public standing, or contemplation. Moreover, in any human action the moral goodness is located in an ever variable mean that is determined in each case by the individual prudent man. It is "the mean not of the object but relative to us" (*EN* II 6, 1106b7). In art or productive science knowledge is what matters most, but in the moral realm the choice of the act, the choosing of it for its own sake, and the performing of it in the way a virtuous man would perform it, are the all-important factors (4, 1105a26-b9). Everything goes, then, as though Aristotle is serious and consistent in the tenet that the starting point of things done is choice and is located in the doer. He proceeds in fact as though the tenet is basic in his conception of practical science.

The answers to the first three questions proposed above should be clear enough from these considerations. Aristotle does indeed mean, not only prima facie but in the very core of his ethical procedure, that every deliberate undertaking is a new beginning, a beginning not determined by anything that preceded it. It does imply that every act of choice results in a determination that springs from itself and not from anything antecedent. It in fact sets up on each occasion a starting point that adds to the order in the universe and that was not previously contained in it. The answers to these three questions are sufficient to account for the radical distinction between theoretical knowledge and practical knowledge in the Aristotelian epistemology.

But what of the answer to the fourth and final question asked above? How can there be any possibility of science and scientific knowledge or demonstration where everything depends not upon fixed truth but upon the ever varying choice of particular individuals? Certainly Aristotle's political philosophy is not relativistic or situational. It is cast in far too public a mold for anything like that. The continued appeal to the public standards of praise and blame as criteria, the regular universalizing of the ethical notions like virtue, justice, or friendship, the syllogistic reasoning in ethical matters, the absence of any conception of private conscience that would be in opposition to public approval[9], all point far beyond an individualistic or private framework. The stand that something condemned by public consent of good men could nevertheless be right for a particular individual does not seem to enter into Aristotle's thinking. Even a case of equity, which corrects the failure of a general law to come to grips with a particular instance, will come under the generic universality of justice[10] and would be agreed to by all good men including the legislator. How, then, is this universality possible when the basis is individual choice?

III

One avenue of inquiry in answer to the last question is opened by Aristotle's quite regular appeal to the nature of things when working out ethical solutions. The approach to the whole moral field in the *Nicomachean Ethics* is mapped in a theoretical consideration of the good. The good is what all things desire or aim at.[11] It is accordingly analogous in regard to the differing individuals who desire it, and it has primary and secondary instances.[12] These conclusions are all metaphysical tenets, and a study of them for their own sake lies outside the scope of moral philosophy.[13] The epistemological precisions developed so carefully in the *Ethics* arise from the nature of the subject matter[14], and not from choice. From an analysis of its nature public standing is shown to lack the depth sought for in the supreme human good[15], and accordingly may for the moment be dismissed from consideration. Money-making or gain is likewise ruled out on account of its nature as a means and not an end.[16] The location of the supreme good in the activity that conforms with the best and most complete virtue is based upon a theoretical study of human nature and its resultant actions.[17] The accompanying needs and conditions are shown to follow from the same ground (*EN* I 7, 1098a18-20; 8, 1098b12-1099b8). The specification of the highest human activity as contemplation also takes place on theoretical grounds.[18] Amusement is rejected as the supreme human goal not only on the moral appeal to correct disposition as was pleasure in the first book of the *Nicomachean Ethics* (5, 1095b19-22), but also because in its own nature it is meant to be a means for the pursuance of other activity.[19] There is one political constitution that is best by nature (V 7, 1135a5), regardless of place or time. There is a natural justice, which though variable, arises from nature and not from convention (1134b18-35). Man is by nature a social animal[20], and some men are meant by nature to be slaves.[21] Pleasure is repeatedly studied throughout the *Ethics* from the viewpoint of its nature.

Enumeration of instances such as these could continue. They are amply sufficient to show that the consideration of the natures of things plays a crucial role in Aristotelian moral thinking. This places it quickly enough outside the category of a simple intuitionism. Even though a person correctly brought up is supposed to see and accept the moral principles right away without any need for knowing the reasons for them (*EN* I 4, 1095b4-13), he is still an eligible student of moral philosophy. He is in fact the one type that is able to pursue the science. There is no question, then, of a curt dismissal of the problem of the acceptance of moral principles by saying that either you seem them or you don't. You are referred to the guidance of more experienced men[22], and you are set at a study of the nature of the good and of the human soul to the extent to which these items of theoretical knowledge are required. In a word, moral knowledge can be checked and deepened and developed by incorporating the publicly accepted and scrutinizable results of the theoretical sciences. Its heavy leaning upon nature gives it in this respect a public setting that should safeguard it against the isolation of merely private decisions. The universe in which human conduct takes place is the same public universe in which men exist and which they share with animals, plants, and inanimate things.

Nevertheless, there are problems. In any of the instances in which nature is consulted for the purposes of moral decision, can the final determination ever be regarded as left to nature. Is it not always made by human choice? May you not prove cogently from a study of the good and of human nature that the supreme human good is contemplation, obtain full agreement from the one with whom you are talking, and yet have him say: "Correct, but it is not for me. I admire anyone who can lead that kind of a life, but for myself I want to do something. I prefer an active life." Even Aristotle, after having so carefully demonstrated that the nature of man requires that the supreme human good be contemplation, and having extolled the contemplative life with the full glow of personal conviction, sees the active life, when lived in accord with the moral virtues, as a secondary instance of *eudaimonia*, that is, of the good or happy life.[23]

No matter how cogently the natures of the things involved show what the supreme human good is, then, an individual apparently remains free to choose something else. He can choose as his supreme good the leading of an active political life, as in the case just considered, and his decision will have the stamp of public approval and be regarded as morally good by the Aristotelian prudent man. It is not hard to extend this reasoning to the choice of a life of pleasure or of moneymaking[24], except that here the Aristotelian ethical approval could hardly be expected. An individual man can be conceived as admitting the cogency of Aristotle's reasoning, and yet placing his supreme good in pleasure for the sake of pleasure or wealth for the sake of wealth. A miser may have no dominating interest in pleasure or political power, and still keep devoting his whole effort to accumulation of money, regardless of the theoretical knowledge that money by its nature is meant for something further. The point at issue is that the knowledge of the nature of things is not the decisive factor in determining one's choice of the supreme good.

Similarly one may be ready to admit that some people are adapted by nature for manual work, and yet find slavery abhorrent. One may be enthusiastically committed to the reasons that make a certain form of government the best of all, and yet hesitate to recommend it for a people whose mentality is not judged susceptible of it. Even for Aristotle the social nature of man does not get the chief credit for political order: "A social instinct is implanted in all men by nature, and yet he who first founded the state was the greatest of benefactors" (*Pol.* I 2, 1253a29-31; Oxford tr.). Nature should play a basic role in the deliberation. But nature does not do the determining. The determining is done by human choice and decision.

Nature, then, by reason of its basic role of object to be considered in the deliberation, provides a public framework in which moral decisions are to be made. To that extent it provides a common setting for ethical thinking. In this way it allows its own universality to permeate the deliberations of the many different individuals and to seep through into the decisions. But the determining remains a matter of individual choice. The good, though coextensive with being[25], is always relative to a desire or other appetitive act. With man, accordingly, the supreme human good is chosen by the individual and is relative to the individual's disposition. That is the main starting point of ethical reasoning. What nature shows to be the best without qualification has to be worked out from that starting point: "in conduct our task is to start from what is good for each and make what is without qualification good good for each" (*Metaph.* Z 3, 1029b6-7; Oxford tr.).

IV

But how? What can assure genuine universality in making the right ethical choices in conformity with the basic natures of things? Aristotle's answer is clear and unhesitating. *Paideia*, meaning education and culture, is what equips the individual to make the right moral decision in each case and to grasp the ethical principles in a way that will allow them to function as premises from which conclusions may be drawn in the manner of an authentic science.[26] Hence the importance of correct habituation from earliest childhood on.[27] Through this habituation are the moral starting points acquired.[28] The habituation consists basically in the three moral virtues of temperance, courage and justice, and the intellectual virtue of prudence. These four basic virtues reciprocally involve each other, and habituate each man to perform his actions in the manner that the good man would decide.[29] In this way the universality and the exactitude appropriate to ethical matters is attained.[30]

The moral virtues, however, are habits that are permeated with the openness of choice.[31] They accordingly are geared to choosing. They do not impose any rigid determination, as a conclusion for instance follows with formal necessity from premises in mathematics. Rather, they dispose and condition the individual to make the right choice. But the final determination of the human action always remains in the power of the agent. It is always something that is chosen, and chosen in each case by the individual. The role of choice remains basic and remains open throughout all its habituation. The habituation does not at all infringe upon the power of the individual to choose.

Is the moral habituation of the individual, though, sufficient to guarantee genuine universality? It seems to be regarded without hesitation by Aristotle as able to do so. Everywhere it receives his full confidence for molding into a common pattern the conduct of individuals correctly brought up under the influence of the surrounding culture. The workings of Greek culture as operative in the environment appear to be taken for granted by Aristotle. The pattern set by them is accepted without question. The pattern will not be rigid or already fixed, like a physical nature or a blueprint or a Platonic Idea. Rather, it will function as a norm that is ever variable and always adapting itself to the continually changing circumstances. It will be a flexible measure that can provide with exactitude for intricate curvings.[32] Accordingly it may be regarded as having genuine universality, though a universality in which nothing is static or immobile.[33] It has, in a word, the universality that is appropriate to the subject matter of moral philosophy.

Is not the role of culture in providing a flexible universality that emerges from individual actions borne out strikingly by modern acquaintance with cultural dynamics and the living structuralism inherent in human language and conduct? Has not contemporary scientific study shown that the education of the individual provides cultural stability, yet in a way that is always open to change? The views of a present day expert sound surprisingly like the conception of *paideia* presupposed by Aristotle for his ethical doctrine: "However, the basic principle involved is clear: *The enculturation of the individual in the early years of his life is the prime mechanism making for cultural stability, while the process, as it operates on more mature folk, is highly important in inducing change.*[34] Consequently, "culture is *both* stable and everchanging"[35], and the presence of "universals in human culture"[36] is not compromised by their lack of theoretical rigidity or absolute application.

Against this background of cultural dynamics as known today, Aristotle's notion of a genuine ethical universal seems refreshingly up-to-date. While in the rout simile of the *Posterior Analytics* (II 19, 100a12-b5) the individual soldiers seem to line up in a fixed order resembling that of the Greek phalanx, a place is left open in the *Analytics* for genuine demonstration in subject matter that holds only "for the most part".[37] The subject matter of moral philosophy is of this type. It allows reasoning from premises that apply to it "as for the most part" (*EN* I 3, 1094b21) to conclusions that hold in corresponding fashion. Instead of lining up the individuals in the set order of phalanx or legion or regiment, it has them advance in the manner of commandos with whom the position of an individual at any particular moment of the attack is left to his own judgment on the spot, yet in a way that represents most effectively the *common* objective.

The correct habituation of the individuals in a common culture can accordingly provide a type of universality that is genuine and yet thoroughly flexible. It allows the individual actions to be instances of an authentic universal, even though each moral decision is unique and dependent upon deliberation that takes account of unrepetitive circumstances. It is dynamic in a way that keeps changing and is always open to further universalization in world culture. That is why Aristotle's ethics "can be applied to Soviet Russia, to medieval Christendom, to India, to New York City".[38] It enjoys a true universality, yet a universality that springs from habituated choice; for the moral virtues either come under the notion of choice or cannot be conceived apart from the factor of choice.[39] Far from interfering with the conception of choice as the starting point of things done, they in fact intensify that tenet.

V

Nature and culture, then, furnish convincing enough grounds for ethical universality in Aristotle's actual procedure. They both contribute towards providing a public and common setting in which moral decisions are made. Yet in all moral thinking they function in a way that leaves individual choice predominant. The individual remains master of his activity. Neither nature nor culture determines his choice. He determines his action himself in each particular instance. Each decision is a new starting point arising in the universe without ancestry and without any way of transferring the responsibility to an antecedent cause. Nothing less than this interpretation seems able to satisfy the radical distinction between starting points already present in the objects of theoretical science, and choice as the starting point of things done.

Choice, accordingly, has to be respected as the ultimate factor in the subject matter of moral philosophy. Yet in Aristotle it functions clearly enough in a manner that cannot be reduced either to an unrestricted relativism or to a descriptive phenomenology. Each act of choice is a highly individual decision. It is likewise a new fact in the universe. But the openness to universality and the immersion in what ought to be are unavoidable for it. They are built-in aspects that are involved in every act of human choice. They are operative in a way far too thoroughgoing to permit the individual to seal himself off hermetically from a common moral order.

These considerations may at first sight seem paradoxical. If choice is genuinely undetermined by anything antecedent to it, why cannot the individual choose to disregard nature and culture and anything that savors of what ought to be done? Why is he not master of his own conduct to the full extent of placing it outside the range of any common norm whatsoever? Why may he not choose to live entirely according to his whims?

The answer found repeatedly in the Aristotelian *Ethics* is the appeal of the goodness appropriate to human actions, a goodness expressed in Greek by the neuter of the adjective that means beautiful in an esthetic context, the *kalon*. It is difficult to render its meaning in the moral setting into English. Perhaps "seemly" is as close as one may come to it. If for the moment one may agree to use "seemly" to express the notion, one may convey the Aristotelian meaning by saying that the seemly presents itself to the human mind with an obligatory force of its own. The obligation is expressed in Aristotle by means of the Greek verb *dei*. It is what ought to be, or what should be. No other reason is given by him. Throughout the realms of the various virtues the motive always is the seemly. Virtuous actions are themselves seemly and are done for the sake of the seemly.[40] The texts read as though every virtuous action has an inherent quality of seemliness, and that the seemliness itself shows the deliberating human individual that he ought to perform this action. The obligation expressed by the verb *dei* arises apparently from the seemliness of the action and from nothing else. Apparently just as today the compelling attraction of purely moral issues in questions of war and civil rights (in contrast to material and national advantages) has been repeatedly seen to be the dominant force in student and other demonstrations, so in Aristotle the seemliness alone gives rise to obligation. Under this aspect the seemliness extends to all the moral starting points and to all morally good actions, whether in regard to means or in regard to end. It is present in each virtuous action, even apart from conscious orientation of the action by the individual to the correct supreme goal.

What can this mean? No explanation is developed in the Aristotelian text. But are not sufficient pieces present to be worked out into a satisfactory account? If each act of human choice sets up an utterly new starting point in the universe, must not an acute awareness of responsibility accompany it and permeate it? The choice is an intellectual action and accordingly is fully aware of itself. It knows that it is doing the deciding and that it consequently is the cause of what follows.[41] It cannot help but be aware of its responsibility. But in this notion is there not a dignity and an eminence that will at once impose themselves upon the mind's consideration? To be an originator in so profound a sense, to be master of a new series of events in the universe, to be responsible for what happens in a way that brings either credit or blame, are aspects that present themselves spontaneously to one's reflection. Do they not suggest an obligation to act in full accord with the dignity involved in choice? Do they not require that the decision be made in a way that will respect the natures of things and the culture in which one lives?

That seems to be the meaning of doing a thing as one ought. The doer in making a choice is himself engaged in an action that manifests to him a particular dignity of his own and draws him to a response corresponding in dignity. He sees what is seemly, what is appropriate, and sees in it an obligation to make his decision in accordance with it. His own engagement in the proposed course of action requires him to decide in a way that corresponds to his own recognized dignity and eminence. He sees that he *ought* to perform the good action, and avoid its contrary. He is not necessitated to make the choice, but he is aware that the one course becomes him in his role of deciding, and the other course does not. In that context the characteristically moral notions, such as dignity, responsibility, obligation, blame, approval, begin to appear.

In this way the characteristic of moral goodness is not something present in nature antecedently to the act of choosing. It does not spring from anything in the nature of things, but from the engagement of choice with a proposed course of action. It is not derived from what already is, but has a beginning that is new and unheralded in each new situation that becomes related to an individual's choice. Nor is it something superimposed upon an already constituted action. Rather, it is something that permeates the action from the very origin of a thing done or a thing chosen. Either it or its opposite, moral badness, characterizes every choice *qua* choice. In the responsibility and dignity of bringing a new direction, no matter how small, into the universe lies the obligatory appeal to do the thing in a befitting way. This would appear to be the explanation of what Aristotle means by doing the seemly for the sake of the seemly, or of doing a thing as it ought to be done.

Under this explanation, of course, moral goodness and moral badness are qualities of a human action. Aristotle explicitly classes the virtues under the category of quality, though in a different division from that of sensible qualities.[42] Virtuous actions correspond to this qualification.[43] In accordance with the quality they can be described as good or bad, as just, temperate, or courageous. Because seemly, they can be described as obligatory. From these viewpoints Aristotle's ethics may be characterized as descriptive. But it is descriptive of moral, not natural, qualities. Nor is it descriptive of facts that prescind or abstract from obligation. On the contrary, it is descriptive of seemliness, a characteristic that in its own self involves obligation. From this viewpoint Aristotle's ethics is seldom, if ever in a primary sense, jejunely prescriptive. It does not try to prescribe action. But it does show that actions of a certain kind are obligatory, and obligatory on account of their inherent seemliness.

VI

In this setting of the seemly and its inevitable obligation, then, is ethical universality to be understood in Aristotle. Just as in the theoretical sphere the individual color perceived by sight is color, and the individual *alpha* scrutinized by the grammarian is an *alpha*[44], so the act of courage that Socrates ought to perform is the act of courage that a man ought to perform. If the reasons for making the decision follow from the specific nature of man or arise from the common culture, the individual decision is open to universal scope. It can engender an ethical norm. Here as in the theoretical order, there is no real separation of individual from universal. The one is the other, regarded in a different way.[45] The universal considerations that arise from physical natures can accordingly exert their influence on the individual decision and allow its normative force to extend to other instances in which those natures similarly enter into the deliberation. The decision, though individual, marks in general the way in which morally good men would perform the action. Choice can likewise be habituated, as the experience of human culture shows. It can be habituated to choose regularly in the way good men choose, and thereby take on the universal aspect that bears on moral subject matter. A man may make the wrong choice, as regards either end or means. But that is not the final word. As long as he has choice he remains always open to a reversal of the decision. The role of natures as they confront his deliberation, and the appeal of the culture in which he has been brought up, continue to exert their dynamic influence and keep him within the ambit of a common moral world.

Ethical universality for Aristotle, consequently, is not something imposed from above or from without upon a manifold of individual decisions. It does not function like a law. Rather, it springs from the very starting point of a human action, of a "thing done". It is inherent in the openness of human choice. Every act of choice, highly individual though it is, faces in its preceding deliberation the natures of things around it and the culture in which it takes place. It thereby faces its own responsibility for bringing something that is radically new into a common universe. It opens out into universality. Aware on the one hand of its dignity as an act not determined by any preceding cause, and on the other hand of the natures and the culture that it faces, it sees in the proposed course of conduct a congruence that may be termed seemliness, or an incongruence that may be called unseemliness. Inherent in the seemliness appears the obligation to act accordingly, in the unseemliness to avoid the action. Nor need one object that the decision can always be made in defiance of nature and culture, ultimately escaping the universality. No, the power of choice still remains open for the individual. It is not done away with by a bad decision. It is still open in future decisions to the influence of natures and common culture. Men are always able to "pray that the things that are good absolutely may also be good for them".[46] Ethical universality is not prescriptive in Aristotle as though it were a law. It is not an imperative.[47] Nor is it on the other hand a quality in nature or derived from anything natural. It does not antecede choice. Yet it emerges from the activity of choice in a way that allows natures and common culture to serve as its grounds.

Does not this notion of the ethical universal sufficiently explain Aristotle's allegedly inconsistent use of the term *proairesis* for both "intention" and "choice"?[48] For him, choice is the basic factor in distinctively human actions, paralleling the role played for natural philosophy by the substantial principles of corporeal things, and the role played for productive philosophy by the plan in the mind of the artificer. If there is to be a science of human actions, then, their basic starting point, choice, must be open to universality. Yet the universality has to be flexible, not rigid. It does not necessitate the action, as natural principles would. The universality required is a type that will assure regularity for the most part and in a roughly consistent way, while always allowing for exceptions. Yet these exceptions, unlike the exceptions in nature, will have to be attributed to deficiencies in human choice.

How will these considerations affect Aristotle's use of the term "choice"? In point of fact, different men appear to choose (*EN* I 5, 1095b20) their supreme goal in different ways.[49] There can hardly be any doubt that men can deliberate about the choice of a life of pleasure, or of public standing, or of contemplation. The whole of the *Ethics* is meant to show why the life of contemplation should be given the preference. On the other hand, the supreme goal may be viewed under the aspect of happiness (I 3, 1095a20). Under this aspect it is not chosen (III 2, 1111b29). No more than the aspect of goodness itself can this general notion of a supreme good be absent in a human action (I 1-2, 1094a1-21). It is present in the action from the nature of things and not from human choice. But definite goals such as public standing or pleasure or intelligence or virtue may be selected for the sake of happiness as well as for their own sake (I 7, 1097b1-6). With the end already willed, choice is made of the means to the ends (III 3, 1113a11-14). The activities of the virtues are concerned with these means and proceed by way of choice, placing even a man's virtuous habituation within his own power (5, 1113b3-21).

So far the Aristotelian doctrine is thoroughly consistent. Both ends in particular (whether ultimate or non-ultimate) and means are objects of choice. But what about the uncontrolled man, who chooses to act rightly, yet acts in a contrary way (*EN* I 13, 1102b18-21)? Is he not actually doing the opposite of what he is choosing?

This situation would be impossible if what Aristotle understands by choice were exactly the same as what is meant today by free will. Aristotle gives no metaphysical explanation of choice. He is concerned with it only as it is observed in the practical sphere.[50] He categorizes the man who lacks self-control as virtuous, in contradistinction to the profligate. But virtue is either a choice or involves choice (II 5, 1106a3-4), and choice rather than actions characterizes a man's moral habituation (III 2, 1111b5-6). As long as a man has virtue, then, his choice is correct. A particular action of the man may not accord with that choice. Aristotle is content to call this moral weakness and to describe it without attempting to explain it. His interest lies in showing, as a solution to certain aporiae, that neither universal knowledge nor practical knowledge[51] is overcome in the action (VII 3, 1146b24-1147b17).

Does not this procedure indicate clearly enough that Aristotle's concern is for choice to function as the starting point of practical science? As the basic feature in distinctively human action, choice has to be habituated by virtue if it is to ground the universality required in a science, and it has to take into consideration the natures of things in its deliberation. Failures can be regarded as accidental to it.[52] The accidental, however, is not the object of any science (*Metaph. E* 2, 1026b3-1027a15). It does not require scientific explanation. But with choice one can always either do or not do, or do right or do wrong (*EN* III 5, 1113b4-14). Choice always remains open to actions against the way it has been habituated. As the starting point of things done, it gives rise to a subject matter in which the universal will hold only for the most part. Approached from this viewpoint, Aristotle's statements about it seem consistent enough as long as his grounds for ethical universality are given their appropriate bearing on the source of moral goodness in human actions.

14. Nature and Ethical Norm
in Aristotle

By way of introduction to discussions in a field so extensive as Aristotelian studies, may I propose a topic of sufficient generality to span the two most important divisions of the Stagirite's philosophy. These divisions are the theoretical and the practical. The theme will be the relation of morality to nature.

In Aristotle,[1] the difference between procedure in the philosophy of nature and procedure in moral philosophy is quite obviously meant to be radical. The starting points for the philosophy of nature are located in visible and tangible things, while those for moral philosophy are found in human free choice. The goal set for the philosophy of nature remains in knowledge just as knowledge, while for moral philosophy the goal is action in the sense of right conduct. Because of starting points and purpose, then, the two disciplines would seem destined to travel entirely different routes. Yet is it at all possible for ethics to dispense with knowledge of nature? Would ethics not be functioning in a vacuum? Are not ethical considerations regularly influenced and conditioned by the natures of the things with which human activity is concerned?

Procedure in moral philosophy, moreover, is syllogistic for Aristotle (*EN* I 3, 1094b19-22). It journeys from premises that hold roughly and for the most part to conclusions that hold in similar fashion. Syllogistic reasoning, however, requires universality at least in its middle term (*APo.* I 11, 77a7-8). In the Aristotelian framework nature is fully able to provide the basis for universality, since physical form (which is nature in the prior sense—*Ph.* II 1, 193b6-8) enables the singular thing to be known in a universal manner, and even allows the same term *eidos* to denote in a multisignificant way the physical form and the specific universal. But if free choice is undetermined by natural antecedents, if it is uniquely individual in each decision and conditioned by nonrepetitive circumstances, how can it furnish any ground for universal norms in ethics? The rule of moral goodness with Aristotle is basically the decision of the prudent man. The moral norm is explicitly "the mean relative to us, this being determined by a rational principle, and by that principle by which the man of practical wisdom would determine it" (*EN* II 6, 1107 a

1-2; Oxford tr.). The mean between excess and defect is the norm of moral goodness for the human act, and this mean is decided in each case by a prudential judgment in accord with ever changing circumstances.

Yet this tenet, though setting aside antecedently "objective" determination, does not seem to give rise to the least savor of a "situation ethics," or of any kind of "subjective" morality. The understanding of a "universal account" (*EN* II 2, 1104a5) for the ever changing subject matter of ethics, the constant universalizing of moral notions such as goodness, virtue, courage, and so on, the regular appeal to public approbation and blame as ethical criteria, the repeated classification of ethics among the sciences, all require that moral philosophy should function in a universal and public framework. But how can individual free choice lay a basis for universal norms?

Aristotle's own answer would ground this universality in culture and education (*paideia*). The correct choice of the moral mean requires proper habituation from earliest childhood (*EN* I 4, 1095b4-13; II 2, 1104b11-13). The habituation makes "all the difference" (*EN* II 1, 1103b25) in regard to moral choice. It equips one to recognize immediately what is right or wrong in a proposed decision, or at least to see the right or wrong when it is pointed out by others. The result is a flexible norm (*EN* II 2, 1104a3-26). Like an instrument to measure the varying surface of a molding (*EN* V 10, 1137b29-32), this norm is always adaptable to the ever changing contours of circumstances. Yet it is genuinely universal in its own non-rigid way. Its type of universality, by way of illustration today, is not comparable to

The even trench, the bristling mound

The legion's ordered line (Macaulay, *Lay's of Ancient Rome*).

Rather, it works in the manner of the commando tactics that allow the individual soldier to take advantage of every shelter and every opportunity according to his own individual judgment on the spot, with far greater contribution towards the common success of the attack.[2]

In this way individual decisions generate patterns of acting that build up a common culture. Do not cultural dynamics, as known today, seem to bear out Aristotle's ethical conception of a stable culture that is nevertheless always in process and change, thoroughly dependent on individual thinking and acting?[3] Likewise, do not the structuralism and the formalism that are found inherent in human language and in the deepest personal experience substantiate this Aristotelian notion, in contrast to a "situation ethics" based on unrestricted existentialism?[4]

With correct habituation, any man is able to make the decision that his fellow citizens will universally regard as correct in moral matters. He can discern the moral goodness (τὸ καλόν) in a proposed course of conduct, because it is in conformity with his lifelong habituation. Accordingly he will act for the sake of that good. The moral good appeals to him in a way that makes it obligatory under the aspect of something that should (δεῖ) be done. So, "not to desert our post nor take to flight nor throw away our arms" (*EN* V 1, 1129b20-21; Oxford tr.) will have an obligatory appeal for the brave man. But to make that ethical judgment in face of the spontaneous urge of nature to stay alive at all costs, the correct upbringing and habituation will be required. The proper moral attitude has to be instilled into citizens from the time of their earliest education, as both Aristotle and Plato insist. This attitude the Romans strove to inculcate with Horace's (*Odes*, III, 2, 13) "dulce et decorum est pro patria mori." It was echoed in nineteenth century England in the lines memorized by every student:

And how can man die better
Than facing fearful odds,
For the ashes of his fathers,
And the temples of his gods" (Macaulay, op. cit.)

On the other hand, its moral appeal and its obligatory suasion is completely missed by one who has been habituated to the notion that it is better to be alive under any ideology whatsoever than be dead. A person so habituated will make the opposite moral decision. From this viewpoint one can see considerable meaning in the proverb that the songs of a nation are more important than its laws.

But is this not circular reasoning? Correct habituation is the result of the good acts one performs. Yet the very notion of "good" in the present moral sense depends upon the judgment of the correctly habituated man. He has to be correctly habituated *before* he can make the right judgment. Correct habituation, as the result of one's individual acts, comes *after* these acts. Each of them, however, presupposes the right judgment, if the act is to be morally good. To perform a morally good act the correct habituation must be already present. But to acquire this habituation, one must first perform the good acts. Correspondingly, habituation is attained through culture and education, but the culture itself is built up as a result of morally good acts on the part of the individuals.

Aristotle, one might reply, takes for granted that Hellenic culture is already there, and that within it ethics as a practical science has its common norms assured. Only for a theoretical investigation would the query which came first arise. Yet the question of origins cannot easily be sidestepped in an overall inquiry. Did not something have to start the culture? All human knowledge originates for Aristotle in the cognition of sensible things. Can ethical knowledge escape this conditioning? Hardly. Besides, there are a number of texts that seem to base moral considerations on natural grounds. Every city state exists by nature (*Pol.* I 2, 1252b30-3l), and man is by nature a political animal (ibid., 1253a2-3). Slavery is justified by Aristotle on the ground that nature adapts some men to work with their bodies under the intellectual guidance of the more gifted (*Pol.* I 2, 1252a31-34). In matters of justice the mean is sometimes determined by nature (*EN* V 7, 1134b24-30).

Yet to interpret these texts in the sense that nature imposes a predetermined law upon human activity would run counter to the origin of moral principles in free choice and not in things. Can the meaning, then, be that nature offers the inclination and the framework for community life, for institutions like slavery, for paying back the exact quantity borrowed, but that these determinations enter into the moral order only when free choice decides they are to be followed in human conduct? This notion seems to be insinuated by the conclusion: "A social instinct is implanted in all men by nature, and yet he who first founded the state was the greatest of benefactors" (*Pol.* I 2, 1253a29-3l; Oxford tr.). Nature, apparently, seems to provide as it were the materials. But the formal entrance into the moral order would be dependent upon the action of a human will.

This would mean, then, that ethics is dependent upon nature for the materials in which it has to work. It has to take the different kinds of materials into consideration in making its decisions. In that way it is able to use the results of the other sciences without making itself subalternate to or subject to any of them. At *EN* I 13, 1102a18-25, Aristotle insists that the moral philosopher must have some theoretical knowledge of the soul, even more than the medical practitioner requires a certain amount of theoretical knowledge in regard to the body and its various organs. This would mean biology and physiology in the medical man not in their entirety nor for their own sakes, but only to the extent necessary for healing the body. Correspondingly the moral philosopher will require as much knowledge of natural philosophy, and presumably of the other theoretical sciences also, as is necessary for guiding human conduct.

Does not the picture as a whole make sufficient sense? All knowledge comes from the sensible world, but it enters the moral order only when free decisions are made about it by the properly habituated man. Nature has its own attractions, its own impulses, its own set determinations. These have to be considered and respected in making correct moral decisions. But they do not dominate or impose laws on human conduct. What makes a determination moral is not anything already established in nature, but the considered choice on the part of a correctly habituated rational being.

15. Aristotelian Ethics, Medicine, and the Changing Nature of Man

I

If we ask how the unrestrained man's ignorance is dissipated and he returns to a state of knowledge, the explanation is the same as in the case of drunkenness and sleep, and is not peculiar to failure of self-restraint. We must go for it to physiology. (Aristotle, *Ethica Nicomachea*, VII 3, 1147b6-9; trans.H.Rackham).

For the ultimate means of catalyzing moral ignorance and restoring moral knowledge in a weak-willed man, Aristotle falls back in this passage of the *Nicomachean Ethics* upon the knowledge of a man's physiological condition. The instance he brings forward is that of a person to whom the eating of sweets is not permitted. Overwhelming appetite for them is pushing the man towards eating a delicacy in front of him, while more considered judgment tells him not to. Since the man is weak-willed, his intellectual inclination to follow his better judgment does not prevail against sense impulse. In this particular instance he goes ahead to enjoy the forbidden object.

The passage does not receive too much attention from commentators on the *Ethics*, as it refers to a solution outside their proper field.[1] Yet it has crucial importance for the understanding of Aristotelian ethics in its relation to medicine and the changing nature of man. For Aristotle, strange as it may perhaps appear at first sight, the ultimate remedy here is not to be looked for in properly ethical considerations. Rather, it is to be sought in the type of knowledge provided by the physiologists. The eating of the delicacy is regarded by him as taking place in moral *ignorance*. In the Socratic tradition of Greek moral optimism a faulty opinion could not be allowed to prevail over knowledge, man's highest and rightfully dominant possession. No man should knowingly be able to do wrong. The judgment that sweets should not be eaten here and now is undoubtedly present in the weak-willed man's intellect. But it cannot be there as knowledge, against this background. It is present only as a corresponding proposition would be in the mind of a drunkard reeling off verses of elevated poetry, or in an ordinary actor reciting epic lines on the stage. It is not related to the inebriate or the actor as his own, and accordingly is not actual moral knowledge. But the weak-willed man is not totally depraved. He did indeed have the moral knowledge before succumbing to the impulse. He still retains the knowledge, though only in an habitual state. As moral knowledge it is dormant and ineffective. From the viewpoint of actuality there is only moral ignorance.

The latent moral knowledge, however, is definitely referred to by the recital of the words and the concomitant presence of the moral proposition in the weak-willed man's consciousness. How is it to be restored to actuality? How may the moral ignorance in which the man acts be broken through? Surprisingly, Aristotle does not invoke any specifically ethical aids. Without further ado he drops the characteristically moral procedure and states bluntly that the method is to be learned from the physiologists.

This way of dealing with weakness of will may at first strike today's reader as somewhat unusual in the setting of Greek intellectualism. Yet a little reflection will show that the whole passage fits appropriately enough into the general framework of the Aristotelian *Ethics*. The first point to note is that the passage is not asking how ethics can help medicine, but rather how physiology, which is applied by medicine, can help ethics in cases such as the one under discussion. This brings up the general question of how medicine is related to ethics for Aristotle. The bearing of the question is quite significant. Ethics is for him the supreme practical science, the science that governs all the other sciences, arts and crafts, and that directs all human conduct (*Ethica Nicomachea*, I 1-2,1094a1-b11). It has the right to call upon any of them, and explicitly upon the knowledge of human nature (*Ethica Nicomachea*, I 13,1102a18-b28), for whatever help it needs.[2] The reason is that for Aristotle ethics directs man towards the highest goal of his being, his supreme destiny. All other purposes in a man's life are subordinate to that end, and are meant to contribute towards its attainment. This supreme goal consists in the highest kind of intellectual life, namely, the exercise of man's highest faculty, the intellect, upon its highest object. Because of this one common goal, ethics for the community (the *polis*) and ethics for the individual coincide. Their purpose, the highest kind of human intellectual life, is exactly the same (*Ethica Nicomachea*, I 2,1094b6-11). All other types of activity are subordinated to its pursuit. They are meant to help towards it. One requisite, of course, is bodily health, the goal of medical interest (*Ethica Nicomachea*, I 7,1097a15-24). In this way, and in this way only, does Aristotle regard medicine as subordinate to ethics.

Aristotle was the son of a practicing medical man ([9], V.1). In accord with the wording of the Hippocratic oath ([23]), 1298, line 13), he may be presumed to have received the medical instruction and training customarily given the sons of a medical practitioner. He regularly speaks of medical knowledge with high respect, and makes accurate use of medical illustrations and similes throughout his writings. Yet his own bent was primarily philosophical. His main interest in practical life centered on the supreme destiny of man, towards which bodily health was but a means and a necessary condition. Against that background the question 'Can ethics be of help to medicine?' would have seemed to him wrongly placed. With Plato (*Republic,* III, 389BC) he would most likely agree that ethics could help keep the patient from deceiving the physician about medical symptoms, and could like rhetoric, (*Gorgias*, 456B) persuade him to submit to the prescribed medical or surgical treatment.[3] But these considerations would be only incidental. Aristotle's overall understanding of the relation between ethics and medicine would place the essential question as 'How can medicine help ethics?' The appeal to physiological knowledge in the case of the weak-willed man would accordingly be but an instance in which the question was found to apply. From this angle the passage quoted at the beginning of the present paper fits neatly enough into the general Aristotelian conception of practical knowledge.

Secondly, the problem here evoked calls for an understanding of Aristotle's notion of practical science itself. For him, the reasoned development of moral knowledge may be called 'practical science' (*Topica*, VI 6,145a15-18) or 'political science' (*Rhetorica*, I 4,1359b10-11;17-18), and is classed under 'practical' in his divisions of the sciences (*Metaphysica*, E 1.1025b18-1026a23; K 7,1064a10-b4). His basic distinction between the kinds of human knowledge lies between the theoretical on the one hand, and the practical and productive on the other. Theoretical knowledge deals with an object just as it stands, detached in itself, before one's intellectual gaze. The grounds of theoretical knowledge are accordingly located entirely within the object itself. The knowledge does not vary with the personal conditions of the agent at the moment. In Euclidean geometry, for instance, the angles of a triangle are and remain equal to two right angles regardless of the changing dispositions of the knowing agent. Whether the mathematician is good or depraved, strong-willed or weak-willed, sick or well, the geometrical theorem remains unaffected.

Moral knowledge, on the other hand, is worked into and imbedded in the habituation of the agent in a way that allows it to be described as going along with his nature.[4] So constituted, it is obviously changeable with the changing conditions of the man. Culture, habituation, physical and psychic conditions will affect it radically. A German boy brought up from childhood in the Hitler Jugend will tell you that he could see things only from a Nazi viewpoint until the bubble burst in the experience of post-war conditions and the outlook of his earlier years was changed completely. People educated in a strictly Victorian atmosphere will alter their moral judgments drastically with absorption into the spirit of mid-twentieth century permissiveness. Prolonged anger or deep sexual passion will gradually change one's judgment about what one should do. Because changing conditions so profoundly affect moral decisions, they are an essential aspect to be reckoned with in dealing with this type of knowledge. Consequently the physiological dispositions may be expected to play an essential part in the development or the restoration of truly moral cognition. That is just what the Aristotelian passage under consideration presupposes. Again it is found to be quite at home in the broad picture of Aristotle's ethics. To go back to the instances before his own eyes (*Ethica Nicomachea*, I 5,1095b14-1096a7), instead of the modern ones used just now to illustrate his meaning, different types of men do things for the ultimate purposes of pleasure, reputation and public standing, or intellectual activity. They are obviously making their judgments in accord with the type of life they lead. Their personal dispositions determine their differing judgments about what is good for them to do.

The third question that arises from the wording of the Aristotelian passage is what the term 'physiologist' meant exactly at the time. As Aristotle uses the word elsewhere ([5], 835b41-49), and as it was used by others in the epoch, it meant 'one who inquires into natural causes and phenomena' ([25], s.v.). Specifically it referred to the type of investigator who studied nature in the tradition that was followed from Thales onward. The object was to explain natural events in the light of their ultimate causes. For Aristotle, nature in this sense necessarily implied change. For him, change in fact pervaded the sensible world like a sort of life (*Physica*, VIII 1,250b14-15) for the things constituted by nature.

By 'physiologist,' then, Aristotle did not mean specifically a medical practitioner. He had at his disposal, and made regular use of ([5], 338a21-53), the precise Greek terms for medical man and the art of medicine. However, in the *Ethics (Ethica Nicomachea*, I 13,1102a21-22) he has in mind 'the more cultured type of medical practicioners,' who have devoted great attention to the knowledge of the body. In the historical setting this could not mean anything else than the study of the human body in the Hippocrtic tradition, which was in turn couched in the natural philosophy of the Presocratics.[5] Nature as envisaged by the Presocratics was the ground for medical discourse.[6] Even the objection of the author of *Ancient Medicine*, XX, against what philosophers and physicians have written about nature, does not bear on any separation of medicine from the ancient physiology but rather on the necessity of correct medical knowledge for the understanding of what nature really is.[7]

But what did 'nature' mean for Aristotle himself in this context? He recognizes a number of senses for the term. Its two basic significations in Greek tradition were the stable constitution of a thing and the thing's growth or development.[8] Against this historical background of both change and permanence, Aristotle seems to take the best of both worlds. He finds the basic philosophical meaning of 'nature' to be the *unchangeable* components of *changeable* things. The components are matter, which lacks all determination just of itself, and form, which provides stable determination. Things constituted by these two components exist 'by nature', for instance, animals and their parts, and plants and simple bodies. Since the matter is able to lose one form and acquire another, natural things have to be changeable things.[9] Other meanings of 'nature,' such as the actual process of growth or development, or substances composed of form and matter, or the essential constitution of a thing, will in this context be philosophically consequent upon the basic notions of matter and form.

In man, this will mean for Aristotle that there is a form called the soul, and matter, which of itself has no specific or individual character. The man, the human being, is the composite of the two. The two, as in any living body, form a unit, a single living thing (*De Anima*, II 1,412a3-b8). Consequently there is in a man but the one substantial being, the one agent, the one human nature that is his from birth to death.

II

What, then, is Aristotle's view on the changing nature of man? Certainly in the framework just probed, the formal component of a man, the soul, is essentially unchangeable. It remains the same in the man from embryonic state till death. It makes him and keeps him a human being throughout his entire existence. It likewise makes him and keeps him the same individual throughout his career.[10]

On the other hand, since motion pervades bodies as a sort of life, there is incessant change in the human composite. A man is changing every moment, waking or sleeping. He is changeable through birth, nutrition, growth, activity and death. Yet from womb to tomb he remains the same substance, the same thing, the same human being. There is no dualism at all here. Body and soul are but the one substance for Aristotle. They are a unit, a single thing, not two existents. The body is not just matter, but the composite of matter and soul. Soul is included in the body as its basic form.[11] To speak of the soul as doing something is but a shorthand way of saying that the man is doing it through his soul or by means of his soul (*De Anima*, 1 4,408b11-15). There is but the one agent, the human composite.

Aristotle, it is true, regularly contrasts soul with body in the way of speaking of his time, which is also the way of speaking in our time. Actions or functions that are wholly conditioned by spatial and temporal considerations, which follow upon the composite being, can readily be attributed to the body. Those that transcend the conditions of space and time can be attributed to the soul, for instance, actions that involve universality or free choice.[12] But in either case it is the same agent, the man, who is performing the activity. He remains the same because his soul does not change in substance, no matter how much it develops in its activities and consequent habituation.

The Aristotelian ethics is developed in the framework of these two aspects of the same man, namely, the unchangeable form and the changeable composite body. Because changeable as a composite, a man is educable. He is able to be trained and habituated from his earliest years. According to the way he is trained and educated, he will form his judgments of conduct. If brought up to live only for sense pleasure, his motivation will hardly rise above the bestial level. If trained to live for glory and reputation, he will be conditioned for war and public life. If educated to place intellectual pursuits above all else, he will for Aristotle be given the correct human orientation. Even if he himself does not have too much bent for intellectual interests in his personal life, but is brought up to respect and do what is right (*to kalon*) in the well-ordered community, he will be living a life that is directed towards ensuring the proper overall conditions for intellectual engagement. In this way he will be living, though of course only on a secondary level, for the truly human goal (*Ethica Nicomachea*, 1 4-5,1095a14ff.;X 7-8,1177a12-1178b7).

Proper education, then, is what habituates a man from childhood to pursue the *kalon*, the right thing. The habituation is envisaged as extending throughout the whole gamut of human endeavors in enabling the correct mean to be known and attained in all conduct. It engenders the virtues of wisdom, justice, temperance, and courage, along with their subordinate qualities. It prompts the deliberation necessary to determine the correct mean for human conduct under the incessantly changing circumstances of the ambient and the varying dispositions of the man himself. In view of these ever changing conditions, hard and fast rules cannot hope to be decisive - the decision in every case depends upon the judgment of the cor-rectly habituated man (*Ethica Nicomachea*, II 6,1107a1-2). He alone can determine the correct mean in each new situation, the mean which is the high point of excellence (a6-8). In some cases this high point will always coincide with one of the extremes, for instance, 'adultery, theft, murder' (a11-12). There is no morally right time or right manner or right person with any of these. They are always wrong. The tenet that moral norms are flexible is itself flexible, and flexible enough to allow for norms that hold absolutely (*haplôs* -a17). The tenet itself is changeable according to the situation. Where the components of the situation add up to theft or murder or adultery, the high point of moral excellence is located in the ex-treme of avoiding them completely. Even in the theoretical order the stand that everything is changeable is untenable in its complete universali-ty, for that would mean that it itself is changeable into its opposite. It thereby, to avoid being self-destructive, allows for something that is un-changeable. Correspondingly the tenet that in the practical order the norms are of their nature flexible has of itself enough flexibility for the admission of absolute norms. Where the morally good and wise man judges that a type of conduct like adultery or murder is always wrong regardless of circumstances, the high point of excellence never varies with the changing ambient. Decidedly Aristotle's views do not come under the notion of the currently popular 'situation ethics.'

From these considerations does not a clear enough picture emerge of the way Aristotle conceives the changing nature of man in relation to ethical knowledge? In its formal element, the soul, man's nature is basically permanent and unchanging. In that regard a man does not make his own nature, and he is unable to change it. He remains always a man, a human being, and always has to be regarded as such. Permanently his nature is intellectual and free, regardless of what may happen to him amid the tragedies of human life. This stands in opposition to much contem-porary existentialist writing, in which a man in contrast to something irra-tional makes his own nature and becomes what he is. But is it not sufficiently obvious that we are free not because we choose to be but because we are so by nature?[13] A man's nature antecedes his choice, and endows him with an aspect of permanence that is not within his power to discard.

Nevertheless, with his nature presupposed, it is man's freedom condi-tioned by deliberation that sets up the moral order.[14] As an agent a man is a composite of soul and body. By nature this composite is changeable. It can be habituated according to the moral and intellectual virtues. If in current language habit is to be regarded as a second nature, the habituation in which correct moral knowledge is ingrained from the earliest years of a man's upbringing may well be termed his changing nature. As the speaking of a language or the playing of a musical instrument becomes ingrained in a person through long and careful habituation, and allows him to adapt gracefully his speech or his performance to the exceedingly intricate themes he may be required to express, so the morally habituated man is equipped to make the correct moral judgment in the incessantly changing circumstances of human life.

But bodily dispositions, both physical and psychic, can change. A man who had no noticeable urge for alcohol or sedatives may gradually develop the opposite disposition towards them. A sudden burst of anger, an overwhelming impulse of greed, a surge of sexual passion, may prompt a man to act against the judgment made on the basis of his lifelong habituation. The impulse runs contrary to the moral habituation, and drives the man in an entirely opposite direction when it comes to predominate. This means that the habituation is no longer actually functioning, and accordingly that the moral knowledge embedded in it is not actual. The man is literally in a condition of moral ignorance. Moral motivation cannot be appealed to. The physical or psychic disposition of the man has to change before there can be question of moral guidance. The study of how this change takes place is not something on the properly moral level. It pertains to the study of the physical and psychic dispositions of the man. That was the province of the ancient 'physiology.' It is no longer a matter of free choice, the ground of the moral order.

Consequently Aristotle, for all his emphasis on correct education from childhood on, could not say with Democritus that 'teaching transforms man, and in transforming him makes his nature' ([8], 69B 33). Rather for Aristotle the basic nature of a man antecedes his education, and provides the combined permanence and changeability required for it. Nor could he acquiesce entirely in the other well-known saying of Democritus: 'Medical science cures diseases of body, but wisdom rids soul of passions' [7,24]. For Aristotle the dichotomy could not be that clear-cut. For him there are situations in which wisdom is powerless to rid the soul of a passion, and recourse must be had to the type of knowledge that is applied by medical science.

III

These reflections should allow sufficient understanding of the passage quoted at the beginning of the discussion. Aristotle's weak-willed man acted through ignorance, because at the moment of going into action he was oriented in actuality towards the delectable object alone. His lifelong habituation, in which his moral knowledge was embedded, had been pushed completely out of actuality by the contrary tendency in the sudden impulse of sense appetite. He could not tend in two completely opposite directions at the same time, once one of the tendencies became fully dominant. His will is not strong enough to resist the take-over by the sense impulse. His moral habituation fades out of actuality, and with it his moral knowledge. Actually — and it is the actuality that matters for his conduct — he is in a state of ignorance.

How is this ignorance to be broken through? Certainly not by moral reasoning or persuasion, for it has rendered moral knowledge inoperative. The immediate cause is physical or psychic. The cause of the ignorance is a change that has taken place in the composite, in the body. The study of it pertains accordingly to the physiologist. To him will belong the task of investigating how the physical and psychic conditions of the man keep changing, with the gradual result that the sense appetite is satisfied or lessened or assuaged and the normal equilibrium of the body is restored. The man's moral habituation and the knowledge it concretizes will no longer be impeded from coming into actuality.

That is the general picture. The passage in question does fit neatly enough into the overall conceptions of Aristotle's moral philosophy. In detail, however, the answers to present-day questions are not found ready-made in his own writings. He is indeed explicit in asserting the obvious fact that the passions and emotions cause bodily changes: '. . . for it is evident that anger, sexual desire, and certain other passions, actually alter the state of the body, and in some cases even cause madness' (*Ethica Nicomachea*, VII 3,1147a15-17; trans. Rackham). But he does not explain in detail how sense impulse prevents moral knowledge from functioning and how the physiologist would account for the subsiding and disappearing of passion. He remains content with a merely factual description of what takes place, and with the assertion that the causal account will be the same as in the cases of sleep and drunkenness.

With regard to sleep we do have a detailed Aristotelian account.[15] Sleep is an affection of the composite of soul and body, in things that are endowed with sense perception (*De Somno et Vigilia*, 1,453b11-454a19). It is 'as it were, a tie, imposed on sense-perception, while its loosening (λυσις) or remission constitutes the being awake' (*De Somno et Vigilia*, 1,454b26-27). So far the parallelism is exact. Sleep, like passion, essentially involves a bodily change that prevents a definite kind of cognition. It consists in a sort of chain or bond that has to be loosened (*cf.* λύεται, *Ethica Nicomachea*, VII 3,1147b6). But here the help from the parellelism seems to end. For sleep, the bond or blocking condition is located in the functional failure of a definite Aristotelian sense faculty, the *sensus communis (De Somno et Vigilia*, 2,455b8-12), a faculty intermediate between external sensations and the imagination.[16] The purpose of sleep is the natural and necessary preservation of animals (b13-28). Its physical cause is 'a sort of concentration, or natural recoil, of the hot matter inwards' (*De Somno et Vigilia,* 3,457b1-2; 458a25-28). None of these three specific explanations will apply in case of weakness of will. The directions in which the detailed accounts should be sought are thereby indicated. But the accounts themselves are not provided in the Aristotelian writings.[17]

IV

The analysis of the passage in question, then, against the general background of Aristotelian ethics, seems to offer a satisfactory enough instantiation of the way that ethics is related to medicine and to the changing nature of man. Ethics regards medicine as an art whose purpose is bodily health ([5], 338a26-30). Bodily health is an integral constituent of a complete life span, and a complete life span is a requirement (*Ethica Nicomachea*, 1 7,1098a18-20; 9,1100a4-5) of the human happiness that constitutes the goal of Aristotelian ethics. Accordingly medicine comes in global fashion under the direction of ethics, and is an aid in attaining the supreme goal for which ethics strives (*Ethica* Nicomachea, I 6,1097a17-24). The extent to which it is to be pursued in the community, and the qualifications required in the persons who are to take it up, fall under the supervision of ethics (*Ethica Nicomachea*, I 2,1094b1-6). At the same time medicine is recognized as a science with its own distinctive method, which accordingly cannot be dictated by any other science no matter how superior.

From these Aristotelian tenets some corollaries pertinent to today's setting may be readily drawn. In general, ethics requires that the practice of medicine be directed to and subordinated to the general human good. This means that the government should promote it and subsidize it to the extent necessary for the welfare of the citizens, and should enforce rules regarding the qualifications of those permitted to practice it.[18] Under the norms of distributive justice and commutative justice, ethics requires that medical practitioners respect all the rights of the patients and render the services to which they are obligated, receiving in return appropriate remuneration for their services. At the same time, outside interference in questions that are to be decided solely from a medical viewpoint would run counter to the Aristotelian conception of method in the sciences.

Further, both ethics and medicine deal with man, a composite of soul and matter. The composite is an essentially changeable nature, changeable through both moral persuasion and physiological alteration. Moral persuasion is effective only up to a point, namely, as long as a man's moral habituation is able to function. When through drunkenness, or mental disease, or overwhelming passion it no longer has actual influence, the physical and psychic factors alone direct a man's action. The situation has to be handled on the physiological and psychological plane. As it is the medical practitioner who puts this type of knowledge into practice, the ready corollary to be drawn is that medicine can here tender essential service to ethical conduct. There is no need to labor this point today. Cures for alcoholism, the prescription of tranquilizers, and the use of other thereapeutic aids for persons who want to follow their better moral judgment, testify to it abundantly.

Today nobody will want to accept the Aristotelian picture in its entirety. The advance in mathematical and experimental science on the one hand, and on the other the different outlooks in modern philosophies and in the Judeo—Christian and Moslem tradition, have drastically changed the ambient in which ethical thinking takes place. The habitat is no longer the closely-knit culture of the Greek city-state. But the insights of the Aristotelian ethics range far beyond the social and physical limits in which they were engendered. To regard them as irrelevant because ancient would be to misunderstand their nature. Their origins lie deep in the innermost recesses of human personality itself. They have in consequence proved capable of fecundating each new ambient as it arises. They may still be made one's own with enthusiasm and with profit.

The *Nicomachean Ethics*, in fact, continues to fascinate students today as few ancient documents can. Its method, because so deeply human, is always very much alive. It is surprisingly capable of adaptation to modern problems, and, as an American philosopher has remarked, it can be applied 'to *any* cultural heritage.'[19] Precisely because of this sensitive universality and vital openness to each new situation, the Aristotelian writings cannot be expected to provide ready-made answers to particular problems in ethics. To look in their pages for cut and dried solutions to modern questions would be to misinterpret fatally the nature of the thinking they develop. They focus on human life, life that keeps changing with man. But because they spring so genuinely from actual human motivation and conduct, they range as wide as human activity itself.

Accordingly, the Aristotelian writings are not geared towards doing a reader's thinking for him in ethical problems. Rather, they inspire and guide him towards penetration into the actual moral situations facing him in real life, towards analyzing them into their components and following them through to the problem's solution. They are never meant to serve as a substitute for personal reflection and hard intellectual work of one's own. What they teach the reader is the much more difficult and more important art of doing his own thinking through each new set of circumstances in an incessantly changing human life. It is in this way that they continue to have relevance and importance for current ethical thinking.

Notes

Notes to Chapter 1

1. Ernest Barker, *The Politics of Aristotle* (Oxford: Clarendon Press, 1946), p.v.

2. Jose Ortega y Gasset, *Man and Crisis*, tr. Mildred Adams (New York: W.W. Norton, 1958), p. 118.

3. The biographical data handed down about Aristotle may be found critically assessed in detail in Ingemar Düring, *Aristotle in the Ancient Biographical Tradition* (Göteborg: Universitas Gothoburgensis, 1957).

4. On the present state of the edition of these fragments, see Paul Wilpert, "The Fragments of Aristotle's Lost Writings," in *Aristotle and Plato in the Mid-Fourth Century*, ed. I. Düring and G.E.L. Owen (Göteborg: Symposium Aristotelicum, 1960), pp. 257-264). The Prussian Academy edition (Berlin: Reimer, 1831-1870) of Aristotle, which gives the page, column and line by which he is usually quoted, prints Valentin Rose's second edition of the fragments (R²), in volume V, page 1474al ff. The Oxford translation, *The Works of Aristotle*, ed. W.D. Ross (Oxford: Clarendon Press and the University Press, 1908-1952) has as its twelfth volume *Select Fragments* giving in English the more important and interesting items.

5. See C.J. De Vogel, "The Legend of the Platonizing Aristotle," in *Aristotle and Plato in the Mid-Fourth Century* (supra, n.4), pp. 255-256.

6. The term "metaphysics" though regularly used by the Greek commentators, is not found in Aristotle. As a title for the Aristotelian treatises it may be traced to within a century of Aristotle's death--see Paul Moraux, *Les listes anciennes des ouvrages d'Aristote* (Louvain: Editions universitaires, 1951), pp. 312-315. On much less substantial indications it has been traced back to Aristotle's immediate pupils. The now popular notion that it was originally an editorial designation coined by Andronicus of Rhodes, in the first century B.C., is a fantasy springing only from the imagination of a young German writer, J.G. Buhle, in a paper published in 1788.

7. *The Life and Letters of Charles Darwin*, ed. Francis Darwin, 3rd edition. (London: John Murray, 1887), III, 252.

8. John Herman Randall Jr., *Aristotle* (New York: Columbia University Press, 1960), p. 248.

9. See supra, n. 8. Cf. Randall, pp. viii; 300. Exploratory coverage of Aristotle's views on language, one of the two areas of relevance signalized by Randall (p. viii), may be found in Miriam Therese Larkin, *Language in the Philosophy of Aristotle* (The Hague & Paris: Mouton, 1971).

Notes to Chapter 2

1. James Gould. "Ryle on Categories and Dualism," *The Downside Review,* LXXVII (1959), 298. The Aristotelian categories had long before, against the Cartesian background, been called "une chose tout arbitraire" by Arnauld, *Logique de Port-Royal,* Ie partie, c. 3; and in the Nominalist tradition they had been spoken as of the "Ten Names" by Locke, *Essay concerning Human Understanding,* III, 10, 14. An historical sketch of the category doctrines up to the modern era may be found in Adolph Trendelenburg, *Geschichte der Kategorienlehre,* in *Historische Beiträge zur Philosophie,* v. I (Leipzig: Bethge, 1846), pp. 196-380.

2. On the term *katêgoria,* see Lambertus M. De Rijk, *The Place of the Categories of Being in Aristotle's Philosophy* (Assen: Van Gorcum, [1952]), Appendix, pp. 89-92.

3. *Tht.,* 167A. Cf. Ast, *Lexicon Platonicum,* II, 171.

4. *Cat.,* 3,1b10-14. The best text is in L. Minio-Paluello, *Aristotelis Categoriae et Liber de Interpretatione* (Oxford: Clarendon Press, 1949). For authenticity and early dating of the *Categories,* see Isaac Husik, "On the Categories of Aristotle," *The Philosophical Review,* XIII (1904), 514-528; "The Authenticity of Aristotle's Categories," *The Journal of Philosophy,* XXXVI (1939), 427-431; L. M. De Rijk, "The Authenticity of Aristotle's Categories," *Mnemosyne,* 4a ser. IV (1951), 129-159. On the various shades of meaning in Aristotle's use of *katêgoria,* see De Rijk, *The Place of the Categories of Being in Aristotle's Philosophy,* p. 91.

5. For Aristotle, equivocals and univocals refer primarily to things, and only secondarily to conceptual expressions and words, as I have tried to show in *The Doctrine of Being in the Aristotelian Metaphysics* (Toronto: Pontifical Institute of Mediaeval Studies, 1951), pp. 49-63. [3rd ed., pp. 107-135, Ed.]

6. *Cat.,* 1,1a1-15. Cf. *Top.,* I 15,106a29-39.

7. *Cat.,* 2,1a16-22. The strongly logical aspect of the category doctrine is clear at *Top.,* I 9,103b29-39, where the categories are described as predicates asserted of an individual man.

8. *Cat.* 2,1a13-24. The parenthesis at 1a24-25 is placed before these lines (a23-24) in the Oxford and Loeb translations.

9. *Cat.,* 2, 1a24-25. "Be" and "exist" stand for the one Greek verb *einai.*

10. *Cat.,* 2, 1a29-b6. The individual substance is here (5,2 all ff.) the primary instance of substance.

11. *Systoichiai, APo.,* I 15,79b7-11; *Sens.,* 7,448a14-16; *PA.,* III 7,670b20-22; *Metaph.,* I 3,1054b35-1055a1; 8,1058a13-14.

12. *Cat.,* 5,3a35-37. For the noun in this sense, see Bonitz, *Index Aristotelicus,* 377b52 ff.; for "*schemata* of predication," 378a32-34.

13. *Cat.,* 2,1a20 ff (*legetai*). Cf. supra, nn. 3-4.

14. *Cat.,* 3,1b10-15. In this way a category is a "division" (*Top.,* IV 1,120b36) of genera and species.

15. In that sense the Latin translation *praedicamentum* became fixed in its Scholastic usage. Hence the English expression "to get into a predicament." Only what was restricted in scope could belong to a category.

16. "Substantia" was the term used by Boethius in his translation and commentary *In Cat. Arist.*, I (*PL*, LXIV, 181ff.), and elsewhere in his logical commentaries. Through Boethius it became the accepted Scholastic translation of *ousia* in designating the first of the categories. Because *ousia* in its logical function is the *subject* of the accidental predicates, the rendition "substance" worked neatly enough in the logical context. *Essentia* had been recognized as the Latin equivalent of *ousia*, and *substantia* was used as an equivalent of *essentia*; see E. Gilson, "Notes sur le Vocabulaire de l'Être," *Mediaeval Studies,* VIII (1946), 152-155.

17. "Entity" seems the safest English translation; "Essence" has come to have other meanings in current Aristotelian discussions. "Being" is not permissible as a translation of *ousia*, since it is the regular translation of the participle *on* and the infinitive *einai*, and so has too general a sense to designate a category: τὸ δ' εἶναι οὐκ οὐσία οὐδενί· οὐ γὰρ γένος τὸ ὄν (*APo.*, II, 7,92b13-14). Being is not a genus for Aristotle, and so is not placed in any category. It is above all the categories, and is common to them all.

18. *Cat.*, 4,1b25-27. The Aristotelian designations for the accidental categories are more concrete—quantum instead of quantity, quale instead of quality, and so on. In particular, "place" means the exact location answering the question "Where?" and "time" means the definite time answering the question "When?"

19. "Position" refers to the disposition of the bodily members, as the examples "lying" and "sitting" (*Cat.*, 4,2a2-3) show. "State" translates the infinitive of the verb "to have." The examples given (a3) are "shod" and "armed." The notion seems that of "having something on," as shoes, clothes, or weapons. These two categories are not mentioned expressly in any of the lists outside markedly logical contexts. A convenient table of the lists in the *Organon* may be found in M. M. Scheu, *The Categories of Being in Aristotle and St. Thomas* (Washington, D.C.: Catholic University of America Press, 1944), p. 12, and of the lists in the other Aristotelian works on p. 22.

20. The list of ten occurs only here in the *Categories* and in the *Topics*, I 9,103b22-23. The passage in the *Topics* mentions explicitly that the kinds of categories are ten in number. Yet there is no indication that Aristotle worked out a number for the categories on any systematic or as it were *a priori* basis, as in Kant. The *Metaphysics* (Δ 28,1024b12-16), though, maintains that no category of being can be resolved into any other.

21. See Diogenes Laertius, *Lives of Eminent Philosophers*, VII, 44; 56-58. Cf. Aristotle, *Int.*, 2,16a19-b18.

22. *Metaph.*, Z 3,1029a20-21; cf. 1,1028a10-b2.

23. For a synopsis of the discussions, see L. M. De Rijk, *The Place of the Categories of Being in Aristotle's Philosophy*, pp. 1-5. De Rijk himself concludes (p. 88) that the logical and ontological sides of the category doctrine are interwoven for Aristotle, with the ontological aspect having the primary role. Cf. pp. 7; 72-74; 83-86.

24. For a discussion of the topic in Avicenna, Thomas Aquinas, and Duns Scotus, see J. Owens, "Common Nature: A Point of Comparison between

Thomistic and Scotistic Metaphysics," *Mediaeval Studies*, XIX (l957), 1-14; and in comparison with Plato's Ideas, "Thomistic Common Nature and Platonic Idea," *Mediaeval Studies*, XXI (1959), 211-223. Roger Albritton, in the symposium "Substance and Form in Aristotle," *The Journal of Philosophy*, LIV (1957), 669, n. 2, expresses a doubt that "Aristotle would have understood any better than I do the suggestion that a thing may be neither universal nor particular." Yet that way of understanding the nature of a sensible thing as just in itself was a commonplace among mediaeval readers of Aristotle, in the wake of Avicenna. It is not at all a question of attributing to the common nature an existence outside the particular and outside the universal, but rather of maintaining that it is the same common nature that has existence *either* as individual in reality *or* as universal in the intellect. In any case, there has to be some aspect that metaphysics and logic touch in common: ". . . a logic that had literally no relevance to . . . what there is, would be about as 'meaningless' an enterprise as the wit of man could devise." J. H. Randall, *Aristotle* (New York: Columbia Univ. Press, 1960), p. 296.

25. See *Metaph.*, M 10,1087a15-21. This text concludes: "But *per accidens* sight sees universal colour, because this individual colour which it sees is colour; and this individual *a* which the grammarian investigates is an *a*" (Oxford tr.). The colour that is particular is also the color that is universal, and the *a* that is individual is likewise the *a* that is universal. The one cannot be seen or known without thereby incidentally knowing the other. This seems quite the same as saying that the nature is the same in both the particular and the universal. It is the same nature that is known actually as individual, potentially as universal. Cf.: "For we know no sensible thing, once it has passed beyond the range of our senses, even if we happen to have perceived it, except by means of the universal *and* the possession of the knowledge which is proper to the particular, but without the actual exercise of that knowledge" (*APr.*, II 21,67a39-b3; Oxford tr.). So at *Metaph.*, Z 10,1036a6-8, the same thing that passes out of actual cognition continues to be known in the universal. At 10,1035b27-3l, "man" and "horse" in their universality are but something composed of a particular form and a particular matter, as taken universally. At 11,1037a5-10, it is likewise the same thing that has the two senses, individual and universal.

26. Henry Veatch, *The Modern Schoolman*, XXX (1953), 150, found this explanation open to the suspicion of reading back into Aristotle lessons learned from the Scholastics. The problem is not that simple. The mediaevals faced the issue in an existential framework. The same nature has a twofold existence, in reality and in the mind, and so of itself neither existence belonged to it. Accordingly neither singularity, which conditioned its existence in reality, nor universality, which conditioned its existence in intellection, pertained to it in itself. Of itself it was neither individual nor universal, but took on these conditions only in the one or the other existence. This existential framework cannot historically be read back into Aristotle. The Stagirite's explanation is given wholly in terms of actuality and potentiality within a formal (as contrasted with existential) order—the one Aristotelian term *eidos* serves for the object of both the potential

knowledge given by the "species" and the actual knowledge by way of "form." Of itself the Aristotelian form is actual. It is multiplied by matter and thereby assumes singularity; it is able to give universal knowledge of the other singulars in which it may be found, and so is potentially universal. The conclusion that of itself it is neither singular nor universal is not drawn in Aristotle. When it is drawn today, it is not drawn because of any grounds found in mediaeval philosophy, but upon grounds present in the Aristotelian text. To this extent there need be no hesitation in agreeing with Francis H. Parker and Henry B. Veatch, *Logic as a Human Instrument* (New York: Harper & Brothers, 1959), p. 52, n. 3, that "the solution of the problem here proposed is certainly implicit in Aristotle." The problem, explained by a doctrine of moderate realism, is that "it is one and the same nature or essence which exists in these dual states or conditions" (*ibid.*, p. 53). The reasoning that what can be both singular and universal is of itself neither, may be learned from the mediaevals. But the mediaevals would be a hindrance rather than a help in discovering why the Aristotelian form is of itself neither singular nor universal.

Because the categories consist of natures common to the treatment of both logic and metaphysics, they may be said to form, in Zeller's words, "the true connecting link (*das eigentliche Bindeglied*), in Aristotle's philosophic system, between Logic and Metaphysics." *Aristotle and the Earlier Peripatetics* (tr. Costelloe and Muirhead, London: Longmans, Green, and Co., 1897), I,273.

27. See Gerard Smith, "Avicenna and the Possibles," *The New Scholasticism*, XVII (1943), 340-357, concerning the metaphysical implications of "this buffer state . . . which is without existence" (*ibid.*, p. 349).

28. Or, in a standard formulation. "It has been erroneously supposed that from the two statements *I am sitting on this chair* and *This chair is a logical construction*, it follows that *I am sitting on a logical construction.*" L. Susan Stebbing, *A Modern Introduction to Logic*, Appendix B (6th ed., London: Methuen & Co., 1948), p. 505. Cf. Aristotle, *APr.*, I 33,47b15-29.

29. *Metaph.*, Z 7,1032b1-14; 11,1037a28.

30. *Metaph.*, Z 13,1038b8-16;16,1041a5.

31. "Here Aristotle definitely breaks with his doctrine in the *Categories* where they were called substances (if only in a *secondary* sense)." L. M. De Rijk, "The Authenticity of Aristotle's Categories," *Mnemosyne*, ser. 4, IV (1951), 146-147. The reason is that "all substantiality has now definitely been denied" to them (*ibid.*, p. 148). Eugène Dupréel, "Aristote et le Traité des Catégories," *Archiv für Geschichte der Philosophie*, XXII (1909), 247, considers the secondary substances of the *Categories* as equated with the forms of the *Metaphysics*, thereby expressing a doctrine directly opposite to the teaching of the latter work.

32. Their identity with each other is expressly denied at *SE*, 22,178a11-12. In the other places in the logical works where they are mentioned together (*Cat.* 4,1b27; *APo.*, I 22,83a22; b17; *SE* 4,166b13-18), they are regarded as distinct from each other in the same way as any category is distinguished from another.

33. ". . . movement is in the mobile thing; for it is the actuality of the mobile, caused by what is able to impart movement, and the actuality of what is able to

impart movement is none other than it. For it has to be the actuality of both, since through potentiality a thing is able to impart movement but is imparting it through actualizing. But what it is able to actualize is the mobile, so that the actuality of both is one; just as the interval of one to two is the same as that of two to one, and the uphill road is the same as the downhill road. For these coincide, though their notions do not." *Ph.*, III 3,202a13-20; cf. a21-b22. Action and passion, accordingly, are identified in reality with motion. In the real world they are one and the same, though in the mind they are grasped by different notions. It is the same situation as the case of the one real road on the hillside. The road may be said to go up or to go down, according to the point from which you view it. The concepts of action and passion are different, but they express one and the same reality, though from different standpoints. Cf. *G C*, I 6,322b18-19; 7,323b1-324b24; 9,326b29-31.

The same doctrine may be found in the *De Anima*: ". . . for the actuality of the agent and of the mobile thing comes to be in the patient. . . . so action (*poiêsis*) and passion are in the patient and not in the agent." *De An.*, III 2,426a4-10; cf. a15-17. It may also be seen in the *Metaphysics*, Θ 8,1050a28-36. At *Metaph.*, Z 4,1029b25, "movement" (*kinêsis*) alone seems to stand for both action and passion in a grouping of the categories, and at *Metaph.*, Δ 7,1017a26 and *Ph.*, V 1-2,225b7-14 (=*Metaph.*, K 12,1068a9-14, action and passion are mentioned in the groupings as though they both together formed but one category set off from the others. In the aporematic treatment at *Metaph.*, B 2,996b18, they are listed separately, however, as in the *Categories* and *Topics*; and likewise at *Metaph.*, Δ 6,1016b7 (cf. *E E*, I 8,1217b29), where the treatment deals with the different ways in which things may be called one. In this latter grouping in the *Metaphysics*, the logical category "state" (*echein*) is also included.

The texts seem sufficient to show that for Aristotle the only real actuality distinguishing a potential moment from an actual moment is the movement itself, and this is found only in the thing that is being moved. The Aristotelian form by its very nature "actualizes" (*energei*—see *Ph.*, VIII 4,255a1-b24; cf. *Metaph.*, Z 7,1032a12-8,1034a8; Θ 8,1050b29-30) if there is no impediment and the proper conditions are present. A man having knowledge, for instance, would be always thinking if nothing hindered him, fire burns unless something is stopping it, light and heavy bodies travel in their respective directions if nothing prevents them, and so on. This doctrine is essential for understanding Aristotle's argument in the eighth book of the *Physics* that whatever is being moved is being moved by another. "Everything is dynamically active," as stated by Corliss Lamont, "A Humanist Symposium on Metaphysics," *The Journal of Philosophy*, LVI (1959), 45, holds for Aristotle of things because of their substantial form rather than on account of the special category of activity.

While from the viewpoint of the *Physics* and *Metaphysics* movement is identified with the category of action and passion, it is treated in the *Categories* (14,15a13-b16) as common to several categories, under which action and passion are not included. Accordingly, in later tradition, it was classed among the *postpredicamenta.* From this standpoint, movement is not found in the category of action and passion (*Ph.*, V 2,225b13-16 and *Metaph.*, K 12,1068a13-16). Further, action (*poiêsis*) may be sharply distinguished by Aristotle from natural production (*Metaph.*, Z 7, 1032a25-27) or from moral activity (*E N*, VI 4,1140a2-6; b3-7; cf. *Metaph.*, E 1,1025b22-24). These variations in the use of terms complicate the study of motion in Aristotle. Moreover, no effort is made by the Stagirite to deal with motion from the aspect of new existence.

34. *Cat.*, 4,1b27; *Top.*, I 9,103b23. *Cat.*, 9-10,11b10-16 is bracketed by Minio-Paluello. All the reality contained in disposition and "state" can be quite easily allotted to the other categories. Logically, however, there seems to be no reason why these and other such predicates should not be accepted as categories; see e.g., the relation in knowledge at 8, 11a20-39.

35. "Quite differently did Aristotle conceive the soul . . . neither identical with the body nor separate from it—therefore to be distinguished from, yet at the same time related to, the body." Richard Hope, *How Man Thinks* (Pittsburgh: University of Pittsburgh Press, 1949), p. 57. For Aristotle (*Metaph.*, Δ 28,1024b10-16), matter and form differ generically in a way that is contrasted with the regular category *schemata.*

36. The difficulties are apparent in the brief treatment of the intellect in *De An.*, III 5,430a10-25. They occasioned the insinuation of Plotinus (*En.*, IV,7,8^5.15-16) that the Peripatetics were constrained to introduce a second soul—the first soul informed the body, but could not fully account for thought.

37. *Metaph.*, Z 3.1029a20; 24. At a23-24, substance is said to be asserted (*kategoreitai*) of this ultimate matter, as the other categories are asserted of substance. Language would have to be strained badly to make such an assertion, e.g., that the ultimate matter is humanized, equinized, lapidized, as it takes on the forms of man, horse, and stone! This is a situation that the logician does not encounter, and he can apply his norms to it only by representing the ultimate matter as "a something."

38. Form and matter are the principles of natural things (*Ph.*, II 1, 192b8-193b20; cf. 2,194a12-13), and *both* are required to constitute a natural thing. So a point is a principle of a line (*Top.*, I, 18,108b26-31; VI 4, 141b6-12), but in itself it has no parts and therefore of itself it does not satisfy the requirement of parts (*Cat.*, 6, 4b25-5a37) that goes with the notion of quantity.

39. . . . qualités réelles en la nature, qui soient ajoutées à la substance, comme des petites âmes à leur corps, . . . *Lettre CCXCIX* (A Mersenne), Apr. 26,1643; *A-T*, III, 648.4-6. Malebranche calls them "little beings": ". . . une infinité de petits êtres distingués réellement de la matière et de la forme; . . ." *Recherche de la Vérité*, VI, 2° partie, c. 2; ed. Flammarion (Paris, 1935), II, 320. Descartes considers these conceptions to be a result of mixing attributes that belong to the body with attributes that belong to the soul. *Lettre CCXLIX* (à l'Abbé de Launay); A-T, III 420.16-25.

40. " 'Brutus killed Caesar' expresses a relation between Brutus and Caesar." Bertrand Russell, *Introduction to Mathematical Philosophy* (London [Allen & Unwin] & New York: Macmillan, 1919), p. 141.

41. "Our actual entities, I specify further, are all either simple qualia, or relations belonging to one of three primitive categories, or some compound of these." Donald Williams "Mind as a Matter of Fact", See this Journal [sic. *Review of Metaphysics*, Ed.: XIII (1959), 203.

42. See St. Thomas Aquinas, *De Ente et Essentia*, c. III; ed. M. D. Roland-Gosselin (reprint, Paris: Vrin, 1948), pp. 24.1-29.30. This doctrine takes as evident that cognitional existence is a genuine existence: " 'Existence' is predicable of every idea and predicate . . . Every idea and predicate occurs at some time, in some one's mind or language." Paul Weiss, *Modes of Being* (Carbondale; Southern Illinois University Press, 1958), p. 202. As Weiss notes in this connection, "we usually think that it is an error to say that a hippogriff exists, even though it may exist in idea" (*Ibid.*). Since existence applies in one way or another to everything that is thought of or mentioned, it itself is too wide in scope to be a category: " 'existence' is not a generic word like 'coloured' or 'sexed.' " Gilbert Ryle, *The Concept of Mind* (New York: Barnes & Noble, [1949]), p. 23. So modes of existence like necessity and contingence (being *per accidens*), and actuality and potentiality, as well as transcendent properties like the true, are placed outside Aristotle's construction of categories; see *Metaph.*, Δ 7,1017a7-b2; E 2,1026a33-b2. Not-being, on the other hand, has senses that parallel exactly the categories of being; see *APr.*, I 37,49a6-9; *Metaph.*, N 2,1089a16-27. Θ 3,1047a32-35 shows how predicates may differ in reality and thought.

43. Ernst Kapp, *Greek Foundations of Traditional Logic* (New York: Columbia University Press, 1942), p. 37, finds that the "original function" of the Aristotelian category construction was "to protect against fallacies and mistakes caused by the similar linguistic form of different predications." See pp. 38-39. Kapp, however, admits (p. 39) that even in the Aristotelian writings themselves the categories are used as "a conveniently compendious inventory of the main aspects of reality." Ryle sees the origin of the Aristotelian category doctrine mostly in questions of ordinary language: "In the main Aristotle seems to content himself with taking ordinary language as his clue to the list of heads of questions, and so of types of predicates." "Categories," in *Logic and Language* (Second Series), ed. A. Flew (Oxford: Basil Blackwell, 1955), p. 66. However, the predicate complements cannot be explained by grammatical types alone, "they must also express proposition-factors of certain logical types" (p. 70). Accordingly, "certain category-propositions will give the required information about the nature of things" (p. 81).

Notes to Chapter 3

1. ". . . any deductive or inductive inference, no matter how much it may be dignified by the prominent place it occupies in the context of genuinely scientific knowledge, is nevertheless wholly dependent upon the factor of universality." Francis H. Parker and Henry B. Veatch, *Logic as a Human Instrument* (New York, 1959), p. 251. Cf. Dewey's remark concerning this topic: " . . . the modern relation being the equivalent of the mediaeval universal," in James M.

Baldwin's *Dictionary of Philosophy and Psychology*, New Edition (New York, 1911), s. v. "Relation," (3), i. Among recent philosophers of science may be found corresponding assertions: "Generalization, therefore, is the origin of science." Hans Reichenbach, *The Rise of Scientific Philosophy* (Berkeley & Los Angeles, 1951), p. 5. "The premises must contain at least one universal law, whose inclusion in the premises is essential for the deduction of the explicandum." Ernest Nagel, *The Structure of Science* (London, 1961), p. 32. The requirement of universality in scientific knowledge abstracts for the moment, as the varied provenance of the above statements would indicate, from the existential status of the universal itself. Judging from the way the discussions on the latter question have taken place, however, one may say "that the *onus probandi* is inevitably on the shoulders of the nominalist, and that both sides know that this is so." D. S. Shwayder, *Modes of Referring and the Problem of Universals* (Berkeley and Los Angeles, 1961), p. 2 (in *University of California Publications in Philosophy*, XXXV).

2. See Plato, *Laches*, 190E-191E.

3. I.e., through reasoning in terms of cause—αἰτίας λογισμῷ (*Meno*, 98A).

4. See Aristotle, *Metaph.*, A 1, 981a15-30. On the medical origin of Aristotle's illustrations in this chapter, see Francis M. Cornford, *Principium Sapientiae* (Cambridge, Eng., 1952), pp. 40-43.

5. See *Metaph.*, M 10, 1087a15-25. Cf. Z 10, 1036a6-8; 15, 1040a1-7; and *Prior Analytics*, II 21, 67b1-5. Alan Donagan, "Universals and Metaphysical Realism," *The Monist*, 47 (1963), 228, n. 17, sees in this interpretation an attributing of mediaeval "Aristotelian" doctrine to Aristotle himself. The criticism seems to presuppose that the Aristotelian "form" and the mediaeval "essence" can be equated. On the general issue, see my comments in "Aristotle on Categories," *Review of Metaphysics*, 14 (1960), 81, n. 26 [see supra. note 26, p. 191, Ed.]. The difficulties of reading into Aristotle any doctrine of "moderate realism" or of "abstraction" of the universal were stressed by the late James I. Conway in "The Meaning of Moderate Realism," *New Scholasticism*, 36 (1962), 141-79. For Aristotle there is in reality no sensible nature whatsoever apart from the singular, though because of its form a sensible thing may be considered universally; see *Metaph.*, Z 10, 1035b27-31, and 11, 1037a5-8. Accordingly Wilfred Sellars, "Grammar and Existence: A Preface to Ontology," *Mind*, 69 (1960), 517, can allow some truth to the suggestion that "Aristotle, by denying the apartness of the universal, is, in effect, recognizing the unsaturated, incomplete or gappy status which is made explicit by the unsaturated abstract singular term 'that x is triangular.' "

6. *Posterior Analytics*, I 13, 78a22-79a16. Acoustical harmonics, as the Greek commentators understood it, was knowledge of the musical intervals by ear, and not by mathematical ratios; see Sir Thomas Heath, *Mathematics in Aristotle* (Oxford, 1949), p. 60.

7. *Metaph.*, K 1, 1059b15-19; *Rhetoric* I 4, 1359b10.

8. *Metaph.*, Γ 3, 1005b2-5. At *Topics* VIII 14, 163b9-11, dialectic is referred to as an instrument (*organon*) for knowledge. Among the Greek commentators,

logic as a whole was called an *organon*. Hence in the late middle ages the title *Organon* was given to the logical treatises of Aristotle.

On the ancient and mediaeval divisions of the sciences, see Joseph Mariétan, *Problème de la classification des sciences d'Aristote à St. Thomas* (Paris, 1901). Divisions and order among the sciences do not necessarily imply or lead to any strict unification of them. This has been shown recently in regard to the classical philosophers: " . . . although any classification involves some theory of the way in which the different kinds of knowledge are related to one another and thus might be said to attribute to them a certain kind of unity. But a review of such classifications shows that the purposes behind them can be totally opposed to one another. Descartes and Leibniz classify only for the purpose of uniting; Spinoza, Malebranche, Locke, or Berkeley do so in order to separate." Robert McRae, *The Problem of the Unity of the Sciences:* Bacon to Kant (Toronto, 1961), p. vii. Aristotle leaves the sciences distinct, in spite of the necessary interrelations of their subject matter.

9. "The whole of logical treatment is concerned with second notions. These are our work, and at our will can be or not be. Therefore they are not necessary but contingent things; and accordingly they do not fall under science, since science is of necessary things only, as has been said." Jacobus Zabarella, *De Natura Logicae* I, 3; in *Opera Logica* (Basle, 1549), col. 7E. My translation. He explains away (I, 5; 10F) the references to logic as a science.

10. Aristotle, *Metaph.*, E 1, 1025b6-24; K 7, 1063b36-1064a15; *Parts of Animals*, I 1, 640a3-4.

11. "But the science possessed by the arts relating to carpentering and to handicraft in general is inherent in their application, and with its aid they create objects which did not previously exist." *Politicus*, 258DE; tr. Harold N. Fowler.

12. Aristotle, *Ethica Nicomachea*, II 4, 1105a26-28.

13. *EN*, II 6, 1107a1-2. Cf. 4, 1105b5-9.

14. *EN* I 4, 1095b4-6; II 1, 1103b23-25; 3, 1104b9-13.

15. *EN* I 3, 1094b11-22. Cf. Plato, *Plt.*, 295A.

16. In contexts other than the distinction of the sciences, the Greek term *aphairesis* is of course used by Aristotle in various accepted senses. On these see M.-D. Philippe, "Abstraction, addition, séparation dans la philosophie d'Aristote," *Revue thomiste*, 48 (1948), 461-66. It is not found in Aristotle, however; for the process by which the universal is formed, see Conway, art. cit. (supra, n. 5), pp. 147-48.

17. On the priority of substance to accidents, see Aristotle, *Metaph.*, Z 1, 1028a31-b2. Cf. Hippocrates George Apostle, *Aristotle's Philosophy of Mathematics* (Chicago, 1952), pp. 13-14.

18. See *Categories*, 6, 4b20-6a35; *Metaph.*, Z 1, 1028a37-b2. Rarely (*Metaph.*, Z 1, 1028a19; 3, 1029a14) does Aristotle substitute the noun Ποδότης for the neuter adjective.

19. *Metaph.*, Z 10, 1036a9-12; H 6, 1045a33-36; K 1, 1059b15-16; M 9, 1085b1-2.

20. So: "Quantity comes to it first, then quality, after that passivities (*passiones*) and motion. So quantity can be thought of in substance before the sensible qualities (because of which matter is called sensible) are considered in it. Quantity, then, according to its essential nature does not depend upon sensible matter but only upon intelligible matter." St. Thomas Aquinas, *The Divisions and Methods of the Sciences* (In *Boeth. de Trin.*, V-VI), tr. Armand Maurer, 3rd revised edition (Toronto, 1963), p. 31 (V, 3, Resp.). Cf. Apostle, pp. 50-52.

21. *Physica*, II 2, 194a7-8. On the mathematical works listed in the original catalogue of Aristotle's writings, see Paul Moraux, *Les listes anciennes des ouvrages d'Aristote* (Louvain, 1951), pp. 111-114; 315. On Aristotle's differentiation of the mathematical from the physical consideration of natural things, see Augustin Mansion, *Introduction à la physique aristotelicienne,* 2e ed. rev. (Louvain & Paris, 1946), pp. 143-95, and, for a shorter discussion, Sir Thomas Heath, *Mathematics in Aristotle*, pp. 11-16.

22. *Physica*, VIII 1, 251a9-252a5; *Metaph.*, Λ 6, 1071b6-10, 1072b3-14.

23. *Metaph.*, E 1, 1026a13-19; K 7, 1064a30-b3.

24. *Republic*, VI, 509D-511E. Mansion, pp. 133-43, reading into Aristotle's distinction of the sciences a doctrine of abstraction and "degrees of abstraction," attributes the difficulties he encounters to a latent Platonism that Aristotle had not succeeded in overcoming. One of the difficulties is the alleged duality (pp. 136-37) in the object of the Aristotelian primary philosophy, namely being *qua* being (understood by Mansion as immaterial by abstraction) and supersensible being (immaterial in reality). I have discussed the more recent developments of this question in *The Doctrine of Being in the Aristotelian Metaphysics,* Foreword to 2nd ed. (Toronto, 1963), pp. 15-22, [3rd ed., pp. 15-35, Ed.]and the overall Aristotelian notion of being on pp. 455-66. [3rd ed., pp. 455-473, Ed.]

A Platonic background for the "crucially important distinctions" of the *hoti* and *dioti* knowledge is seen by John Wild, *Plato's Theory of Man* (Cambridge, Mass., 1946), p. 202, n. 56. They are regarded as "developments of Plato's notions of the upward path (*quia* and the downward path (*propter quid*)." — Again, however, the parallelism does not hold exactly. One kind of Aristotelian *quia* knowledge is through a remote cause, that is, on the downward path from cause to effect.

25. *Parts of Animals*, I 1, 639b6-641a17. Cf. *Ph.*, II 9, 200a33-b7.

26. "*Because* man is such and such, *therefore* the process of his formation must be such and such and must take place in such a manner; first this part is formed, then that. And similarly with all the things that are constructed by Nature." *PA*, I 1,640b1-4; tr. A. L. Peck. For texts identifying formal and final cause, see Bonitz' *Index Aristotelicus*, 753b28-32.

27. *PA*, II 1, 647b4-7. Cf. III 4, 665b34-666b25.

28. Jacques Maritain, *Science et sagesse* (Paris, 1935), p. 76.

29. *PA*, I 5, 645a5-16. Cf.: " . . . to enter upon our researches concerning animals of every sort and kind, knowing that in not one of them is Nature or Beauty lacking." *Ibid.*, a21-23; tr. Peck.

30. *PA*, I 1, 639a1-10. On Aristotle's conception of a general education, see E.-L. Fortin, "The Paradoxes of Aristotle's Theory of Education in the Light of Recent Controversies," *Laval théologique et philosophique*," 13 (1957), 248-60. In point of fact, modern scientific progress acquired its momentum through sciences that Aristotle explicitly recognized not as natural philosophy but as mathematical investigation, for in the sixteenth and seventeenth centuries "the scientific revolution is most significant . . . in the fields of astronomy and mechanics." Herbert Butterfield, *The Origins of Modern Science*, New Edition (London, 1957), p. 84. In regard to the acceleration of falling bodies, Butterfield comments: " . . . whether Aristotle himself held the views . . . is irrelevant, however, as at any rate the Aristotelians of the seventeenth century held these views." *Ibid.*, p. 83. Clearly enough, though, some blame goes back to Aristotle himself. The reason why the Peripatetic tradition failed to develop mathematicized sciences of nature is traceable to Aristotle's own attitude towards the study of nature in spite of the deeper exigencies of his conception of the sciences.

31. I.e., in answer to the four questions proposed by Kant, *Logik*, Einleitung III; in *Werke* (Berlin & Leipzig, 1923), IX, 25. Cf. *Critique of Pure Reason*, B866-867.

32. Henry Margenau, *Open Vistas* (New Haven, 1961), p. 3.

33. John Herman Randall, Jr., *Aristotle* (New York, 1960), p. 300.

Notes to Chapter 4

1. See Aristotle, *Metaph.*, Z 3, 1029a 20-30. The technical term used by Aristotle for matter was the Greek '*hylê*' or 'wood'. He seems to have been the first to coin a term for this notion, though the philosophic use of '*hylê*' for materials in general was prepared by Plato at *Ti.*, 69A, and *Phlb.*, 54C. In modern times the overall approach to the scientific notion of matter is hardly different; e.g.: "By the building materials I mean what we call matter, . . . ordinary matter is constructed out of two types of ultimate things called "electrons" and "protons." " C. G. Darwin, *The New Conceptions of Matter*, London, 1931, p. 8. Aristotle, however, is approaching the question on a level that does not lead to electrons and protons but to very different principles; cf. Appendix. For texts, see Bonitz' *Index Aristotelicus*, 652b 49-51; 785a 5-43.

2. See *Cat.*, 5, 2a 13-14; 2b 13.

3. *Cat.*, 5, 2b 4-6; 15-17. In a metaphysical context, on the other hand, the form and not the composite was primary substance, as at *Metaph.*, Z 7, 1032b 1-14; 11, 1037a 28. On the category mistake occasioned by this twofold use of 'primary substance' in Aristotle, see my article "Aristotle on Categories," *The Review of Metaphysics*, 14, (1960), 83-84. [See *supra*, pp. 19-20, Ed.]

4. See Aristotle, *Metaph.*, Γ 3, 1005b 2-5.

5. *Metaph.*, Z 3, 1029a 23-24; Oxford tr.

6. *Metaph.*, H 2, 1043a 15; Oxford tr. On this doctrine, and Aristotle's use of the expression 'primary matter' in connection with it, see W. D. Ross, *Aristotle's Metaphysics*, Oxford, 1924, 2, 256-57. 'Primary matter' is found in various senses

at *Ph.*, II 1, 193a 29, *GA*, I 20, 729a 32, and *Metaph.*, Δ 4, 1015a 7-10. 'Matter' in its chief or primary sense, however, meant for Aristotle the substrate of generation and corruption (*GC*, I 4, 320a 2-5), even though the designation 'primary matter' never seems to have been limited by him to that sense. The therapy required by the concept's genesis has to be kept applied in representing the absolutely undetermined matter as that of which things are composed. Such matter is not individual, like any of the materials of which a house is composed. Still less is it something universal, for the universal is subsequent to the individual in Aristotelian doctrine. Rather, it is below the level at which individuality and universality appear. Considered just in itself, it has nothing to distinguish it as found in one thing from itself as found in another. From this viewpoint it parallels the common nature of Duns Scotus, which of itself had nothing to distinguish it as found in Socrates from itself as found in Plato (see Duns Scotus, *Quaest. Metaph.*, 7, 13, no. 21; ed. Vivès, 7, 421b. In contrast to the Scotistic common nature, however, the Aristotelian basic matter lacks all formal determinations, and so not only individual determinations). The absolutely undetermined matter is accordingly one through the removal of all distinguishing characteristics. It is wholly formless in the *Physics* (I 7, 191a 8-12) as well as in the *Metaphysics*. In this sense only, may it be regarded as common. When actuated, it differentiates by its very nature in making possible the spread of the same form in parts outside parts and the multiplication of singulars in a species. In that way it is an individuating principle without being of itself individual. As the substrate of substantial change, it may be said—with the appropriate therapy—to change from one form to another. So doing, it shows itself to be really distinct from its forms, since it really persists while the forms really replace each other. But it is not therefore a really distinct being from the form. In the individual there is but the one being derived from the form to the matter and the composite. Thus any single thing is differentiated from a "heap" (*Metaph.*, Z 17, 1041b 7-31). Subsidiary forms, for instance those indicated in water by the spectra of hydrogen and oxygen, would accordingly be accidental forms for Aristotle, and in a substantial change would be replaced by new though corresponding accidental forms.

7. *Metaph.*, H 2, 1043a 5-7; Oxford tr.

8. *Metaph.*, Z 3, 1029a 20-21; Oxford tr.

9. See Descartes, *Principia Philosophiae,* 2, 4-9; *A-T,* 8, 42.4-45.16 (9^2, 65-68).

10. For Aristotle, predication of being is made through reference to the primary instance of being. Even the negation of being, namely "non-being", is asserted in this way. See *Metaph.*, Γ 2, 1003b 5-10.

11. *Metaph.*, Z 3, 1029a 24-26; Oxford tr. 'Positively' refers here to determination; cf. a21.

12. "The referend of a demonstrative symbol (i.e. a word used demonstratively) is *the object directly presented to* the speaker. The referend of a descriptive phrase is a *property, or set of properties.*" L. Susan Stebbing, *A Modern Introduction to Logic*, London, 6th ed., 1948, p. 499. On the technical term 'referend', cf.: "We shall find it convenient to use the word 'referend' to stand for *that which is signified.*" *Ibid.*, p. 13.

13. See *Ph.*, I 7, 189b 30-191a 7. The analysis of change or motion is made by Aristotle without dependence on the notion of time. Rather, motion is first defined, and then the notion of time is worked out in terms of motion, that is, as the numbering of motion in respect of prior and subsequent (*Ph.*, IV 11, 219b 1-2). Since Kant the tendency has been first to establish the notion of time, and then to describe motion in terms of relation to time; e.g.: "Change thus always involves (1) a fixed entity, (2) a three-cornered relation between this entity, another entity, and some but not all, of the moments of time." Bertrand Russell, *Principles of Mathematics*, Cambridge, Eng., 1903, *1*, 469.

14. *Ph.*, III 1, 201a 8-9.

15. See *Cael.*, I 2, 268b 26-29; *GC*, II 1, 329a 2-8; 8, 334b 31-335a 23.

16. *Metaph.*, Z 16, 1040b 5-16.

17. *Ph.*, I 7, 190b 4-5. Cf. *GA*, I 18, 722b 3-5, and St Paul's simile, *I Cor.*, 15: 36.

18. See *Ph.*, I 2, 184b 25-185a 16.

19. *Ph.*, I 7, 191a 7-12; Oxford tr.

20. See Arthur Stanley Eddington, *The Nature of the Physical World*, Cambridge, Eng., 1928, pp. ix-xi. Cf.: "The whole reason for accepting the atomic model is that it helps us to explain things we could not explain before. Cut off from these phenomena, the model can only mislead, . . ." Stephen Toulmin, *The Philosophy of Science*, New York, 1953, p. 12.

Notes to Chapter 5

1. In the *Meno* (77A), Plato has κατὰ ὐλοὺ to explicate adverbially his regularly used notion of *what* something *is*, in contrast to its singular instances. In the *Republic* (III 392DE), κατὰ ὅλοὺ expresses the consideration of a poem as a whole in contrast to its particular sections or verses. Against this background there is no difficulty in understanding the technical Aristotelian word *katholou* as basically a prepositional phrase with adverbial force. On this topic see Kurt von Fritz, *Philosophie und sprachlicher Ausdruck bei Demokrit, Plato und Aristoteles* (Leipzig, 1938), p. 65. The adverbial use, he notes, is by far the more frequent.

2. Confrontations of these two sharply opposed trends in Greek thought may be seen in P. Merlan, "Isocrates, Aristotle and Alexander the Great," *Historia* (Wiesbaden), vol. 3 (1954), pp. 60-81; and in W. I. Matson, "Isocrates the Pragmatist," *The Review of Metaphysics*, vol. 10 (1957), pp. 423-427.

3. See Aristotle, *Anal. Post.*, II 19, 99b34-100b5; *De An.*, III 7-8, 431a14-432a9.

4. On the union of necessity and universality in the Aristotelian conception of scientific knowledge, see Suzanne Mansion, *Le Jugement d'Existence chez Aristote* (Paris, Louvain, 1946), pp. 18-107, esp. p. 95. On the difference between the Aristotelian setting for this question and the modern background that comes from Hume and Kant, see Francis H. Parker, "Traditional Reason and Modern Reason," *Philosophy Today*, vol. 7 (1963), pp. 235-244.

5. For the opposite view, namely, that the Aristotelian universal duplicates the sensible concrete reality, see Chung-Hwan Chen, "Universal Concrete, A Typical Aristotelian Duplication of Reality," *Phronesis*, vol. 9 (1964), pp. 48-57. This duplication, it is understood, "will cause the Aristotelian metaphysical system to break down" (*ibid.*, p. 57). The alleged dilemma that for Aristotle the real, because singular, is not knowable, and the knowable, because universal, is not real, has been revived recently by Whitney J. Oates, *Aristotle and the Problem of Value* (Princeton, 1963), pp. 180-183. Oates regards the solution given in *Metaph.*, M 10, 1087a15-21, as "Aristotle's extra, and unsuccessful, effort to solve it" (*ibid.*, p. 181). Aristotle's own statement of this aporia in regard to the first principles is found at *Metaph.*, B 6, 1003a5-15.

6. *Metaph.*, Δ 26, 1023b30-32; Oxford tr.

7. *Metaph.*, Z 10, 1035b27-30; Oxford tr., except "what" for "terms which" at b28.

8. *Metaph.*, Z 11, 1037a5-7; Oxford tr.

9. On the soul as form of the body, see *De An.*, II 1, 412a19-b6.

10. On the universal as given in sensation, see *Anal. Post.*, II 19, 100a17-b5; *Metaph.*, M 10, 1087a19-20.

11. cf.: " . . . that which, being a 'this', is also separable—and of this nature is the shape or form of each thing" (*Metaph.*, Δ 8, 1017b24-26; Oxford tr.); " . . . the formula or shape (that which being a 'this' can be separately formulated)" (*ibid.*, H 1, 1042a28-29); " . . . when . . . the predicate is a *form* and a 'this', the ultimate subject is matter and material substance." (Θ 7, 1049a34-36); " . . . the nature, which is a 'this' or positive state towards which movement takes place" (Λ 3, 1070a11-12); " . . . form or essence, which is that precisely in virtue of which a thing is called 'a this' " (*De An.*, II 1, 412a8-9; Oxford tr.).

12. "By form I mean the essence of each thing and its primary substance" (*Metaph.*, Z 7, 1032b1-2; Oxford tr.); " . . . there is a formula of it with reference to its primary substance—e.g., in the case of man the formula of soul" (*ibid.*, 11, 1037a28-29).

13. The two notions may be found confused in modern discussions, e.g., "Many philosophers have claimed that in addition to the objects met with in sense experience there exist entities of an entirely different and more esoteric kind, technically designated as 'universals'. According to this claim there are, in addition to such things as tables and white sheets of paper, the utterly different and less well-known objects tableness and whiteness." Morris Lazerowitz, "The Existence of Universals," *Mind*, vol. 55 (1946), p. 1.

14. That a problem does arise from this distinction, however, may be seen from the careful and protracted consideration given to it by St. Thomas Aquinas, *De Ente et Essentia*, c. II, ed. Roland-Gosselin, pp. 10.20-23.7.

15. *Anal. Post.*, I 11, 77a7-8; Oxford tr.

16. Texts may be found listed in Bonitz, *Index Aristot.*, 243 Δ 279a22-25; Mansion, *op. cit.*, p. 94, n. 1.

17. See *De An.*, III 4, 429a18-22; b21-25. Cf. I 2, 405a13-17; b19-21.

18. *De An.*, III 4, 429b5-8; 30-31 (mind); 8, 431b20-29 (soul).

19. *De An.*, III 5, 430a19-20; 7, 431a1-2. Cf. I 4, 408b13-15.

20. "The underlying nature is an object of scientific knowledge, by an analogy. For as the bronze is to the statue, the wood to the bed, or the matter and the formless before receiving form to any thing which has form, so is the underlying nature to substance, i.e., the 'this' or 'existent'" (*Phys.*, I 7, 191a7-12; Oxford tr.).

21. *Phys.*, II 1, 193a29-30. It is called "ultimate subject" at *Metaph.*, Δ 8, 1017b24.

22. *Metaph.*, Z 10, 1035a7-9; tr. Richard Hope.

23. See texts *supra.*, n. 9.

24. *Metaph.*, Z 8, 1034a4-8; Oxford tr. Cf. 7, 1032a24-25. For the sense of same in species, see Bonitz, *Index Aristot.*, 218a43-52.

25. *Metaph.*, Z 17, 1041b25-28; H 2, 1043a2-7.

26. "For knowledge, like the verb 'to know', means two things, of which one is potential and one actual. The potency, being, as matter, universal and indefinite, deals with the universal and indefinite; but the actuality, being definite, deals with a definite object—being a 'this', it deals with a 'this'. But *per accidens* sight sees universal colour, because this individual colour which it sees is colour; and this individual *a* which the grammarian investigates in an *a*." *Metaph.*, M 10, 1087a15-21; Oxford tr.

27. "Another question is naturally raised, viz., what sort of parts belong to the form and what sort not to the form, but to the concrete thing. Yet if this is not plain it is not possible to define any thing; for definition is of the universal and of the form." *Metaph.*, Z 11, 1036a26-29. Cf. " . . . for the formula that gives the differentiae seems to be an account of the form or actuality, while that which gives the components is rather an account of the matter." H 2, 1043a19-21; Oxford tr.

28. So, for St. Thomas Aquinas (*Contra Gentiles*, II, 93) there can be only one separated substance in one species, because there is no matter to multiply singulars in it. For Duns Scotus, *Quaest. in Metaph.*, VII, 13, no. 21 (ed. Vivès, VII, 421b), the humanity that is in Socrates and humanity that is in Plato would coalesce in reality if the individuating differences could *per impossibile* be struck away, because in that case there would be nothing to cause differentiation in their common nature "humanity." For Aristotle, "same in form" and "same in species" can readily coincide in the one Greek expression, since, on account of the type of causality exercised by the form, the singulars are one in species *because* they are one in form.

29. This feature of Aristotle's though was expressed neatly by Octave Hamelin: "La forme explique tout le reste et se suffit a elle-même." *Le Systéme d'Aristote* (Paris, 1920), p. 405.

30. See *Metaph.*, Z 10, 1036a9-12; 11, 1036b35-1037a5; H 6, 1045a33-36; K 1, 1059b14-20.

31. II 19, 100a12-b5.

32. *De An.*, III 5, 430a14-17; Oxford tr.

33. See text *supra*, n. 22. Cf. *Metaph.*, Z 10, 1036a6-8; 15, 1040a2-5; *Anal. Pr.*, II 21, 67a39-b3.
34. For the three see *De An.*, II 12, 424a17-24; III 8, 432a9-10; III 4, 429b21-22 and 430a7-8 respectively.
35. At *De An.*, II 12, 424a18-19 (Oxford tr.), a sense in general is described as "what has the power of receiving into itself the sensible forms of things without the matter." Yet at III 8, 432a9-10; Oxford tr., the phantasms are distinguished from the contents of sense-perception because—now in contrast to the latter—they are without matter: "for images are like sensuous contents except in that they contain no matter" (Oxford tr.). This would indicate in the phantasms a grade of immateriality not possessed by the contents of sense-perception. Further, mind is described (III 4, 430a7-8) as a power of attaining its objects without matter, implying a still higher grade of immateriality in cognition.
36. This paper was read at the meeting of the Western Division, American Philosophical Association, Chicago, May 1, 1965. Afterwards the chairman of the panel, Richard McKeon, called attention to the different ways in which the universal is regarded by Aristotle in his various *methodoi*. The consideration is important, and should always be kept in mind in the interpretation of the treatises, especially in regard to the ever variable way in which the universal functions in ethical matters. Nevertheless, a common feature throughout is that the universal is predicated of or belongs to the particulars. This can be verified for the theoretical treatises by a glance at Bonitz, *Index Aristot.*, 356b4-25, and for the *Ethics* by a passage like *E.N.*, V 7, 1134b18-1135a8. The present paper has been concerned with a metaphysical inquiry into the grounds in general that make possible the common predication throughout the areas covered by the various *methodoi*.

Notes to Chapter 6

1. "Substantia igitur generalissimum genus est; hoc enim de cunctis aliis praedicatur, ac primum hujus species duae sunt, corporeum et incorporeum . . ." Boethius, *In Porphyrium Commentaria*, III; *PL*, LXIV, 103A.
2. *Phys.* I. 1, 184a 10-16. Cf. *An. Post.* I. 2, 71b 19-23; *Metaph.* A 1, 981a 24-b 6; E 1, 1025 b 6-7; K 7, 1063b 36-37. A discussion of this theme at a greater length may be found in my paper "The Aristotelian Conception of the Sciences," *IPQ*, IV (1964): 200-16. [See *supra* chpt. 3, pp. 23-34, Ed.]
3. *Phys.* I. 1, 184a 16-23. Cf. *An. Post.* I. 2, 71b 29-72a 5; *Metaph.* Z 4, 1029b 3-12; *Eth. Nic.* I. 4, 1095b 2-4.
4. *Phys.* I. 1, 184a 23-24. At *An. Post.* II. 13, 97b 28-29, the assertion is, verbally at least, just the opposite: διὸ δεῖ ἀπὸ τῶν καθ' ἕκαστα ἐπὶ τὰ καθόλου μεταβαίνειν.
5. *Metaph.* Z 10, 1035b 27-30; 11, 1037a 5-10. In the Aristotelian texts, the one thing seems described as known in two different ways. There does not seem to be any duplication of objects. The universal way of knowing the sensible thing,

however, is seen as a duplication by Chung-Hwen Chen, "Universal Concrete, A Typical Aristotelian Duplication of Reality," *Phronesis* IX (1964): 48-57. On the adverbial force of the Aristotelian word "universal," see Kurt von Fritz, *Philosophie und sprachlicher Ausdruck bei Demokrit, Plato und Aristoteles* (Leipzig, etc., 1938), pp. 40, 65.

6. Paul Tannery, "Sur un point de la méthode d'Aristote," *AGP*, VI (1893): 468. What seems to be the opposite is in fact stated in the text quoted supra, n. 4.

7. "It is a complete mistake to ask how concrete particular fact can be built up out of universals." Whitehead, *Process and Reality* (New York, 1929), p. 30.

8. *In Phys.*, 17.25-18.3. Cf. 10.23-11.24; 13.1-12.

9. Alexander, *In Metaph.*, 246. 10-13; 661. 33-39. Asclepius, *In Metaph.*, 232. 4-11. Cf. Simplicius, *In Phys.*, 19. 5-7.

10. Note to Wicksteed tr., ad loc., in the Loeb *Classical Library*. In the instance from *De Gen. et Corr.* II. 4, 331a 20, brought forward as an illustration, καθόλου seems used in its regular sense.

11. *Aristotle's Physics*, p. 457. Passage quoted supra.

12. Cf. ἠρεμήσαντος τοῦ καθολου 100a 6-7); πρῶτον . . . καθόλου (a 16); and τὰ ἀμερῆ . . . καὶ τὰ καθόλου (b2).

13. Simplicius, *In Phys.*, 16. 17-20; Philoponos, 11. 12-18; 19. 16-19. Cf. Themistius, *In Phys.*, 2. 8-9.

14. At *MM* II. 11, 1211a 18-23 it is found used for notions as wide as those of the constituents of friendship: "the good, and being, and well-being" (Oxford tr.).

15. Text supra, n. 4.

16. See Simplicius, *In. Phys.*, 17. 1-5.

17. Ibid., line 4.

18. πρόκειρος καὶ τοῖς πολλοῖς —ibid, pp. 16. 34-17.1.

19. References supra, n. 13.

20. *Metaph.*, Z 3, 1029a 20-25. A further discussion of the process by which the notion of absolutely formless matter is reached may be found in my paper "Matter and Predication in Aristotle," in *The Concept of Matter*, ed. E. McMullin (Notre Dame, 1963), pp. 79-93. [See *Supra* chpt. 4, pp. 35-47, Ed.]

21. E.g., Whitney J. Oates, *Aristotle and the Problem of Value* (Princeton, 1963), pp. 58-59.

22. Τοῦτο μὲν οὖν ἔι τις δύναιτο καὶ πιθανώτερον 'απολογιζέσθω.—Simplicius, *In Phys.*, 19. 17-18.

Notes to Chapter 7

1. *De An.*, III 8,431b21-23; Oxford trans. Cf. 2,425b25-426a28; 4,429a22-24; a27-29; b30-31; 430a3-8; 5,430a14-21; 7,431a1-3; b16-17. On 6,430b23-24, see G. Rodier, *Aristotle: Traité de l'âme* (Paris: Leroux, 1900), II, 485-486; P. Siwek, *Aristotelis Tractatus de Anima* (Rome: Desclée, 1965). ad loc. (p. 338).

2. *De An.*, I 4,408b13-15; Oxford trans. Cf. III 8,432a1-3. The agent here, just as in the building of a house, or in weaving, is the composite of form and matter.

On the use of the aorist at 431b20-21 to mean a recapitulation that is just beginning, see W. D. Ross, *Aristotle: De Anima* (Oxford: Clarendon Press, 1961), p. 308.

3. *De An.*, II 1,412b4-6. A discussion of the nature of this definition may be found in my paper "Aristotle's Definition of Soul," in *Philomathes*, ed. Robert B. Palmer & Robert Hamerton-Kelly (The Hague: Martinus Nijhoff, 1971), pp. 125-145. [See *supra* chpt. 10, pp. 000-000, Ed.]

4. *De An.*, III 7,431a1-6; Oxford trans. Cf. 5,430a19-21.

5. *De An.*, III 4,429b5-10; 430a2-3. C. *Metaph.*, Λ 9,1074b35-36. Richard Norman, "Aristotle's philosopher-God," *Phronesis*, 14 (1969), 71, concludes that in separate substance the self-thinking "is nothing different from what we do when we think in the abstract." This conclusion would seem to require that the Aristotelian separate substances become identical cognitionally with material things, from which they would abstract universal notions.

6. *De An.*, II 12,424a17-24. On the reception of forms for human intellection, see III 4,429a15-18. On the "proportion" required for sensation, see III 2,426a27-b8. Ross, p. 265, finds *logos* at a27-28 to mean a relation of percipient to object. However, at a31 it expressly means the sensation that is dissipated by either excess or deficiency in the stimulus. The notion that the specific character of the substance is not attained by the sense is easy enough to understand. The eye, for instance, sees the white grains scattered on the table without discerning whether they are salt or sugar. The point in finding the design apart from the gold or the iron seems meant merely to illustrate the reception of forms by percipients who are physically different from the original substrates of those forms.

7. Within a species the singulars are differentiated by their matter. See *Metaph.*, Z 8,1034a7-8. Reception of a form "with the matter" (*De An.*, II 12,424b3) is not cognitional. The plant, for instance, "becomes warm" when acted upon "with the matter." It does not perceive the heat. This use of "with the matter" stands in quite apparent contrast to "without the matter" (a18-19), and accordingly shows that "matter" in the phrases refers to material possession of form.

8. See *Metaph.*, Δ 8,1017b15-16; Z 17,104b17-28; H 2,1043a2-26.

9. *De An.*, III 8,432a1-3; Oxford trans. S.H. Rosen, "Thought and Touch," *Phronesis*, 6 (1961), 132, rightly designates this assertion as "a passage of central importance." Both soul and the received form are instruments by which cognitional being for the distant object is brought about in the cognitive agent. What is immediately perceived or known is accordingly the object itself. The difficulty that during the time of the transmission of the signals the object may have ceased to exist disappears, for the form itself is timeless and brings the object into new existence in the percipient. The form as instrumental, though, is known only subsequently, through the study of natural philosophy. On the meaning of "form of forms" (432a2) see Ross, p. 309.

10. For references to Aristotle's statements on these media, see Friedrich Solmsen, *Aristotle's System of the Physical World* (Ithaca, N.Y.: Cornell University Press, 1960), pp. 195-196.

11. On this cognitional primacy of the external sensible thing, as developed by Thomas Aquinas, see my article "The Primacy of the External in Thomistic Noetics," *Eglise et Théologie*, 5 (1974), 189-205. A very different development of the basic Aristotelian notions, however, may be seen in another medieval thinker, for whom intellection is cut off from the aspect of being: "If the intellect, therefore, insofar as it is an intellect, is nothing, it follows that neither is understanding some existence" — *Master Eckhart: Parisian Questions and Prologues*, Q. II, trans. Armand Maurer (Toronto: Pontifical Institute of Mediaeval Studies, 1974), p. 51. Eckhart's view is discussed in comparison with modern conceptions of "the negativity of consciousness" by John D. Caputo, "The Nothingness of the Intellect in Meister Echkart's 'Parisian Question'," *The Thomist*, 39 (1975), 85-115. Caputo (p. 109) explains that for Eckhart the essence of cognitive form "is not to be itself but to let what is 'other' or 'without' (*extra*) be." Instead of cognition as a way of being, the two are set in stark contrast to each other: "To the extent that 'cognitive being' is being it is not cognitive; to the extent that it is cognitive is not being" (Caputo, p. 99). The result is that one still has to face "the fundamental problem, indeed mystery, of knowledge, viz., the problem of how the knower is carried beyond himself into the object of knowledge" (p. 115). Epistemologically, that problem should never arise in an Aristotelian setting.

Notes to Chapter 8

1. . . . ἡ μὲν αἴσϑησίς ἐστι τὸ δεκτικὸν τῶν αἰσϑητῶν εἰδῶν ἄνευ τῆς ὕλης, οἷον ὁ κηρὸς τοῦ δακτυλίου ἄνευ τοῦ σιδήρου καὶ τοῦ χρυσοῦ δέχεται τὸ σημεῖον, λαμβάνει δὲ τὸ χρυσοῦν ἢ τὸ χαλκοῦν σημεῖον, ἀλλ' οὐχ ᾗ χρυσὸς ἢ χαλκός. ὁμοίως δὲ καὶ ἡ αἴσϑησις ἑκάστου ὑπὸ τοῦ ἔχοντος χρῶμα ἢ χυμὸν ἢ ψόφον πάσχει, ἀλλ' οὐχ ᾗ ἕκαστον ἐκείνων λέγεται, ἀλλ' ᾗ τοιονδί, καὶ κατὰ τὸν λόγον. . . . τὰ φυτὰ οὐκ αἰσϑάνεται, ἔχοντά τι μόριον ψυχικὸν καὶ πάσχοντά τι ὑπὸ τῶν ἁπτῶν αὐτῶν· καὶ γὰρ ψύχεται καὶ ϑερμαίνεται· αἴτιον γὰρ τὸ μὴ ἔχειν μεσότητα μηδὲ τοιαύτην ἀρχὴν οἵαν τὰ εἴδη δέχεσϑαι τῶν αἰσϑητῶν, ἀλλὰ πάσχειν μετὰ τῆς ὕλης. Aristotle, *De An.*, II 12,424a17-b3. Ross, *Aristotle: De Anima* (Oxford: Clarendon Press, 1961), p. 265, sees the change from iron to bronze as "an indication of haste," suggesting lack of clarity in the whole passage. The Greek commentators did not seem to object to variation in the examples—Philoponus (*In De An.*, p. 437.14) adds "silver." The passage calls for careful study on the part of the reader, but it does not suggest any hesitation in regard to meaning. It is sharply and firmly phrased.

2. See Aquinas, *De Ente et Essentia*, c. II; ed. Roland-Gosselin, p. 12.5-23.7, with notes on background.

3. . . . ἀληϑές ἐστιν εἰπεῖν τὸ εἶναι αὐτὴν δύναμιν ψυχῆς δι' αἰσϑητηρίων τινῶν δεκτικήν τε καὶ κριτικὴν τῶν αἰσϑητῶν εἰδῶν χωρὶς τῆς ὑποκειμένης αὐτοῖς ὕλης. Alexander of Aphrodisias, *De Anima*, ed. Ivo Bruns (Berlin: G. Reimer, 1887), p. 60.3-6). Alexander is understanding *aisthêsis* as a faculty or power of the soul (cf. Aristotle, *De An.*, II 12,424a27-28), though the term can easily pass over into its

other meaning for Aristotle (5,417a12-13), that of the activity of sensing. Alexander (p. 60.10-11) also calls the sense powers "forms" of the body. On Alexander's place in the Aristotelian epistemological tradition, see Paul Moraux, *Alexandre d'Aphrodise* (Paris: E. Droz, 1942), pp. xv-xix; Giancarlo Movia *Alessandro di Afrodisia* (Padua: Antenore, 1970), pp. 23-28.

4. ὑκάοτη μὲν οὖν αἴοϑησις τοῦ ὑποκειμένου αὐτῇ αἰοϑητοῦ ἐστιν αἴοϑησις, οὐσα ἐν τῷ αἰοϑητηρίῳ οὐχ ᾖ σῶμα ἐκεῖνο, ἀλλ' ᾗ ἔχει τὴν τοιάνδε δύναμιν. Alexander, p. 60. 14-16. The meaning of *aisthêsis* passes over from the meaning of power to the meaning of activity, insofar as sensation is in the organ in accord with the sentient power it possesses.

5. ὅτι γὰρ οὐχ ὡς ὕλη δέχεται τὰ πάϑη ἡ ὄψις ἐναργές. ὁρῶμεν γὰρ ὅτι οὐ γίνεται ἡ ὄψις μέλαινα καὶ λευκή, ὅταν ἐκείνων αἰοϑάνηται. Alexander, p. 62.3-5

6. καὶ γὰρ εἰς ταύτας αἱ ποιότητες μὲν διικνοῦνται, ἡ δὲ ὕλη καὶ τὸ ὑποκειμενον ἔξω. πάοχειν μὲν οὖν λέγονται αἱ αἰοϑήσεις ὑπὸ τῶν αἰοϑητῶν, πολὺ δὲ τὸ πάϑος διάφορον ἢ ὡς πάσχει τὰ ἄψυχα, μᾶλλον δὲ ἀναίσϑητα σώματα· αἱ υὲν γὰρ αἰοϑήσεις λέγονται πάσχειν ὑπὸ τῶν αἰοϑητῶν ἔξω μενούσης αὐτῆς τῆς ὕλης, τοῦ δὲ εἴδους μόνου κινοῦντος τὸ αἰοϑητήριον, . . . αἱ δὲ αἰοϑήσεις οὐχ ὕλαι γίνονται τῶν αἰοϑητῶν· οὐ γὰρ λευκαίνεται ἡ αἴοϑνσις οὐδὲ μελαίνεται οὐδὲ βαρύνεται ἢ ὀξύνεται, ἀλλ' ὁ πολλάκις καὶ εἰρηκαμεν καὶ ἐροῦμεν, τὸ εἶδος ὑποδέχεται μόνον καὶ τὸν λόγον. διὸ καὶ εἰς κρίοιν καὶ εἰς ἀντίληψιν τελευτῶσιν· ὕλη γὰρ οὐδεμία δύναται κρίνειν τὸ ἐγγινομένον εἶδος· ἀσύνετον γάρ τι καὶ ἄκριτον καὶ ἀνατίληπτον ἥ γε ὕλη. ὁ λόγος μέντοι καὶ τὰ ἄλλα καὶ λόγον κρίνει καὶ εἶδος εἴδους ἀντιλαμβάνεται, εἶδος δὲ ἡ αἴοϑησις καὶ λόγος τοῦ πρώτου αἰοϑητηρίου· δύναμις γὰρ αυτου ἐστι καὶ μορφή. Themistius, *In Libros Aristotelis de Anima Paraphrasis*, ed. Richard Heinze (Berlin: G. Reimer, 1899), pp. 77.33-78.14. The last lines here are very explicit. The sense is a form because it is a power or faculty. It comes therefore under Aristotle's (*Cat.*, 8,9a14-27) second division of the category of quality. This makes it an accidental form. Insofar as it is a form it is the power of grasping or apprehending the form of the sensible thing without matter. No effort, however, made by Themistius to show how that hypostatizing of sentient and sensible forms is possible within the Aristotelian doctrine that what acts and undergoes is the composite.

7. . . . ἡ αἴοϑησις δυνάμει οὖσα ὅπερ τὸ αἰοϑητὸν ἄγεται εἰς ἐνέργειαν ὑπ'αὐτοῦ· καὶ γάρ ἐστιν ὅπερ εἰκεῖνο. . . . καϑόλου γὰρ οὐδὲν πάσχον ὑπό τινος τὴν ὕλην τὴν τοῦ ποιοῦντος δέχεται. ἀλλὰ τὸ εἶδος το εν αὐτῷ . . . εἰ γὰρ καϑὸ χρυσῆ ἢ σιδηρᾶ ἡ σψραγίς, ὡμοίωτο αὐτῇ ὁ κηρός, γένεσις ἄν ἦν καὶ ψϑορᾷ, . . . ἀλλὰ κατὰ μόνον τὸ εἶδος, λέγω δὲ αὐτὴν τὴν αἰοϑητικὴν δύναμιν. ἐπεὶ καὶ τὸ σῶμα πάσχει ὑπὸ τῆς ϑερμότητος, πάσχει δὲ καὶ ἡ ἀπτικὴ αἴοϑησις, ἀλλ' οὐ τὸ αὐτὸ πάϑος· αλλ' ἡ μὲν αἴοϑησις ὑπὸ μόνου τοῦ εἴδους τοῦ ϑερμοῦ πέπονϑε γνωστικῶς . . . Philoponus, *In Aristotelis de Anima Libros Commentaria*, ed. Michael Hayduck (Berlin:G.Reimer,1897), pp.437.6-438.13. The Aristotelian identity of sense and what the sensible thing is, in the actuality of cognition, is given strong emphasis in the opening lines of the above text.

8. . . . εἰ καὶ πάσχει ὑπὸ τῶν αἰοϑητῶν, οὐχ οὕτω πάσχει.ὥσπερ τὰ αἰοητικὰ κατὰ τὸ εἶδος πάσχοντα καὶ οὐ κατὰ τὴν ὕλην, ἀλλὰ πάσχει μετὰ τῆς ὕλης, τουτέοτιν ὑλικῶς

καὶ σωματικῶς. Philoponus, p. 440.20-23. In this regard R. D. Hicks, *Aristotle: De Anima* Cambridge: University Press, 1907), p. 419, notes the difference between the view that takes the matter to be that of the agent, and the view that takes it to be that of the patient. But he approaches the difference from a merely physiological viewpoint.

9. δέχεται δὲ τὰ εἴδη ἄνευ ὕλης· οὐ γὰρ εἶδος ἀλλ'εἰδοπεποιημενον ἅπαν ἐστὶν αἰσθητόν. ὥσπερ δὲ ἔστι κατὰ τὸ εἶδος, οὕτως αὐτὸ καὶ λέγει ἡ αἴσθησις κατὰ τὸ εἶδος, καὶ γινώσκεται κατ, αὐτό. καὶ τὸ αἰσθήτηριον οὖν τὴν τοῦ εἴδους δέχεται ἔμψασιν καὶ ἡ αἴσθησις κατὰ τὸ εἶδος ἐστῶσα τὸ αἰσθητὸν γινώσκει. Simplicius, *In Libros Aristotelis de Anima Commentaria*,ed. Michael Hayduck (Berlin: G. Reimer, 1882), p. 166.28-32. On references to Philoponus in Simplicus, see Adrien Pattin, *Simplicius: Commentaire sur les Catégories d'Aristote.* Traduction de Guillaume de Moerbeke (Paris: Beatrice-Nauwelaerts, 1971), p. ix, n.2. Cf.:ἡ ἐν αὐτῷ ἐνεργεῖ ζωὴ . . . , Simplicius, p. 166.22-23. See also ibid., lines 13-15.

10. . . . ὡς ἀύλως καὶ γνωστικῶς καθαρῶς τοὺς λόγους αὐτῶν ἀποματταμένης, . . κιὰ καθόλου πᾶν ποιοῦν τοῦ μὲν εἴδους μεταδοίη τῶ πάσχοντι, τῆς ὕλης δ' οὔ· υἱα γὰρ αὕτη καὶ κοινή. Sophonias, *In Libros Aristotelis De Anima Paraphrasis*, ed. Michael Hayduck (Berlin: G. Reimer, 1883), pp. 102.29-104.13. The last remark means that the matter of the thing is changed and that of the thing into which it is changed is one and common to both. For references in Aristotle to the matter remaining one and the same while undergoing change, see Bonitz, *Ind. Arist.* 785a16-19. At GC, I 7,324b6-7, Aristotle compares it to a genus, which remains the same in differing instances. The comparison with a genus gave Averroes occasion to note that unlike a genus the matter is common through lack of all form and accordingly of distinguishing characteristics. See Averroes,*In XII Metaph.*,14 (Venice: apud Juntas, 1574), fols. 300v2-301r1. This further development of the notion of pure potentiality would work rather against the purpose of Sophonias. It would allow the matter in the agent to be indistinguishable just in itself from the matter in the patient. Sophonias' intent is to show that the matter in the patient had not been that of the agent, just as the wax in Aristotle's simile is substantially one and the same wax both before and after impression by the signet ring, and is common to both states.

11. On his influential distinction between a thing's nature and the ways it exists in the sensible world and in the mind, see Avicenna, *Metaph.*, V,1-2. Cf.: "Essentiae vero rerum aut sunt in ipsis rebus: aut sunt in intellectu." *Logica*, I, fol. 2r2 (Venice,1508). " . . . esse quod habent res in intellectu." Ibid.,fol.342. " . . . sensus enim de hoc quod eam intelligit non est nisi quia forma existit in ea: . . . Formas autem memoratas et formatas esse in aliquo non est ipsas apprehendere, sicut formas sensibiles esse in aliquo non est sensus: unde corpora in quibus sunt formae sensibilium non sunt apprehendentia . . . " *Liber de Anima*, ed. S.Van Reit (Louvain & Leiden: Brill,1968-1972), II (IV-V), 147.18-148.1.

12. "Si enim reciperet eas cum materia, tunc idem esse haberent in anima et extra animam." Averroes, *Commentarium Magnum in Aristotelis De Anima Libros*, ed. F. Stuart Crawford (Cambridge,Mass.:Mediaeval Academy of

America,1953),p.317.15)17. Averroes brought to the fore the consideration that no third thing resulted from the cognitonal union of knower and known: " . . . quod enim componitur ex eis non est aliquod tertium aliud ab eis sicut de aliia compositis ex materia et forma." Ibid.,p.404.506-507.

13. "Agens autem agit per suam formam, et non per suam materiam; omne igitur patiens recipit formam sine materia. . . . Dicendum igitur, quod licet hoc sit commune omni patienti, quod recipiat formam ab agente, differentia tamen est *in modo recipiendi*. . . . Et per hunc modum, sensus recipit formam sine materia, quia alterius modi esse habet forma in sensu, et in re sensibili. Nam in re sensibili habet esse naturale, in sensu autem habet esse intentionale et spirituale." Aquinas, *In II de Anima*, lect.24, Pirotta nos. 551-553. Cf. *De Veritate*, II, 2c. Aristotle (*De An.*, II 5,417b23) has no hesitation in saying that the universals exist in their own way in the mind. Yet he prefers to emphasize that the individual sensible thing is not in the soul (III 8,431b29). The difference of viewpoint is apparent.

14. ". . . unde et Commentator dicit in III *de Anima*, quod non est idem modus receptionis quo formae recipiuntur in intellectu possibili et in materia prima; quia oportet in intellectu cognoscente recipi aliquid immaterialiter. Et ideo videmus, quod secundum hoc in eis natura cognitionis invenitur." *De Ver.*,II,2c. Cf. XXIII, 1c, and "Patet igitur quod immaterialitas alicuius rei est ratio quod sit cognoscitiva; et secundum modum immaterialitatis est modus cognitionis." *Summa Theologiae, I,14,lc.*

15. See Josef Gredt, "De Unione Omnium Maxima inter Subjectum Cognoscens et Objectum Cognitum," *Xenia Thomistica*, ed. P.S. Szabó (Rome: Angelicum,1925),I,303. On the vocabulary used to express the notion "immaterially" in this context (objective, intentionaliter, non-compositive, ut alienas), see ibid.,pp.303-305.

16. "Ad argumentum autem illorum dicimus Aristotelem et hic et ibi de sensu confuse loqui, quia adhuc non est cognita ipsius sensus natura, ibi quidem respexit animam, quae ratione judicationis agere dicitur, et ita activa causa est huius alterationis, quae dicitur sensatio, hic vero respicit organum, quod manifestum est esse illud, in quo fit sensatio. Proinde hoc dicitur pati, recipit enim species, quod est pati, deinde receptam in organo speciem anima iudicat, quod est agere, non igitur ageret nisi passio praecessisset." Jacobus Zabarella, *In III Aristot. Libros de Anima* (Frankfurt, L.Zetzner,1606), col. 481DE.

17. Aristotle had already outlined the doctrine that the sentient subject becomes qualitatively assimilated to the sensible object: "As we have said, what has the power of sensation is potentially like what the perceived object is actually; that is, while at the beginning of the process of its being acted upon the two interacting factors are dissimilar, at the end the one acted upon is assimilated to the other and is identical in quality with it." *De An.*, II 5, 418a3-6 Oxford trans. Yet Philoponus (437.6-8; text supra, n.7) regards Aristotle as having been already saying that the sense is potentially what the sensible thing is. Qualitative assimilation is of course there, and serves as the required build-up for the doctrine that perci-

pient and thing perceived are completely, and not just qualitatively, identical in the actuality of cognition. But the complete identity is required for the reasoning to the immaterial reception of form.

18. *De An.*,III 2,425b23-24; 12,434a29-30. Cf. 4,429b13-22; 430a3-4; 6,430b30-31; 8,432a9-10. See also *P.A.*, I 1,640a31-32; *Metaph.* Λ 3,1070a15-17.

19. *De An.*, III 2,425b25-31; 4,429b30-430a7; 5,430a19-20; 7, 431a1-4; 8,431b21-28.

20. *E.N.*, X 4,1174a14-b14. Cf. "activity of immobility," VII 14,1154b27. See also *De An.*, III 7,431a7.

21. *Soph. Elench.*,22,178a9-11; *Metaph.*, Θ 6,1048b18-35.

22. On this topic, see my article "La forma aristotélica como causa del ser," *Revista de Filosofía* (México), 10 (1977), 267-287.

23. *De An.*,III 7,431a1-6; cf. 5,430a19-21.

24. *De An.*, III 8,432b21-23; Cf. 2,425b25-426a28; 4,429a22-29; b30-31; 430a3-8; 7,431a1-3; b16-17.

25. This Aristotelian problem of self-knowledge may be found discussed in my article "A Note on Aristotle, *De Anima* 3.4,429b9" *Phoenix*, 30 (1976),107-118. [See in this volume pp. 99-108,Ed.]

Notes to Chapter 9

1. See critical apparatus in Paul Siwek, *Aristotelis Tractatus De Anima* (Rome 1965), *ad loc.* The only variants are the alternate form of the reflexive pronoun in a few manuscripts, and the omission of the adverb τότε in two.

2. The history of the Greek commentators on Aristotle, except for a few scholarly studies on individual authors, has still to be written. Paul Moraux, in the first volume of *Der Aristotelismus bei den Griechen* (Berlin 1973), has offered the commencement of a study projected as far as the cessation of the tendency to be "orthodox," a tendency that Moraux (xvi) sees ending about the middle of the third century A.D. This "tendency toward orthodoxy" (*ibid.*) reached its high point in Alexander of Aphrodisias, and ended before Porphyry. Accordingly Aristotelians "of the strict observance" are not to be looked for among the Neoplatonist interpreters (xvi-xvii). As regards the present question, these observations of Moraux throw light on the radical difference between Alexander and the Neoplatonist commentators in the understanding of intellectual self-knowledge. On the commentaries on the *De Anima* prior to Alexander, see Moraux, 132-136; 172-176; 207-208.

3. "Incidentally," or "accidentally," in the Greek κατὰ συμβεβηκός, means in Alexander (p. 86.22) that the intellect's knowing of something else is a thing that has occurred (συμβεβηκέναι) to it, and in that sense is "accidental" to it. The self-awareness depending upon this occurrence is correspondingly "accidental," or "incidental," in Alexander's explanation. His use of the notion *per se* calls for close attention. The ἔιδη λαμβάνειν καθ'αὑτά at p. 86.17 refers to the forms "by themselves" in the sense of "apart from matter" (see pp. 86.29-87.23), while the καθ αὑτόν at p. 86.21 means that it belongs to the very nature of the human in-

tellect to know the forms of other things directly. Since in the Aristotelian context the form is the intelligible content of the thing, and the matter just in itself is unknowable, Alexander can refer to the forms as the objects known, quite as the universal is the object known.

Zabarella, *In III Arist. Libros de anima* (Frankfurt 1606) cols. 781D-783A (3, text. 8), defends Alexander's interpretation of the self-awareness as concomitant and not direct, against the Neoplatonic view of Simplicius. Zabarella (col. 782D) uses the Scholastic contrast of *spiritaliter* with *realiter* to explain the difference between cognitional identity and real identity. But he does not mean, as R. D. Hicks, *Aristotle De Anima* (Cambridge 1907) 485, would suggest: "Experience shows that the mind thinks other things without any self-consciousness." Zabarella's words are "*saepe intellectus noster alias res cogitat sine ulla suiipsius cogitatione*" (col. 782D), but the context shows the meaning to be that the intellect does not confuse the self and the object with each other. It does not understand itself to be really the same as the horse, and when it judges the horse to be different from the donkey it does not judge that it (the intellect) is different from itself. The meaning is clearly that the intellect knows other things without putting into them anything of what it knows about itself. But Aristotle's doctrine, as well as Alexander's interpretation of it, must require that self-awareness accompany every act of human intellection, without any exception. Zabarella's (col. 782C) point was merely to show that this self-awareness is not direct. The situation vis-à-vis Aristotle is well expressed in the observation "in thinking of something the mind is conscious of itself thinking it," in Richard Norman, "Aristotle's philosopher-God," *Phronesis* 14 (1969) 72, even though contrary to Norman's conclusion one may hold that self-knowledge in the separate substances is not "the same activity that human minds perform when they engage in abstract thought" (67).

4. Bywater, "Aristotelia II," *Journal of Philology* 14 (1885) 40-41.

5. " . . .überzeugend . . . hergestellt." F. Susemihl, "Bericht über Aristoteles . . . ," *Jahresbericht über die Fortschritte der classischen Alter-tumswissenschaft* 42 (1885) 240.

6. "*Contextus* (b7) omnino exigit, ut in b9 legatur δι' αὑτοῦ . . . " Paul Siwek (above, n. 1) 328. Norman (above, n. 3) 65, though writing after the publication of the Ross and Siwek texts, adheres to the traditional reading, expressly declining to accept the emendation.

7. See above, n. 3. The Cartesian epistemology, in which mind is known to itself in priority to and with greater evidence than bodies (Descartes, *Prin.* 1.11; A-T. 8.,8.17-19), likewise remains in sharp confrontation with the basic Aristotelian tenet that only in the knowledge of external sensible things is the human intellect able to know itself. The Aristotelian tenet requires that something else be more present to the cognition than the cognition is to its own self. In this regard Descartes, in spite of his aim to separate the notion of mind from that of material things, seems to conceive the notion of cognition after the model of something material, which of course is more present to itself than is any other material thing.

8. Bywater's reference to *De An.*, 2.5, 417a24-28, shows beyond doubt that he is correct in using "at will" to express the meaning of "of himself" at 429b7. It was similarly interpreted by Aquinas as "*cum vellet*" and "*cum voluerit*" (*In III de An.*, lect. 8, no. 701), and by Zabarella as "*quando vult*" (*In de An.*, 3, text. 8, cols. 778E-779B).

9. The further actualization of the habitual state is correctly called "actual knowing" by Ross (292). "Thinking," on the contrary, does not usually require the qualification of "actual," since it denotes rather the actual exercise of thought. The one Greek verb νοεῖν is used for both.

10. The model may be seen in the description of soul as first actuality in the body (*De An.* 2.1, 412a9-b6). It actuates the matter of the body in stable fashion, in contradistinction to the further actualization found in passing activities such as thinking. In the Scholastic tradition this became standardized as the distinction between "first actuality" and "second actuality."

11. Norman (above, n. 3) 65, refers to the habitual possession of the forms and the actual exercise of thought as "two kinds of thinking." There is no difficulty of course in the Greek in understanding them as two different kinds of νοῦς or νοεῖν. Nor is there any hesitation in English in calling them two different kinds of knowing. But in ordinary use "thinking" seems to refer to the activity. Cf. above, n. 9.

12. On the two readings at 430a22, see Siwek, 333. The opposition of these readings to each other does not affect the present point, for in either case the difference between the two kinds of intellection remains the same. Aristotle himself does not use the notion "direct" to qualify the knowledge he contrasts with the concomitant self-awareness in human cognition. But Alexander's προηγομένως (p. 86.21) seems best translated by "directly." Norman (above, n. 3, 72) expresses it as "primarily." This would suggest The Aristotelian πρώτως and would seem to relate the two kinds of cognition as primary and secondary instances. That does not appear to be Aristotle's intent in saying that an act of cognition is of something else though concomitantly of itself. There is but the one act of cognition, focusing on the object but simultaneously aware of itself. It is hard, in fact, cognition, except in the temporal sense that a new act of cognition may now be focused upon the self. But that is not the question here. The Aristotelian meaning is rather that self is always concomitant with the object upon which the cognition focuses, on account of the identity of the two in the act of knowing. Alexander's (p. 86.21-22) ranking of the two as *per se* and *per accidens* implies a relationship of primary and secondary from that angle, but here the force of the *per accidens* is that acts of human cognition *happen* to have taken place (see above, n. 3). It leaves intact the tenet that self-awareness is essential to and necessarily involved in every act of cognition. Alexander (p. 22.16-18) had already used the contrasted terms προηγουμένως and κατὰ συμβεβηκός to describe the body being moved *per se*, and its form *per accidens*. This is heardly a relationship of primary and secondary movements. Rather, it describes the way one and the same movement is attributed in different fashion to two subjects, somewhat as the seated passenger shares *per accidens* the motion of the ship. Zabarella (cols. 782C; 783BD),

however, understands Alexander to mean a relationship of *principaliter-secundario* and *antecedenter* or *praecedenter-postquam*. The objects are contrasted as *primum* or *primarium*, and *secundarium* (783E). They may be found contrasted in this terminology by Aquinas (*ST* 1.87.3 c), but in the sense of the objects of two different acts of cognition. So John of St Thomas, *Ars Logica* 2.23.3, in *Cursus Philosophicus*, ed. B. Reiser (Turin 1930) 1.741-746, can regularly use the term "direct" for the cognition of objects and yet refer (742b32-34) to it in contrast to the knowledge of self as object with the words *primo . . . secundario*. The annoying confusion is avoided if with Hicks (above, n. 3, 485) the concomitant cognition is described as taking place "indirectly," in contrast to the way the cognition focuses "directly" upon an object.

Notes to Chapter 10

1. " . . . in all demonstration a definition of the essence is required as a starting-point, so that definitions which do not enable us to discover the derived properties, or which fail to facilitate even a conjecture about them, must obviously, one and all, be dialectical and futile." *De An.* 1. 1. 402b25-403a2 (Oxford tr.). Cf. *An. Post.* 1.4. 73b26-74a3 for the geometrical model, the demonstration of the attribute of equality to two right angles for the angles of a triangle.

2. *De An.* 1. 1. 402b3-5. The expression "human soul" is used also at *Pol.* 3. 15. 1286a19. "Nutritive soul," "sensitive soul," and "intellective soul" occur more frequently; see Hermann Bonitz, *Index Aristotelicus*[2] (Berlin, 1870), 865a3-35.

3. *De An.* 2. 1. 412a4-6 (Oxford tr.). The role of definition, accordingly, is to express the essence—in this case what soul in general is.

4. *De An.* 2. 1. 412a9-11; cf. a22-26. Cf. "change from not-working to working" at 4.416b2-3 (Oxford tr.). The notion of "actuality" (ἐνέργεια) in this context seems to imply operation, in such a way that something can be an entelechy without "actualizing" itself. Accordingly it is safer here to use the word "entelechy" or "perfection" to translate *entelecheia*, and to leave "actuality" for rendering "*energeia*," even though elsewhere the two words may be found used interchangeably as noted by George A. Blair, "The Meaning of 'Energeia' and 'Entelecheia' in Aristotle," *International Philosophical Quarterly*, 7 (1967), pp. 101-117. See especially the reference on p. 102, n. 4. At *De An.* 2. 2. 414a8-10, in a context in which knowledge and health are viewed as the actuality of an efficient cause (a11-12), the qualification "and, as it were, an actuality of the recipient" is used.

5. Both generic and specific traits signify the *kind* of substance, and to that extent are qualitative within the category of substance. See *Cat.* 5. 3b18-21.

6. A discussion of this topic may be found in my paper, "Matter and Predication in Aristotle," in *The Concept of Matter*, ed. Ernan McMullin (Notre Dame, Ind., 1963), pp. 79-93. [See *supra* chpt. 4, pp. 35-47, Ed.]

7. Z 12. 1038a19-26. The ultimate differentia is regarded as containing all the other differentiae, just as "two-footed" contains "endowed with feet" (a32-33).

8. See *supra*, n. 4.

9. *Ph.* 8. 4. 255b3-4; b21-23.

10. E.g., *"actus autem secundus est operatio,"* Aquinas, *ST* 1. 48. 5c. However, Aquinas uses *"perfectiones secundae"* to mean acquired or infused habits, such as virtues. See *In I Sent.*, d. 39, q. 2, a. 2, ad 4m (ed. Mandonnet, 1. 934-935). But in both uses really distinct accidents are meant, as superadded entities in contrast to the first actuality or the first perfection. Aquinas' existential approach requires new being for a previously non-existent operation.

11. *De An.* 2. 1. 412b6-9. Cf. *Metaph.* H 6. 1045a7-b24.

12. *De An.* 2. 1. 413a5-7. Cf. 2. 413a31-32; b24-27.

13. *De An.*, 2. 1. 413a8-9. In 3. 5. 430a12-15, an intellect that seems to act as an efficient cause is introduced. But the theme is not developed. Alexander, *In De An.*, ed. I. Bruns (Berlin, 1897), pp. 15, 9-26 and 20, 26-21, 12, rejects the notion of soul as pilot. Themistius, *In De An.*, ed. R. Heinze (Berlin, 1899), p. 43. 27-30, sees, however, the separate intellect in the comparison of pilot with ship. Philoponus, *In De An.*, ed. M. Hayduck (Berlin, 1897), p. 225, 29, allows it to be understood in the same way regarding "parts of the soul" in the plural, the "parts" being the intellective powers (p. 225, 31; cf. p. 227, 29-32). For Simplicius, *In De An.*, ed. M. Hayduck (Berlin, 1882), p. 95, 26-27, the "parts" are the theoretical and practical powers. A discussion may be found in R. D. Hicks, *Aristotle, De Anima* (Cambridge, 1907), pp. 319-321.

14. *De An.* 2. 1. 412b25-26. In this respect organic compounds synthesized in a laboratory, at least as at present understood, would not meet Aristotle's description of "organic body." On the tenet that what is potentially something is the material that is immediately disposed for it, as brass for a statue and wood for a casket, see *Metaph.* Θ 7. 1049a8-24.

15. *De An.* 2. 1. 413a9-10. "Sketch" is from painting, "rough model" from sculpture. On the mixed metaphor, see J. A. Stewart, *Notes on the Nicomachean Ethics* (Oxford, 1892), I, p. 17. A longer discussion of the situation may be found in H. Cassirer, *Aristoteles' Schrift "Von der Seele"* (Tübingen, 1932), pp. 21-47. The project implied seems to be the working out of the definition from the dull, lifeless, inexpressive stage of the clay model to the vigor and verve that was wrought into the finished marble by the Greek sculptors, and that has been eulogized in Macauley's lines:

The stone that breathes and struggles,
The brass that seems to speak:—
Such cunning they who dwell on high
Have given unto the Greek (*The Prophecy of Capys. 28*).

16. See Euclid 6. 13; cf. 2. 14. Euclid need not be put back far enough in the century to allow Aristotle to have read his work. The common heritage of Greek mathematics would suffice for the use of this example.

17. The remote cause is nonetheless named a "cause" (*An. Post.* 1. 13. 78b24; b28-29) in this context. The neuter and feminine forms of "cause" in the Greek are used interchangeably, in accord with the gender of the noun to which they refer; see 78b17. On the requirement that the "strict cause" fit exactly, cf. "On

the other hand, any isoceles triangle has its angles equal to two right angles, yet isoceles triangle is not the primary subject of this attribute but triangle is prior." *An. Post.* 1. 4. 73b38-39 (Oxford tr.). For a discussion of the *De Anima* framework in terms of ὅτι versus διότι, see Philoponus, *In De An.*, p. 225, 37-227, 26; F. A. Trendelenburg, *Aristotelis De Anima*² (Berlin, 1877), pp. 276-279.

18. *An. Post.* 1. 13. 78b12-13. Cf. *De An.* 2. 2. 413a11-13; *Ph.* 1. 1. 184a10-23; *Metaph.* Z 4. 1029b3-8.

19. See *supra*, n. 12. The problem is faced in *De An.* 3. 5. 430a10-25, but without satisfactory solution, and has caused unending difficulty in the Aristotelian tradition.

20. *De An.* 2. 2. 413b26-27 (Oxford tr.). This way of speaking lends color to the charge by Plotinus, *En.* 4. 7. 8⁵. 15-16, that the Peripatetics are forced to introduce another soul or mind to enable a man to think, since the first soul enabled him only to have a living body.

21. *De An.* 2. 2. 413b29-31. Cf. 4. 415a16-22, where the order of this knowledge is shown to be from objects to functions to faculties.

22. *De An.* 2. 414a7-10. The ᾧ of the traditional text at a7, though bracketed by Hett and Ross after Bywater, is retained by G. Rodier, *Aristote, Traité de l'Ame* (Paris, 1900), and P. Siwek, *Aristoteles, Tractatus de Anima* (Rome, 1965). On the question, see R. D. Hicks, *Aristotle, De Anima* (Cambridge, 1907), p. 328.

23. On this notion, see *supra*, n. 14.

24. *De An.* 2. 2. 413a15. Cf. *supra*, n. 17.

25. *De An.* 2. 2. 414a10. The same Greek term for "recipient" is used in a context in which the soul may remain impassive while receiving a form in cognition: "The thinking part of the soul must therefore be, while impassible, capable of receiving the form of an object; that is, must be potentially identical in character the object." *De An.* 3. 4. 429a15-16 (Oxford tr.). The notion of "recipient," accordingly, should not be too facilely identified with that of "matter" or of "subject" in this context. The traditional Scholastic explanation of cognition, in fact, was that the things known were received by the faculty *immaterially* and *objectively*, in contrast to materially and subjectively, and therefore were received as forms into form, and not as forms into matter. See Josef Gredt, *Elementa Philosophiae Aristotelico-Thomisticae*⁷ (Freiburg i. Breisgau, 1937), I, pp. 356-360. At the same time there is the other sense (*De An.* 3. 5. 430a10-24) in which intellect is passive and like matter.

26. *Aristotle, De Anima* (Oxford, 1961), p. 220. Ross correctly states that Aristotle's "real way out" is to class soul as a first entelechy. This contrasts it with "matter," but not necessarily with "recipient," in accord with what has been said in the preceding note. Ross, however, considers that "first entelechy" would contrast it with "recipient" as well as with "matter."

27. *De An.* 2. 2. 414a13-14 (Oxford tr.). Cf. "the body is the subject or matter" at 1. 412a18-19. I had completed this paper before reading the illuminating article of Rosamond Kent Sprague, "Aristotle *De Anima* 414a4-14,"

Phoenix 21 (1967), pp. 102-107. Mrs. Sprague's norm for interpreting Aristotle here seems unquestionable, that it is *"prima facie* unlikely that he would prepare the way by means of illustrations implying the opposite of what he intended to say" (p. 102). However, looking forward to lines a14-28, can one really have "no doubt that Aristotle would have completed the scheme" (p. 103) in a way that would parallel soul with the context's acceptance of knowledge and health (p. 104)? This inference seems to presume that "recipient" has to be equated with "matter" or "body". But in establishing the emphatic position of πρώτως (*in the most primary sense*, p. 104), and its backward reference to the definition worked out in the preceding chapter ("that the soul is actuality," p. 106), and in exploring the Platonic background, Mrs. Sprague's study is an exceptionally welcome contribution to the understanding of this difficult problem.

Against Ross and Sprague, T. M. Robinson "Soul and Definitional Priority: *De An.* 414a4-14," [*Apeiron*, 4 n. 1 (1970) 340-344, Ed.] suggests that "primarily" at 414a13 may have no particular reference to the sense involved in the expression "first entelechy." After examining the various senses of priority in Aristotle, Robinson finds abundant signposts that "priority from the point of view of strict definition" fits the situation. Since the object of definition is form, the (ontological) conclusion is allowed that soul be a form. This interpretation keeps the relation of soul to knowledge at 414a5-6 from looking "like an odd man out," but it involves Aristotle in the witting or unwitting "exploitation of the ambiguity between ontological and definitional priority" embedded in the notion "primarily." For the bearing on my own interpretation, see *infra*, n. 30.

Greek commentators tend to understand "primarily" here as applying to form in relation to the secondary role played by matter in the constitution of the physical thing. See Alexander, p. 31, 10-22; Philoponus, p. 245, 28-32; Sophonias, *In De An.*, ed. M. Hayduck (Berlin, 1883), p. 50, 11-12.

28. *De An.* 2. 2. 414a17-27. On the notion "appropriate matter," see *supra*, n. 14. On the difficulty in placing matter under the notion "that by which we live," see Simplicius, p. 104, 3-13. On the general progress made in the definition, see Rodier, *op. cit.*, II, p. 208, *ad* 414a18.

29. Hicks, *op. cit.*, p. 331, sees a "logical flaw" in this formulation. Just as "such as we have described" (p. 312) at *De An.* 2. 1. 412a21, meant "a natural body potentially having life," so, Hicks maintains, the Greek term should have the same reference at 2. 414a28. But this seems to take for granted that no progress has been made in the elaboration of the definition throughout chapter two of the second book. If "such as we have described" now means the potential or material component required by the formal principle through which we primarily live and perceive and think, the description has taken place in terms of notions grasped reflexively in internal experience, and not through externally observed living bodies. Instead of "that which has the capacity to be endowed with soul" (Hicks, p. 59), the notion referred to would be "the type required by the primary capacity to vegetate, perceive, and think," insofar as each of these activities is a specific instantiation of the general notion of life.

30. T. M. Robinson, *op. cit.*, *supra*, n. 27. Robinson's careful study of the various senses of "primary" in Aristotle, and of Aristotle's own attitude towards the multisignificant notion, reveals a setting in which the term in a given instance could do double duty. That the main intention here is "definitional priority" does not rule out, in Robinson's view, the insertion of "ontological priority" to By the same token, "primarily" could here express definitional priority and at the same time imply the notion of "immediate cause" as in "primary" at *An. Post.* 1. 13. 78a25-26. Likewise, backward reference to "first entelechy" at *De An.* 2. 1. 412b5-6, would be compatible with an implication of the sense of "primary" in the *Analytics*. But in both cases some pertinent indications in the text would be required to establish the presence of the additional sense. Such indications, however, are lacking.

31. See *Part. An.* 1. 1. 640a33-b4; cf. 639b14-30. Aristotle, however, was aware of the difficulties of determining in practice what the form actually is in a particular case, as is apparent from *Meteor.* 4. 12. 389b28-390a20. On human ignorance of real essences, see Locke, *Essay*, III, 6, 2-27.

32. A discussion of this topic may be found in my paper "The Grounds of Universality in Aristotle," *American Philosophical Quarterly*, 3 (1966), pp. 162-169. [See *supra* chpt. 5, pp. 48-58, Ed.]

33. Malebranche, reacting against the Cartesian fundamental tenet that the mind has a clear and distinct idea of itself and its activity, showed (*De la Recherche de la Verité*, III, 2e partie, c. 7, no. 4; *Entretiens sur la Métaphysique et sur la Religion*, II, 10) that in this respect it has only an interior sentiment that gives but imperfect knowledge. An idea of the soul would allow psychology to be done *more geometrico*: "mais si nous voyions en Dieu l'idée qui répond à notre âme, nous connaîtrions en même temps ou nous pourrions connaître toutes les propriétés dont elle est capable; comme nous connaissons (ou nous pouvons connaître) toutes les propriétés dont l'étendue est capable, parce que nous connaissons l'étendue par son idée." *Récherché, loc. cit.* For Aristotle, *Metaph.* Λ 9,1074b35-36, human knowledge and sensation are only concomitantly of themselves. Knowledge of the self and its activities, according to this tenet, should be parasitical upon the knowledge of the external sensible object, and open to clear analysis only in terms of sensible things.

34. Strictly speaking, it is the *man* who feels and perceives and thinks, and he does so through the soul — *De An.* 1. 4. 408b1-15.

35. For an interpretation of Aristotle's metaphysics as thoroughly aporematic, see Pierre Aubenque, *Le Problème de l'Être chez Aristote* (Paris, 1962). The topic of the agent intellect in *De Anima* 3. 5. 430a10-25, so important for the considerations of the present article, is an undoubted instance of a key problem left in the state of *apora*. But one should be careful about drawing generalizations from this and a few other instances, no matter how great the overall importance of these latter may be.

The present paper has benefited greatly from seminar discussions held by the Classics and Philosophy departments of the University of Toronto during the winter term of 1967-68, especially from the contributions of J. A. Philip, T. M. Robinson, D. Gallop, and A. C. Pegis.

Notes to Chapter 11

1. *Phys.* I 7, 191 a 7-12; Oxford tr. Cf. II 1, 193 a 31-b 3. Unless otherwise stated the texts of Aristotle will be quoted in the Oxford translation.

In the *Physics*, the material principle of bodies is designated merely as "matter". Elsewhere Aristotle (*PA* I 1, 640 b 5; *GA* III 11, 762 b 1) does use the expression "material principle" (ὑλικὴ ἀρχή), though in the sense of matter in general. The difficulty today is that "matter" suggests something that is a body. The matter of which Aristotle is speaking in the present text, however, as Simplicius (*In Phys.*, pp. 229.4-230.12) emphasized, has to be kept carefully distinguished from the notion of a body. A body necessarily has determinations, while its material principle has none. Since in the present context Aristotle is treating of matter explicitly as a principle of bodies, the least confusing way of expressing the notion seems to be "the material principle of bodies". So Philoponus can regard Aristotle as speaking here of "the material principle" (εἰπὼν οὖν τὴν ἀρχὴν τὴν ὑλικήν, *In Phys.* 167.26). "Natural bodies" (φυσικὰ ρώματα) and "sensible bodies" (αἱσθητὰ σώματα), of course, regular Aristotelian ways of referring to the composites of which this matter is a principle; see Bonitz, *Ind. Arist.*, p. 742 a 38 - b 22.

2. *Met. Epsilon* 1 1026 a 27-29; *Kappa* 7, 1064 b 9-14.

3. N. Lobkowicz, in a "Comment" in *The Concept of Matter*, ed. E. McMullin (Notre Dame, Ind., 1963), p. 116, expresses a current (see infra, n. 11) doubt that matter as primary substrate in the *Physics* and the absolutely undetermined matter of the *Metaphysics* are the same reality. Lobkowicz notes "that Aristotle never made an attempt to clarify this point". But was any such attempt really necessary? The basic determination of any natural thing is the determination it must first receive in the category of substance. Without that determination it cannot have any other. Yet the primary substrate is the underlying subject of change within this category: "Plainly then, if there are conditions and principles natural objects and from which they primarily are or have come to be—have come to be, I mean, what each is said to be in its essential nature, not what each is in respect of a concomitant attribute—plainly, I say, everything comes to be from both subject and form" (*Phys.* I 7, 190 b 17-20). The Greek commentators had no difficulty in seeing that this substrate within the category of substance was of itself entirely formless; see Themistius, *In Phys.*, p. 27.6-7; Simplicius, p. 229.12-14; Philoponus, p. 162.29-31. Aristotle's procedure, in fact, is not to take two definitions and ask if they have the same referent. Rather he reaches the primary substrate in the *Physics*. The passage in the *Metaphysics* (*Zeta* 3, 1029 a 1-25) regards the composition of bodies from matter and form as already established, and shows that the primary substrate has none of the categorial determinations. This text in the *Metaphysics* does not read as though the primary matter can be reached through an analysis of predication. On the contrary, the

text *assumes* that primary matter is already known as the basic substrate of bodies, and broaches the *problem* why it is not the primary instance of substance, since the basic substrate is to be considered as the ultimate subject of predication. Accordingly there need be no hesitation in agreeing fully with Professor Lobkowicz (p. 118) that one has "to know *in advance* that there is a matter different from all substantial form" in order to approach this problem of predication. Likewise there is no possibility of numerical sameness in the primary matter before and after a substantial change. Without form, primary matter cannot even be pointed out; see Simplicius, pp. 217.14-15; 229.18. In itself it is not able to be an object of referring or of ostensive definition.

The further contention (Lobkowicz, p. 120) about matter, that "in order to maintin the continuity of the substratum, it must be assigned some actuality", hinges on whether change within the category of substance really takes place. An actual subject would mean that there is no generation, in the sense of substantial change, but only the kinds of change that Aristotle (*Met. Alpha* 3, 983 b 7-17) attributed to the Presocratics. Accepting substantial change as the starting point, however, the argument in its conclusion requires an entirely potential substrate, a substrate that of itself has no actuality whatsoever. Accordingly, as purely potential, it does not exhibit any "determinations which permit me to identify it" (Lobkowicz, ibid.). As the continuing substratum throughout the change, it can be known only insofar as substantial change is known. On matter in general as knowable for Aristotle only in relation to the thing of which it is the subject, see Wolfgang Wieland, *Die aristotelische Physik* (Göttingen, 1962), p. 64. Cf.: "Man kann es immer nur dadurch bestimmen, daß man angibt, *wofür* es Substrat ist . . ." Ibid., p. 135.

4. Cf.: "Again, some things are one in number, others in species, others in genus, others by analogy; . . . things that are one in species are all one in genus, while things that are so in genus are not all one in species but are all one by analogy; while things that are one by analogy are not all one in genus." *Met. Delta* 6, 1016b31-1017a3. Cf. *PA* I 5, 645b26-28.

5. On the force of καϑόλου as adverbial, see Kurt v. Fritz, *Philosophie and sprachlicher Ausdruck bei Demokrit, Plato und Aristoteles* (Leipzig, etc. [1938]), p. 65.

6. See also *GC* I 3, 317b13-319b5; *Meta. Eta* 1, 1042a32-b3; *Lambda* 2, 1069b9-34.

7. On this necessary role of the universal in demonstration, see *An. Post.*, I 11, 77 a 5-9. On the analogous notion functioning as a middle term, see ibid. II 14, 98 a 20-23; 17, 99 a 15-16. G. L. Muskens, *De vocis* ΑΝΑΛΟΓΙΑΣ *significatione ac usu apud Aristotelem* (Groningen 1943), p. 30, concludes: "Identitatem analogicam eadem esse dignitate qua genericam in scientiis demonstrativis hoc loco interum affirmat, et hoc omissa explicatione, quippe quod procul dubio sit." Cf. ibid., p. 92. On pp. 15-18 the passages in the *Physics* that make use of analogy are listed.

8. John Stuart Mill, *A System of Logic*, III, 20, 2. So, in the "sens propre" of reasoning by analogy, similarity of Mars with Earth in climate and atmosphere "a

conduit à augmenter la conviction que Mars est habité par des êtres vivants ainsi que la terre"—J. Lindenbaum Hosiasson, "Induction et Analogie", *Mind*, L (1941), 352; cf. p. 364. This would seem akin to the argument from "example" (*paradeigma*) in Aristotle (*An. pr.* ii 24, 68 b 38 - 69 a 19; *Rhet.* II 20, 1393 a 22 - 1394 a 18), since its middle term lacks sufficiently established universality. The crucial difference between it and Aristotelian analogy may escape recognition if one hastily infers that similarity of relations outside mathematics can yield only probable conclusions: e.g., "Between this 'Aristotelean' analogy, and analogy in the modern sence, there is no essential difference." P. Coffey, *The Science of Logic* (London, etc., 1912), II, 161. On the other hand, for a conception of four-term analogy "from which an algorithm may be derived for finding a fourth term (which need not be unique) given the other three", see Mary B. Hesse, "On Defining Analogy", *Proceedings of the Aristotelian Society*, LX (1959-1960), 79; cf. pp. 92-100. In *Models and Analogies in Science* (London and New York, 1963), pp. 70-74. Miss Hesse distinguishes between the types of analogy in question and the relation of proportionality. The distinction applies in the modern understanding of analogy. For Aristotle, on the contrary, the relation of proportionality was what the term "analogy" itself expressed. The range of the term has to be widely extended in order to denote what is uppermost in the currently accepted notions of analogy; e.g. "Here I shall take 'analogy' in its broadest sense to refer not merely to proportional analogy (a : b :: c : d) but to any mode of reasoning in which one object or complex of objects is likened or assimilated to another . . . " G. E. R. Lloyd, *Polarity and Analogy* (Cambridge, Eng., 1966), p. 175. The result, however, is that in practice the current conceptions become restricted to instances of the Aristotelian paradigm: "The paradigm represents what we should call argument from analogy." Ibid., p. 406.

For the view that philosophical analogies, in a misuse of ordinary words, "recombine known words in an unfamiliar way while trading on their familiar meanings", see Margaret Macdonald, "The Philosopher's Use of Analogy", *Essays on Logic and Language*, ed. Antony Flew (Oxford, 1951), p. 82. The application of this notion of analogy to the Aristotelian problem of matter may be seen on pp. 85-87 and 92-94, ibid.

9. See A. Wolf, in *Encyclopaedia Britannica* (14th ed.), s. v.

10. *Met. Zeta* 10, 1036 a 8-9. Cognition for Aristotle (*De an.* II 12, 424 a 17-24; III 8, 431 b 26 - 432 a 3) takes place when the *form* of the thing known is in the knower.

11. Since human cognition does not take place without sensible images, a substrate has to be represented to the mind as a substance endowed with quantity, sensible qualities, and the other categorial determinations. These determinations have to be precisively excluded, one by one, through additional acts of intellection, as at *Met.ˉ Zeta* 3, 1029 a 20-26. J. de Vries, "Zur aristotelisch-scholastischen Problematik von Materie und Form", *Scholastik*, XXXII (1957), pp. 164-167, saw difficulties in identifying this metaphysical concept of matter with the physical concept of ultimate substrate for generation, and regarded the problem as left unsolved by Aristotle. On this question, see supra, n. 3. It is true,

as E. McMullin, "Matter as a Principle", *The Concept of Matter* (Notre Dame, Ind., 1963), p. 189, remarks, that though matter appears to be indeterminate "this point is never explicitly made in the *Physics*". Cf. McMullin's misgivings in "Four Senses of Potency", ibid., p. 315. But does not the conclusion follow clearly enough from Aristotle's assertions in the course of the *Physics* itself?

For a general survey of the problem regarding the unitary character of the Aristotelian concept of matter in its various functions, see Francisco Ramos, *La doctrina Aristotelica de la materia prima* (Quito, 1964), pp. 177-340.

12. "The universal is more knowable in the order of explanation, the particular in the order of sense: for explanation has to do with the universal, sense with the particular." *Phys.* I 5, 189 a 5-8.

Simplicius (*In Phys.*, p. 226.25-227.22), seeing in the Pythagorean Timaeus a common source for Plato's teaching on the receptacle and Aristotle's on matter, from the viewpoint both of doctrine and of expressions, has accordingly to face the problem why Plato (*Tim.* 52 B) used "spurious reasoning" to characterize what Aristotle means here by knowledge through analogy. See also Philoponus, *In Phys.*, p. 162.31-163.12. A discussion of this topic may be found in Luis Cencillo, *Hyle: Origen, concepto y funciones de la materia en el Corpus Aristotelicum* (Madrid, 1958), pp. 72-78.

13. Cf. "When we analyze an object, a particular, a τόδε τι, with respect to what it is and the various reasons or 'causes' why it has come to be what it is, Aristotle assumes that our analysis, the structure we have erected in our λόγος or our reason, and the structure in the objective thing *correspond*." Whitney J. Oates, *Aristotle and the Problem of Value* (Princeton, 1963), p. 59.

14. "For elsewhere, as for instance in house building, this is the true sequence. The plan of the house, or the house, has this and that form; and because it has this and that form, therefore is its construction carried out in this or that manner. . . . Thus we should say, because man is an animal with such and such characters, therefore is the process of his development necessarily such as it is . . . and after a like fashion should we explain the evolution of all other works of nature." *PA* I 1, 640 a 15 - b 4. For Aristotle the form is the physical perfection of the material thing, and accordingly is the purpose that nature is striving to attain. Hence formal cause and final cause are easily regarded as coinciding with each other, as at *Phys.*, II 7, 198 a 22-27.

15. *Met. Zeta* 7, 1032 a 24-25; Hope tr. The Oxford translation has "the so-called 'formal' nature, which is specifically the same (though this is in another individual); for man begets man." The meaning is that which is called nature from the standpoint of form, is the same in the different individuals. J. Warrington translates: " . . . the so-called 'formal nature', which is specifically the same as the nature of the thing generated; for man begets man." Tredennick: "which has the same form as the thing generated."

16. *Met. Zeta* 7, 1032 a 20-22. For a presentation of the argument from the plurality of individuals in a species, see Fernand Renoirte, *Eléments de critique des sciences et de cosmologie*, 2e éd. (Louvain, 1947), pp. 220-222.

17. On the development of this argument in the middle ages, with texts quoted

from Aquinas, Bonaventure, and Giles of Rome, see John O'Neill, *Cosmology* (London, etc., 1923), I, 121-122. For a further development in terms of the spatiotemporal continuum, see Renoirte, pp. 223-228.

18. See text cited supra, n. 16. On potentiality as the operative feature in the other two arguments, cf.: "Donc l'essence des individus de la même espèce n'est pas détermination pure; elle comporte un principe de détermination et un principe de déterminabilité." Renoirte, p. 220. "L'essence d'un être matériel doit comporter deux principes d'être, un principe de détermination et us principe de déterminabilité. . . . L'essence d'un être qui dure successivement doit donc être composée de principes d'être. Ceux-ci doivent justifier à la fois et la détermination et la déterminabilité de la substance matérielle. On appelle matière première le principe de déterminabilité, . . ." Ibid., pp. 227-228. However, neoscholastic discussions of the various arguments, e. g. Peter Hoenen, *The Philosophical Nature of Physical Bodies*, tr. David Hassel (West Baden Springs, Ind., 1955), pp. 4-16, have not been concerned with looking for a common operative feature running throughout them all, and accordingly have not emphasized the common role played by the notion of potentiality. On the level of natural philosophy, as should be apparent from all that has just been said, potentiality functions as a genuine principle of explanation and enlightenment. On the level of experimental science, in contrast, it is not of any help.

19. *Met. Lambda* 9, 1074 b 18-35. Separate substances are pure actuality, in accord with Aristotle's (ibid., 6, 1071 b 20-22) teaching that they exist without matter. Final causality is the only type of causality mentioned (7, 1072 b 3-14) for them. Elsewhere (*Phys.*, III 3, 202 a 14-20; *De an.* III 2, 426 a 4-10) the actuality and the perfection of an efficient cause is located in the patient. Accordingly efficient causality would be incompatible with the self-contained perfection of immaterial being. The complete containment of separate substance within itself just as itself, in contrast to parts and effects, could hardly be emphasized more strongly.

20. "Water and air are, and are generated, 'from' each other, but not in the way in which bricks come 'from' a house and again a house 'from' bricks . . . " *Phys.* I 4, 188 a 15-17. Cf. 7, 190 a 32 - b 9.

21. I am indebted to Professor Herbert Hingert for carefully reading the first draft of this paper, and for his helpful suggestions that have been incorporated into the final draft.

Notes to Chapter 12

1. ". . . still another part of natural philosophy, which sets forth the purposes (*fines*) of things. So far it is without name, though it is most noble and most useful. It could be called 'Teleology.' " Christian Wolff, *Logica*, Discursus Praeliminaris, no. 85. My translation.

2. See *The Encyclopedia of Philosophy*, ed. Paul Edwards (New York, 1967), s.v.

3. *Metaph.*, Δ 4, 1014b16-1015a19.

4. *Metaph.*, E 1,1025b18-1026a29; K 7,1064a10-b14. Even in this context, however, Aristotle shows no hesitation in intermingling the older and wider meaning of the term *physis*, e.g., 1026a20; 1064a35-37; b 11.

5. *Ph.*, VIII 1,250b14; Oxford tr.

6. *Metaph.*, Z 10,1036a8-9.

7. *Ph.*, II 1,192b8-193b6.

8. *De An.*, II 1,412a12-b6. Cf. 2,414a12-19. Aristotle speaks of the vegetative, sentient, and intellective soul (see instances in Bonitz' *Index Aristotelicus*, 865a6 ff). "Human soul" is found at *Pol.*, III 15,1286a19.

9. *De An.*, III 4,429a10-18.

10. *De An.*, III 5,430a10-25. The entire passage is quite enigmatic, but the assertion (a24-25) that the passive intellect is perishable is explicit and formal.

11. *Ibid.*, a22-23. Cf. *Ph.*, I 9,192a34-36.

12. Further discussion of the general problematic here may be found in my study *The Doctrine of Being in the Aristotelian 'Metaphysics,'* 2nd ed. (Toronto, 1963), pp. 22-26. [3rd ed. rev., pp. 1-67, Ed.]

13. "And since 'nature' means two things, the matter and the form, of which the latter is the end, and since all the rest is for the sake of the end, the form must be the cause in the sense of 'that for the sake of which,' " *Ph.*, II 8,199a30-32; Oxford tr. For other texts, see Bonitz, *Ind. Arist.*, 753b24-39.

14. *De An.*, II 4,415b16-20; Oxford tr.

15. *P A* I 1,640a15-18; Oxford tr. Cf. *Ph.*, II 7,198b2-9.

16. *P A*, I 1,640b1-4; Oxford tr.

17. *Metaph.*, M 5,1079b24-27.

18. *APo.*, II 19,100a13-14. The occasion was the question how the soul could universalize the objects of sense perception. Aristotle's answer was that this is the way the soul is constituted, namely as something able to account for the manifest results.

19. *P A*, II 1,647b4-7; Oxford tr. Cf. III 4,665b31-666b25.

20. *Cael.*, I 2-4,269a2-271a33. Cf. *Ph.*, VIII 10,267a21-b25.

21. This is discussed by Locke, *An Essay Concerning Human Understanding*, III, 6, 2-27, in terms of his distinction between real and nominal essences. Aquinas from first to last in his writings insists that human intelligence does not penetrate the specific differentiae of bodies. Not only does he make no exception for rationality as a specific differentiae in man, but in a couple of texts (*De Ver.*, X, 1, ad 6m; *De Spir. Creat.*, a. 11, ad 3m) he expressly mentions it as an instance of this general failure to penetrate specific natures. Paul Kristeller, *Le Thomisme et la Pensée Italienne de la Renaissance* (Montreal & Paris, 1967), pp. 42-47, notes how in medieval and renaissance Italy the study of Aristotelian philosophy was geared to the study of medicine, and not to that of theology as in the Paris where Aquinas had flourished. There need not be too much wonder, then, that the Aristotelianism encountered by Galileo was so entirely uninfluenced in this regard by the more careful attitude of Aquinas.

22. E.G., *APo.*, I 13,78b34-79a16; *Metaph.*, Λ 8,1073b3-38.

23. See *APo.*, I 14,79a18-20; *Ph.*, II 2,193b25-194a12.

24. *Supra*, n. 21.

25. E.g., at *De An.*, II 2,414a4-14.

26. *De An.*, II 4,415a26-b2; Oxford tr. See also *Pol.*, I 2,1252a28-30.

27. Cf. *Cael.*, I 9,279a17-30; *G C*, II 10,336b27-337a7; *Metaph.*, Θ 8, 1050b28-30 (text infra, n. 30).

28. *De An.*, II 4,415b3-7; Oxford tr. See background in Plato, *Symp.* 207D. Across the centuries an echo may be heard in "he lives on, indeed, in his children, he lives on in his name, he lives not on in his own person." John Henry Newman, *The Second Spring*, ed. Francis P. Donnelly (New York, 1911), p. 22 (no. 2).

29. "That, too, is why all the other things—the things, I mean, which are reciprocally transformed in virtue of their 'passions' and their 'powers of action,' e.g. the 'simple' bodies—imitate circular motion. For when Water is transformed into Air, Air into Fire, and the Fire back into Water, we say the coming-to-be 'has completed the circle,' because it reverts again to the beginning." *G C* II 10,337a1-6; Oxford tr.

30. *Metaph.*, Θ 8,1050b28-30.

31. *Cael.*, II 2,285a29-30. Cf. I 7,275b25-26; *Ph.*, VIII 9,265b32-34.

32. See *Metaph.*, Λ 7,1072a24-b14; 10,1075a11-25.

33. *E N*, I 2,1173a4-5; Oxford tr. Cf. *Metaph.*, Λ 10,1075a23-25.

34. *Pol.*, I 8,1256b15-20; Oxford tr.

35. *Ibid.*, b20-26.

36. The discussion of slavery at *Pol.*, I 4,1253b23 ff., is introduced under the topic of property and the acquisition of property.

37. *Pol.*, I 2,1252a31-34; Oxford tr.

38. *Pol.*, I 2,1252b7-9; Oxford tr. A similar attitude on this point may be seen expressed in Isocrates, *Second Letter to Philip*, 4-5, showing that the deep cleavage in views on theoretical philosophy did not affect this practical standpoint.

39. *Pol.*,.I 3,1253b21-22; Oxford tr.

40. *Pol.*, I 5,1254a23-24 and 1255a1-3; Oxford tr.

41. *Pol.*, I 4,1254a5-17. Cf. *E N*, VIII 11,1161b3-5.

42. *Pol.*, VII 16,1335b20-21.

43. *E N*, V 11,1138a9-14.

44. *E N*, IX 4,1166a1-19.

45. See *De An.*, III 4,429a10-11.

46. *Enneads*, IV, 7, 8 ⁵.15-16.

47. *Anabasis*, V, 8, 8-11.

48. *Pol.*, VII 16,1335b24-26; Oxford tr.

49. *E N*, X 8,1178a9-22.

50. See T. A. Goudge, "Salvaging the Noosphere," *Mind*, 71 (1962), 543-544.

51. *Discours de la Méthode*, 5; A-T, VI, 55.29-56.9. For Aristotle, the graded levels allow form to play a proportionately greater role in the inanimate, plant, and animal kingdoms respectively, with corresponding increase in the obviousness of the teleology; See *Meteor.*, IV 12,390a2-b2.

Notes to Chapter 13

1. *EN* III 2, 1111b8-13. Cf. *EE* II 10, 1225b26-27; 1226b21-22; *MM* I 11, 1187b7-18. This restriction suffices to locate choice in the aspect of soul described as having rationality (*to logon echon* – *EN* I 13, 1102a28; 1103a2). In that passage the morally virtuous man is said to choose the right direction even in an act of moral weakness, just as the paralytic chooses (1102b19) to move his limbs in a different direction from the way they are actually going. But an action performed through moral weakness is definitely blameworthy (*EN* VII 1,1145b10; 4, 1148b6; cf. 8, 1151a24-28). Must it not therefore be something chosen, just as any other action for which a man is responsible. The charge of inconsistency in Aristotle's use of *proairesis* has accordingly been raised. Pierre Aubenque, *La Prudence chez Aristote* (Paris 1963), pp. 119-143, in a penetrating and comprehensive study of the background of *proairesis* in preceding Greek thought, finds in Aristotle's discussions a "dualité de contextes, de problématiques et, finalement, de *sens*" (p. 119). The result in Aristotle, he claims, is inconsistency and contradiction due to a double use of *proairesis*, 1) as a "disposition concernant l'intention" and 2) as choice in "la structure de l'action" (p. 119). For instance: "La suite des idées est ici peu naturelle et, pour finir, parfaitement in-intelligibile, si l'on ne reconnaît pas qu'interfèrent ici deux problématiques ... " (p. 124). Only the realization that the problem side is twofold, 1) the technical use of *proairesis* in the Academy and 2) the popular use of the term, will finally allow "un sens acceptable" (p. 138, n. 2) to be given to Aristotle's treatment of the overall theme. The double background accordingly enables one, in Aubenque's view, to see how Aristotle can leave choice (in the popular sense) out of consideration when regarding virtue as a *hexis proairetikê*: "il ne songe nullement à l'analyse, qui est aujourd'hui celle du livre III, sur le choix délibéré" (p. 119). – This conception of Aubenque's would allow *proairesis* to be translated as "choice" only in contexts where it has the popular sense. Elsewhere it would have to be translated as "intention" or "disposition" when it has the Academic meaning.

G. E. M. Anscombe, 'Thought and Action in Aristotle', in *New Essays on Plato and Aristotle*, ed. R. Bambrough (London 1965), p. 143, finds inconsistency if one understands "that any case of something being determined by deliberation at all is a case of choice, as seems to be suggested by the formulation 'what is decided by deliberation is chosen' ". In spite of different possible defenses, " 'choice' cannot do all the work Aristotle wants to make it do" (p. 150). – Again the question arises whether *proairesis* may always be translated by "choice" in these contexts. Ross, while translating it by "will" at *Metaph. E* 1, 1025b24, notes at *EN* III 2, 1111b5 that it is "a very difficult word to translate. Sometimes 'intention', 'will', or 'purpose' would bring out the meaning better; but I have for the most part used 'choice'." But in view of Aristotle's clear distinction between *proairesis* and *boulêsis (EN* III 2, 1111b19-30), the translation merely by "will" does not seem permissible, though Burnet claimed, in *The Ethics of Aristotle* (London 1900), p. 131, that *proairesis* "is really what we call the will, though the idea is, generally speaking, foreign to Aristotle's thought in this form." On the other hand, W. H. Fairbrother, "Aristotle's Theory of Incontinence", *Mind* VI (1897),

362, had claimed that "the 'Will', as we understand it, was not an Aristotelian conception at all". Difficulties in translation, then, are to be expected. But may not one take the translation "choice", e.g. as in Apostle's *Aristotle's Metaphysics* (Bloomington, Ind. 1966) at *E* 1, 1025b4, and see if it can be consistently applied throughout the contexts of virtue and self-control in the *Ethics*?

2. *EN* III 5, 1113b3-14; *EE* II 10, 1226a26-28; *MM* I 17, 1189b6-8. Cf. *EN* III 2, 1111b26-30; *EE* II 10, 1225b34-37; 1226b16-19; *MM* I 11, 1187b7-18.

3. *Metaph. K* 7, 1064a10-b3; *Top.* VI 6, 145a15-18; VIII 1, 157a10-11. In Plato (*Plt.* 258CE) the sciences that Aristotle names "productive" are called "practical". Hence Aristotle can also use a merely twofold division, theoretical and practical at *Metaph. α* 1, 993b20-23 (cf. *De An.* I 3, 407a23-25; *Pol.* VII 14, 1333a24-25), or theoretical and productive at *Metaph.* A 2, 982b9-11, Λ 9, 1075a1-3, *EE* I 1, 1214a8-14, and can class moral philosophy under the "productive" division at *EE* I 5, 1216b10-19.

4. See texts *supra*, n.1. Cf.: "Now all essences are by nature first principles of a certain kind, owing to which each is able to generate many things of the same sort as itself, for example a man engenders men, and in general an animal animals, and a plant plants. And in addition to this, obviously man alone among other animals initiates certain conduct – for we should not ascribe conduct to any of the others." *EE* II 6, 1222b15-20; tr. Rackham (Loeb.). See also *EN* VI 2, 1139a18-20. *MM* I 11, 1187b7-8 mentions also inanimate things as not said to "do", in this sense of conduct.

5. See texts *supra* n. 3, and the Platonic background in *Plt.* 258DE. While both the practical and the productive go beyond mere knowledge, only the productive sciences give rise to products that are something other than the action itself (*EN* VI 5, 1140b6-7; cf. other texts listed in Bonitz, *Ind. Arist.* 631a31-34). At *EN* I 1, 1094a3-6 and a16-18 the Platonic hearers are gently initiated to the contrast.

6. *EN* I 4, 1095b4-13; 7, 1098b2-4; II 1-2, 1103a14-1104b3.

7. *EN* I 13, 1103a3-9. The theme is developed throughout *EN* II-VII.

8. "Virtue, then, is a habit concerned with choosing, and found in the mean relative to us, which is determined through a rational standard and as a prudent man would determine" (*EN* II 6, 1106b36-1107a2). The virtuous man himself is as it were the rule (canon) and measure of moral truth on each occasion (III 4, 1113a31-33).

9. "Nowadays we must find it difficult to imagine how entirely *public* was the conscience of a Greek. (In fact, the early Greeks never conceived anything like the personal conscience of modern times.)" Werner Jaeger, *Paideia*, tr. G. Highet, 2nd ed. (New York 1945), I, 9.

10. *EN* V 10, 1137b8-11. Similarly the definition of a particular kind of injustice falls within the generic definition, at 2, 1130a32-b1.

11. *EN* I 1, 1094a2-3; 4, 1095a14-15; X 2, 1172b35-1173a5. Cf. *MM* II 7, 1205b35-36.

12. *E* I 6, 1096a23-29; b8-30. Cf. *E* I 8, 1217b25-40; *MM* I 1, 1182b16-1183a24; 2, 1183b19-1148a8.

13. *EN* I 6, 1096b30-35; cf. 13, 1102a13-26; *MM* I 1, 1182a28-30.

14. "... in accord with the subject matter" – *EN* I 3, 1094b12; 7, 1098a27-28. "... in the nature of the object; for the material of conduct is radically of this kind" – V 10, 1137b18-19. See also VI 4, 1140a1-23.

15. *EN* I 5, 1095b23-33. Cf. X 8, 1178a9-22.

16. *EN* I 5, 1096a5-7. Cf. IV 1, 1120a5-15.

17. *EN* I 7, 1097b24-1098a20. Cf. *EE* II 1, 1219a1-39; *MM* I 4, 1184b31-36.

18. *EN* X 7, 1177a12-1178a8. Cf. *Metaph.*, Λ 7, 1072b14-30; 9, 1075a2-10.

19. *EN* X 6, 1176b27-1177a1. Amusements are also desirable for their own sake, b9-10.

20. *EN* I 7, 1097b11; IX 9, 1169b18-19. Cf. VIII 12, 1162a17-19. See also *Pol.* I 2, 1253a2-3; III 6, 1278b19; *et al.*

21. *Pol.* I 5-6, 1254a17-1255b15. The contrary view (3, 1253b21-22) was that the distinction between freeman and slave was made by law and not by nature. Aristotle takes this opposed view into consideration, but remains firm in his tenet that by nature some men are free and others are slaves (5, 1254a23-24; 1255a1-3).

22. *EN* I 4, 1095b8-13; VI 11, 1143b11-14. Cf. I 8, 1098b9-29. Though not a criterion of theoretical truth, common sense may in this way be regarded as an important factor in judging practical truth.

23. *EN* X 8, 1178a9. This does not locate the supreme good for Aristotle himself even secondarily in public standing, but in the virtue (I 5, 1095b26-31) on which public standing is based.

24. See *EN* I 4, 1095a20-25; 5, 1095b19-20; 12, 1101b27-31; X 2, 1172b9-18; *EE* I 2, 1214b6-9. The money-making life was one of the three types attributed traditionally to the teaching of Pythagoras – see Diogenes Laertius, VIII 8.

25. *EN* I 6, 1096a23-27; *EE* I 8, 1217b25-40; *MM* I 1, 1183a9-12. On the good as transcendental, in the sense of extending throughout all the Aristotelian categories, see Henry Veatch, "Non-Cognitivism in Ethics", *Ethics* LXXXVI (1966), 109-114. Yet in Aristotle the notion 'quality' extends outside the category designated by it. It is used of substantial differentiae (*Cat.* 5, 3b18-20; *Metaph.* Δ 14, 1020a33-b2) and of good and bad actions, especially (*Metaph. loc. cit.*, b24-25) in the case of choice. On the qualification of virtuous actions, see *EN* II 1, 1103a31-b23; 4, 1105a17-b10; IV 1, 1120a23-24.

26. *EN* I 3, 1094b19-22. "Science" is used at *MM* I 1, 1183a33-36; *Top.* VI 6, 145a15-18; *Rh.* I 4, 1359b10-18.

27. *EN* II 1, 1103b23-25. Cf. X 1, 1172a20-25.

28. *EN* I 3, 1095a3-9; 4, 1095b7-8; 7, 1098b4; II 4, 1105a26-b18. If a man's disposition is contrary to that of virtue, the moral starting points or first principles of conduct do not become manifest to him: "The first principles of action are the end to which our acts are means; but a man corrupted by a love of pleasure or fear of pain, entirely fails to discern any first principle, and cannot see that he ought to choose and do everything as a means to this end, and for its sake; for vice tends to destroy the sense of principle." *EN* VI 5, 1140b16-20; tr. Rackham. This is said in express contrast to the mathematical principles (b13-16),

which appear always the same regardless of the individual's disposition at the time.

29. *EN* I 8, 1099a13-24; II 6, 1106b36-1107a2. On the reciprocal involvement of prudence and the moral virtues, see *EN* VI 13, 1144b17-1145a6; X 8, 1178a16-19; *EE* III 7, 1234a28-30.

30. *EN* I 3, 1094b11-25; II 2, 1104a3-11. For Aristotle the highest type of scientific exactness is that of the highest type of wisdom – *EN* VI 7, 1141a16-17; *Metaph. A* 2, 982a12-b10. A discussion of the type of universality appropriate to ethics may be found in my article "The Ethical Universal in Aristotle", *Studia Moralia* (Rome), III (1965), 27-47.

31. *EN* II 5, 1106a3-4. At *EE* II 7,1223a21-23, virtue and vice are said to be *defined* by voluntary character and choice.

32. See *EN* V 10, 1137b29-32. The reason given here is that the object to be measured is itself indefinite. For the Platonic background, see Plato, *Plt.* 294B-295B.

33. *EN* II 2, 1104a4. For Plato (*Plt.* 294B), likewise, nothing in human conduct is at rest.

34. Melville J. Herskovits, *Cultural Dynamics* (New York 1964), p. 25.

35. *Ibid.*, p. 6.

36. *Ibid.*, p. 62. See also Herskovits, *Cultural Anthropology* (New York 1965), pp. 111-116.

37. *APo.* I 30, 87b19-25. Cf. *Metaph. E* 1, 1025b6-13; 2, 1027a20-21.

38. J. H. Randall, Jr., *Aristotle* (New York 1960), p. 248.

39. See *supra*, n. 31. It is hard to see how this conception of virtue as involving choice in its very notion could have been absent from Aristotle's mind when he defined virtue as a *hexis proairetikê* (*EN* II 6, 1106b36). At least the process by which moral virtue is shown to be acquired in *EN* II 1-2 seems clearly the process over which choice has control in *EN* III 5 and *EE* II 6, 1222a15-1223a20. On Aubenque's view, see *supra*, n. 1.

40. *EN* III 7, 1115b12-13; IV 1, 1120a23-24. On the seemly as qualitative, see *supra* n. 25 and *infra*, n. 42.

41. "We deliberate about things that are in our control and are attainable by action (which are in fact the only things that still remain to be considered; for Nature, Necessity, and Chance, with the addition of Intelligence and human agency generally, exhaust the generally accepted list of causes)." *EN* III 3, 1112a30-33; tr. Rackham. Intellection is aware of itself as well as of its object – *De An.* III 4, 430a2-4. On man as responsible (*aitios*) for things done through choice, see *EE* II 6, 1223a2-19.

42. *Cat.* 8, 8b25-35. The virtues accordingly fall under the first subdivision of quality. Sensible qualities, on the other hand, come under the third subdivision, *ibid.* 9a28-b27. On moral good as qualitative, see *Metaph.* Δ 14, 1020b23-25. In the Aristotelian context there is no justification for calling it a "queer" quality.

43. See *EN* II 1, 1103a31-b23; 4, 1105a17-b10.

when medicine itself has been properly comprehended, but till then it is quite impossible." *On Ancient Medicine*, XX; trans. William H. S. Jones. Cf. Jones ([25], pp. 42-43).

44. *Metaph.*, *M* 10, 1087a15-21; cf. *Z* 10, 1036a6-8; *APr.* II 21, 67b1-5.

45. See *Metaph. Z* 10, 1035b27-30; 11, 1037a5-7; cf. Δ 26, 1023b30-32. A discussion of this point and of the way the natures of things ground universality for Aristotle may be found in my article "The Grounds of Universality in Aristotle", *American Philosophical Quarterly* III (1966), 162-169. [cf. *supra*, ch. 5, pp. 48-58, Ed.]

46. *EN* V 1, 1129b5-6; Oxford tr. Cf. *EE* VIII 15, 1248b26-27. On the notion of an *ethos* as something to be prayed for, see Pindar, *Nemean Odes*, VIII, 35-36. At the same time, the necessity of using physiological means to overcome practical ignorance is insisted upon by Aristotle, *EN* VII 3, 1147b6-9. Both psychological and physiological means seem required by the nature of practical knowledge as something ingrown into one's way of living and acting. On the latter notion, see *infra*, n. 51.

47. Prudence is for Aristotle a virtue "that gives commands" (*epitaktikê*), in the sense that its goal is "what one *should* do or not do" (*EN* VI 10, 1143a8-9). Cf. *EE* II 1, 1220a9, and the Platonic background in *Phlb.* 260B-261B. But moral goodness or seemliness (*to kalon*) is something that antecedes the imperative, since for its sake the action is to be done. It is accordingly for Aristotle much more than a disguised imperative. It is prior to the imperative, and is presupposed by any imperative for a morally good action. From this viewpoint a norm is an indicative rather than imperative. It is completely open to scientific description: "No, a normative science, if it remains true to its proper nature and function, must be quite as descriptive in its way as the so-called descriptive sciences are in theirs." Henry Veatch, "Concerning the Distinction between Descriptive and Normative Sciences", *Philosophy and Phenomenological Research* VI (1945), 285. Misunderstanding may be avoided by using instead of "normative science" the Aristotelian expression "practical science", which, as Veatch (p. 284) notes, is "the more traditional and in many ways the more felicitous term".

48. See *supra*, n. 1. The import of the Aristotelian notion of choice never seems to have entered into the Western tradition of moral philosophy. Aubenque, *La Prudence chez Aristote*, p. 127, observes that *proairesis* in the sense of choice was destined to remain "sans lendemain" in the history of philosophy, and Miss Anscombe, in Bambrough's *New Essays*, p. 150, wonders about the unfulfilled possibility it left open for a term "proheretic".

49. See references *supra*, n. 24. For *proairesis*, see *EE* I 2, 1214b7; *Metaph.* Γ 2, 1004b25.

50. Aristotle shows no concern with the ultimate historical origin of the practical order. The modern approach tends to ask which came first, the culture that makes possible the grasping of the moral principles, or the moral activity that makes possible the culture. In the Aristotelian framework the answer seems to be that there is no first. Art and philosophy are regarded (*Metaph.* Λ 8, 1074b10-14) as repeatedly perishing and being rediscovered, as though this were an instance of the eternal series of generations demonstrated in *Ph.* VIII 1-6.

51. Plato's "practical" knowledge had to be inherent (*symphyton* - *Plt.* 258E) in the actions. The term seems echoed in Aristotle's use of *symphyênai* at *EN* VII 3, 1147a22. With this one might also compare *EN* X 8, 1178a14-16, where moral

virtue is said to be "bound up" (Oxford tr.) with the passions.

52. Aubenque, p. 142, reduces the failure to the contingence found in the real world by Aristotle. But this view does not seem to respect the radical Aristotelian distinction between the starting points of physical things and the starting points of things done. Rather, the contingence lies in choice as the origin of conduct, and is not reducible to nature. In contrast to Aristotle, the Cartesian preoccupation is to reduce human knowledge to a single philosophical science, with one common root. In the Aristotelian framework no such reduction is possible.

Notes to Chapter 14

1. See *Metaph.*, E 1, 1025b18-24; K 7, 1064a10-18; α 1, 993b19-21; EE I 1, 1214a1-14.

2. Further discussion of this type of universality may be found in my article "The Ethical Universal in Aristotle," *Studia Moralia*, III (1965), 27-47. Cf. D. J. Allan, "Aristotle's Account of the Origin of Moral Principles," *Proceedings of the XIth International Congress of Philosophy* (Amsterdam & Louvain, 1953), XII, 120-127; and "The Practical Syllogism," in *Autour d'Aristote*, Recueil d'études offert à A. Mansion (Louvain, 1955), 325-340.

3. On this topic see Melville J. Herskovits, *Cultural Dynamics* (New York, 1964), esp. pp. 4-7; *Cultural Anthropology* (New York, 1965), esp. pp. 111-116.

4. On structuralism, see the double issues devoted to the topic by the *Revue Internationale de Philosophie*, XIX (1965), nos. 3-4, and *Yale French Studies*, XXXVI-XXXVII (1966).

Notes to Chapter 15

1. Later in the period of the Greek commentators the anonymous scholiast, in *Commentaria in Aristotelem graeca*, XX ([19], p. 422.9-24) likened the case to a physiological explanation of a drunken grammarian's inability to do his professional work, since rising vapors caused by his condition cloud his mind. Only when the vapors are dispersed is he able to pursue his science. On the scanty information about dates and capacities of this scholiast, see H. Paul and F. Mercken [27].

In the middle ages Aquinas [3] was content to observe that the body is changed (*transmutatur*) by passions such as lust or anger. This physical transformation has to go if there is to be a return to a sound mentality. Other than that, Aquinas just noted that the explanation does not belong to ethics but has to be learned from the physiologists, that is, from those engaged in the study of nature.

In modern times, C. L. Michelet [28] reproduced the Greek scholiast's short commentary to serve as explanation. Sir Alexander Grant [24] referred to Sextus Empiricus ([42], VII, 129-130) for the Heraclitean notion of sleep, translating *agnoia* not as 'ignorance' but as 'oblivion.' John Alexander Stewart, in his invaluable *Notes on the Nicomachean Ethics* [34], mentioned Grant's reference to Sextus, recalled the account of sleep and waking in *De Somno et Vigilia* (see infra, n. 15), and suggested that the Greek scholiast's statements on drunkenness imply a recollection of that Aristotelian passage. John Burnet [6] noted that the problem is being dismissed by Aristotle from ethical treatment, but that 'to us, of course, it is just the fundamental question.' Burnet referred to *De Somno et Vigilio* for the explanation, and to the case of drunkenness in the pseudo-Aristotelian *Problemata* (III 13, 873a1), and to Aristotle's understanding of pleasure. Harold H. Joachim [22] interpreted the *agnoia* not as 'absence of knowledge,' since that could not be morally condemned, but as 'error.' Jules Tricot in his translation [35] refers to *De Somno et Vigilio* just for 'indications' of an explanation. William F. R. Hardie [18] mentions it in similar fashion. Olof Gigon [15] sees intent to distinguish ethical treatment from physiological research through reference to the special literature on drunkenness and sleep. René Antoine Gauthier and Jean Yves Jolif [14] likewise regard the passage as 'une fin de non recevoir: la question posée relève d'une discipline qui n'est pas la nôtre,' but they refer only to the Greek scholiast's account, which they regard as probably taken from the Aristotelian explanation of sleep.

On the other hand Franz Dirlmeier [10] maintains that Aristotle certainly does not cite *De Somno et Vigilia*, and that he is hardly thinking of Heraclitus but rather of researchers like Diogenes of Appolonia. Muirhead (1900), Marshal (1909), Weldon (1930), Plebe (1957), Warrington (1963), Günther Bien (1972) and others give no special attention to the passage.

A survey of the commentators, accordingly, does not yield any firm information on the physiological processes by which the weak-willed person is restored for Aristotle to moral integrity. Regarding the transmitted text itself, however, there is no special difficulty. It has no variants important enough to demand attention. On the question about the authenticity of the chapter in which it occurs, see Walsh [36]. The passage may be accepted today without hesitation as authentic. But the notion 'physiologist' has to be taken in a much wider sense than in its current use. It had a different background (infra, n. 5). A number of English translations merely retain the Greek term. Aquinas (supra) used the term but offered an explanation that would be immediately apparent to his readers, namely, a person versed in the Aristotelian study of nature. Similarly William Wilkinson [37] gave the Latin translation 'qui de natura rerum disputant.' The notion would include what today comes under the competence of the psychologist. The 'physiologist,' remarks the Greek scholiast ([19], p. 422.13-14) in regard to the present passage, has expert knowledge about what part of the *soul* and which of its faculties are being affected.

2. In this way it exercises the highest authority and functions as 'the most architectonic' discipline (*Ethica Nicomachea*, I 2, 1094a26-27). In the middle ages Abelard [1] could apply to the others the metaphor of 'waiting-women' in relation to ethics, a metaphor taken from the Judeo-Christian tradition from Philo on to describe the relation of all the others to Scriptural knowledge.

3. On the exercise of verbal therapy in ancient Greece, see Pedro Laín Entralgo

[17]. Actually, Laín Entralgo (pp. 241-242) acknowledges this type of therapy 'never came to have real existence' in the Hippocratic tradition, the kind of medicine that Aristotle would regard as 'scientific.'

4. Συμφυῆναι (*Ethica Nicomachea*, VII 3, 1147a22). Cf. Plato (*Statesman*, 258DE), where the knowledge of carpentry and crafts in general is regarded as 'inborn' (σύμφυτον), as though existent in the craftman's activities, in contrast to theoretical sciences like arithmetic, which are not embedded in activities of that kind. Werner Jaeger [21] remarks: "Aristotle would not recognize as valid our modern objection that it (ethics) is indeed a science, but only insofar as it is theory." Aristotle means it to be a science insofar as it is practical. It is the sovereign science 'that employs all the others as its tools' (p. 55).

5. See Laín Entralgo ([11], pp. 139-148. Cf. pp. 39-42). The natural philosophy of the Presocratics ranged globally through areas that today are assigned to psychology as well as to the various natural and life sciences.

6. In this regard Laín Entralgo ([11], p. 148) quotes the Hippocratic work *On Places in Man*, ed. Littré VI, 278: 'The *physis* of the body is the principle (*archê*) of the *logos* in medicine.' The *archê*, in a context like this, meant the starting point from which the entire scientific treatment (*logos*) proceeded.

7. "I also hold that clear knowledge about natural science can be acquired from medicine and from no other source, and that one can attain this knowledge when medicine itself has been properly comprehended, but till then it is quite impossible." *On Ancient Medicine*, XX; trans. William H. S. Jones. Cf. Jones ([25], pp. 42-43).

8. On the etymology, which allows both meanings, see Hjalmar Frisk [12]. There are a number of penetrating studies on the history and development of the notion, e.g., Lovejoy [26] and Holwerda [20].

9. Aristotle (*Physica*, II 1, 192b8-193b21). Cf. I 7, 190b29-191a12; *Met.* Δ 4, 1014b16-1015a19.

10. See "form, in virtue of which individuality is directly attributed" (*De Anima*, II 1, 412a8-9; trans, W. S. Hett). Cf. *Metaphysica*, Z 3, 1029a28-30. On the natural teleology implicit in the Aristotelian vital form, see the 'Prologue aristotélicien' in Gilson [16].

11. The notion of soul as a physical part of the whole man is peculiarly Aristotelian, and is something that Western tradition has found very difficult to grasp. The dominant conception has been either dualistic, reaching its extreme in Descartes and satirized by Ryle as the ghost in the machine, or Neoplatonic, in which body in general was regarded as being in soul [30].

12. In this regard the Aristotelian contrast of soul and body as agents becomes much more clearly articulated in Aquinas, who had to think deeply against the Christian background of flesh warring against spirit. A discussion on the topic may be found in my article [29].

13. This point is tellingly made by Alberto Galli [13].

14. For Aristotle, choice (*proairesis*) is the source of first principle (*archê* – cf. supra, n. 6) of practical science (*Metaphysica*, E 1, 1025a22-24) and of moral con-

duct itself (*Ethica Nicomachea*, VI 2, 1139a31). Against this Aristotelian background Aquinas [2] is able to regard moral philosophy as dealing with an order set up by human reason in voluntary actions.

15. The Latin title, used in the Oxford translation, is *De Somno et Vigilia*. It is often referred to today as *De Somno*. It is commonly accepted as genuine, and there is no serious reason to doubt its authenticity. The reasons in its favor are solid, and the only modern rejection of it along with the other *Parva Naturalia* is based on Zürcher's unacceptable chronology of the Aristotelian writings. On the topic see Paul Siwek [33].

16. For the historical background of the *sensus communis* in this Aristotelian meaning of the phrase, see John Isaac Beare [4].

17. The Pseudo-Aristotelian *Problemata*, XXVII, 1-7, 947b12-950a16, discusses the physiological accompaniments of fear, courage, temperance, intemperance, self-restraint and its lack, but not the therapeutic manipulation of them to restore moral equilibrium. W. H. S. Jones ([23], I xiii-xix) notes the tendency of the Hippocratic writers to describe the course of the symptoms rather than to mention the cures applied. One does not find the precise physiological account desired here.

18. For a discussion of the way professional medical conduct was maintained in ancient Greek times, see Jones ([24], pp. 32-37).

19. See Randall [31].

The concluding paragraphs of this paper have been somewhat revised in the interests of focus upon points brought out in the commentary and in the subsequent discussion from the floor. I appreciate Professor Spicker's remarks and concerns, am in substantial agreement with them, and regard them as furnishing a valued complement to the points dealt with in my paper. The differences seem to be only in the nuancing. For instance, Professor Spicker draws attention to the 'tacit premise' that 'the end of medicine is not only health but the improvement of individual moral conduct' (p. 148). This is implicitly Aristotelian, as long as the 'not only . . . but' is correctly understood to mean for Aristotle that the form of a material thing contains its own orientation to something more ultimate. Like 'honor and pleasure and intelligence and every excellence' (*Ethica Nicomachea* I 7, 1097b2), health is sought for its own sake *and* for happiness. There is no question here of two things that 'are added up together' (b 17). In any non-ultimate end such as 'health' (*Metaphysica*, α 2, 994a9) the ultimate end is always being sought, according to the characteristic Aristotelian teleology (a8-10; b9-16). Medicine thereby concentrates on health only, but in so doing and *without added* orientation has as its purpose human happiness. No 'additional obligation' (p. 148) is thereby imposed. To say that medicine's 'ultimate purpose . . . cannot be anything other than the *health* of the patient' is true for Aristotle only with the understanding that health itself is meant by its very nature for happiness.

The physician's task, then, is to bring about the health of the patient. With that health, the patient works out his own happiness. It is hard to see how any 'paternalism' is involved, either on the part of ethics or on the part of medicine. The sovereign authority of ethics over the practice of medicine is in the Aristotelian view no more paternalistic than the right of expropriation in regard to the private property owner. In either case the sovereign authority bears on full-fledged citizens, not on minors, and is exercised only for the common good, not for lesser interests. On the other hand the power of medical intervention to affect moral judgment (p. 150) does not justify medical *hubris* or usurpation of moral sovereignty any more than does the medical power to damage or destroy life physically by means of poisons. In neither case is 'paternalistic' authority exercised over minors, but wrongly assumed moral sovereignty over human life. The right of each patient to do his own thinking and work out his own happiness has to be safeguarded. The physician contributes towards this by promoting health. Could a man who had been rendered physically or psychically incapable of thinking for himself in face of governmental programming and engineering to be considered by any stretch a healthy person? For Aristotle the proper function of a man is to lead a self-sufficient life in which the man's intelligence is dominant (*Ethica Nicomachea*, 17, 1098a1-17; X 7, 1177a12-1178a8). At least in the Aristotelian setting a bodily condition in which this function is rendered impossible can hardly be considered human health, the goal of the physician's art.

Bibliography of Joseph Owens C.Ss.R., M.S.D.

1946

1. "An Aristotelian Text Related to the Distinction of Being and Essence," *Proceedings of the American Catholic Philosophical Association*, 21 (1946), 165-172.

1948

2. "Up to What Point is God Included in the Metaphysics of Duns Scotus," *Mediaeval Studies*, 10 (1948), 163-177.

1949

3. "Report of a Recent Thesis Defended at the Pontifical Institute of Mediaeval Studies," *Mediaeval Studies*, 11 (1949), 239-245.

1950

4. "The Reality of the Aristotelian Separate Movers," *The Review of Metaphysics*, 3 (1950), 319-337. Reprinted in *Readings in Ancient and Medieval Philosophy*, ed. James Collins (Westminster: Newman Press,1960). 75-81.

1951

5. *The Doctrine of Being in the Aristotelian Metaphysics* (Toronto: Pontifical Institute of Mediaeval Studies,1951), xi-461 pp. with Introduction by Etienne Gilson.
6. "Theodicy, Natural Theology, and Metaphysics," *The Modern Schoolman*, 28 (1951), 126-137.

1952

7. "Comments on Mr. Anderson's Theses," *The Review of Metaphysics*, 5 (1952), 467-469.
8. "The Conclusion of the *Prima Via*," *The Modern Schoolman*, 30 (1952/53), 33-53; 109-121; 203-215. Reprinted in *St. Thomas Aquinas on the Existence of God*: Collected Papers of Joseph Owens, ed. John R. Catan (Albany: State University of New York Press, 1980), 142-168.

1954

9. "A Note on the Approach to Thomistic Metaphysics," *The New Scholasticism*, 28 (1954), 454-476.
10. "The Special Characteristics of the Scotistic Proof that God Exists," *Analecta Gregoriana*, 67 (1954), 311-327.

1955

11. "The Causal Proposition - Principle or Conclusion?," *The Modern Schoolman*, 32 (1955), 159-171, 257-270; 323-339.
12. "The Intelligibility of Being," *Gregorianum*, 36 (1955), 169-193.
13. "Our Knowledge of Nature," *Proceedings of the American Catholic Philosophical Association*, 29 (1955), 36-86.

1957

14. *St. Thomas and the Future of Metaphysics* (Milwaukee: Marquette University Press, 1957), 97 pp., The Aquinas Lecture, 1957. 2nd printing 1973.
15. "Common Nature: A Point of Comparison between Thomistic and Scotistic Metaphysics," *Mediaeval Studies*, 19 (1957), 1-14.
16. "The Number of Terms in the Suarezian Discussion of Essence and Being," *The Modern Schoolman*, 34 (1957), 141-191.
17. Review: Joseph Endres, *Der Mensch als Mitte* (Bonn, 1956), *The Modern Schoolman*, 34 (1957), 144-146.

1958

18. "The Accidental and Essential Character of Being in the Doctrine of St. Thomas Aquinas," *Mediaeval Studies*, 20 (1958), 1-40. Reprinted in *St. Thomas Aquinas on the Existence of God*: Collected Papers of Joseph Owens, ed. John R. Catan (Albany: State University of New York Press, 1980), 52-96.

1959

19. *A History of Ancient Western Philosophy* (New York, Appleton-Century-Crofts, 1959. Reprinted Prentice Hall Publishing Company, 1959), xv-434 pp.
20. "The Interpretation of the Heraclitean Fragments," *An Etienne Gilson Tribute*, ed. C. J. O'Neill (Milwaukee: Marquette University Press, 1959), 148-168.
21. "Thomistic Common Nature and Platonic Idea," *Mediaeval Studies*, 21 (1959), 211-223. Reprinted in *Bobbs-Merrill Reprints in Philosophy* (1969), Phil. 152.

1960

22. "Aristotle on Categories," *The Review of Metaphysics*, 14 (1960), 73-90. Reprinted in *Aristotle*: The Collected Papers of Joseph Owens, ed. John R. Catan (Albany: State University of New York Press, 1981), 14-22.

23. "Diversity and Community of Being in St. Thomas Aquinas," *Mediaeval Studies*, 22 (1960), 257-302. Reprinted in *St. Thomas Aquinas on the Existence of God*: Collected Papers of Joseph Owens, ed. John R. Catan (Albany: State University of New York Press, 1980), 97-131.

24. Review: William F. Lynch, *An Approach to the Metaphysics of Plato through the Parmenides* (Washington, D.C., 1959), *The New Scholasticism*, 34 (1960), 134-136.

25. Review: John Hermann Randall, *Aristotle* (New York, 1960), *The New Scholasticism*, 34 (1960), 520-523.

1961

26. "St.Thomas and Elucidation," *The New Scholasticism*, 35 (1961), 421-444.

27. "Unity and Essence in St. Thomas Aquinas," *Mediaeval Studies*, 23 (1961), 240-259.

1962

28. "Analogy as a Thomistic Approach to Being," *Mediaeval Studies*, 24 (1962), 302-322. Reprinted in *Bobbs-Merrill Reprints in Philosophy* (1969), Phil. 151.

29. "Aquinas on Infinite Regress," *Mind*, N.S., 71 (1962), 244-246. Reprinted in *St. Thomas Aquinas on the Existence of God*: Collected Papers of Joseph Owens, ed. John R. Catan (Albany: State University of New York Press, 1980), 228-230.

1963

30. *An Elementary Christian Metaphysics* (Milwaukee: Bruce Publishing Company, 1963), xiv-384 pp.

31. *The Doctrine of Being in the Aristotelian Metaphysics* (Toronto: Pontifical Institute of Mediaeval Studies, 1963, 2nd ed. rev.).

32. "An Aquinas Commentary in English," *The Review of Metaphysics*, 16 (1963), 503-512.

33. "Elucidation and Causal Knowledge," *The New Scholasticism*, 37 (1963), 64-70.

34. "Concept and Thing in St. Thomas," *The New Scholasticism*, 37 (1963), 220-224.

35. "Existential Act, Divine Being, and the Subject of Metaphysics," *The New Scholasticism*, 37 (1963), 359-363.

36. "Comment on Czeslaw Lewjewski: The Concept of Matter in Pre-Socratic Philosophy," *The Concept of Matter*, ed. Ernan McMullin (Notre Dame, Indiana: Notre Dame University Press, 1963), 57-58.

37. "Matter and Predication in Aristotle," *The Concept of Matter*, ed. Ernan McMullin (Notre Dame, Indiana: Notre Dame University Press, 1963), 79-93, pb ed.; hd ed. 99-115. Reprinted in *Aristotle*: The Collected Papers of Joseph Owens, ed. John R. Catan (Albany: State University of New York Press, 1981), 35-481.

38. "St. Thomas and Modern Science," *The Transactions of the Royal Society of Canada*, Fourth Series, 1 (1963), 283-293.

39. "The Unity in a Thomistic Philosophy of Man," *Mediaeval Studies*, 25 (1963), 54-82.

40. Review: Pierre Aubenque, *Le Problème de l'Être chez Aristote* (Paris, 1962), *Gnomon*, 35 (1963), 459-462.

41. Review: Thomas C. O'Brien, *Metaphysics and the Existence of God* (Washington, D.C., 1960), *The New Scholasticism*, 36 (1963), 244-246.

1964

42. "The Analytics and Thomistic Metaphysical Procedure," *Mediaeval Studies*, 26 (1964), 83-108.

43. "The Aristotelian Conception of the Sciences," *International Philosophical Quarterly*, 4 (1964), 200-216. Reprinted in *Aristotle*: The Collected Papers of Joseph Owens, ed. John R. Catan (Albany: State University of New York Press, 1981) 23-341.

44. "The Causal Proposition - Principle or Conclusion," *Readings in Metaphysics*, ed. Jean Rosenberg (Westminster, Newman Press, 1964), 188-189.

45. "Interrogation of Paul Weiss," *Philosophical Interrogations*, ed. Sydney and Beatrice Rome (New York, 1964), 266, 287, 288, 301, 302, 311.

46. "The Limitation of Being by Essence," *Readings in Metaphysics*, ed. Jean Rosenberg (Westminster: Newman Press, 1964), 276-278.

47. Review: Giovanni Reale, *Il concetto di filosofia prima e l'unità della Metafisica di Aristotele* (Milano, 1961), *The New Scholasticism*, 38 (1964), 254-256.

1965

48. "The Ethical Universal in Aristotle," *Studia Moralia*, 3 (Rome, 1965), 27-47.

49. "Quiddity and the Real Distinction in St. Thomas Aquinas," *Mediaeval Studies*, 27 (1965), 1-22.

50. "The Real Distinction of a Relation from its Immediate Basis," *Proceedings of the American Catholic Philosophical Association*, 39 (1965), 134-140.

51. Review: Ebehard Jungel, *Zum Ursprung der Analogie bei Parmenides und Heraklit* (Berlin, 1964), *The Modern Schoolman*, 43 (1965), 78-80.

52. Review: Whitney J. Oates, *Aristotle and the Problem of Value* (Princeton, 1963), *The New Scholasticism*, 39 (1965), 376-379.

53. Review: Frederick J. Roensch, *The Early Thomistic School* (Dubuque, 1964), *The International Philosophical Quarterly*, 6 (1965), 144-145.
54. Review: Friedrich Solmsen, *Aristotle's System of the Physical World* (Cornell, 1960), *The New Scholasticism*, 39 (1965), 545-547.
55. "Abstracts," *The Monist*, 49 (1965), 670.

1966

56. "Aquinas and the Proof from the 'Physics'," *Mediaeval Studies*, 28 (1966), 119-150.
57. "The Dissolution of an Electicism," *Pacific Philosophy Forum*, 5 (1966), 80-84.
58. "The Grounds of Universality in Aristotle," *The American Philosophical Quarterly*, 3 (1966), 162-169. Reprinted in *Aristotle*: The Collected Papers of Joseph Owens, ed. John R. Catan (Albany: State University of New York Press, 1981), 48-58.
59. "Presidential Address: Scholasticism - Then and Now," *Proceedings of the American Catholic Philosophical Association*, 40 (1966), 1-12.
60. "Abstracts," *The Monist*, 50 (1966), 304.

1967

61. "Actuality in the 'Prima Via' of St. Thomas Aquinas," *Mediaeval Studies*, 29 (1967), 26-64. Reprinted in *St. Thomas Aquinas on the Existence of God*: Collected Papers of Joseph Owens, ed. John R. Catan (Albany: State University of New York Press, 1980), 192-207.
62. "Aristotle," *The New Catholic Encyclopedia*, 1 (New York, 1967), 809a-814.
63. "The Causal Proposition Revisited," *The Modern Schoolman*, 44 (1967), 143-151.
64. "Christian Philosophy and Contemporary Man," *The Ecumenist*, 5 (1967), 19-22.
65. "Greek Philosophy," *The New Catholic Encyclopedia*, 6 (New York, 1967), 732a-736a.
66. "Heraclitus," *The New Catholic Encyclopedia*, 6 (New York, 1967), 1046a-1047a.
67. "Parmenides," *The New Catholic Encyclopedia*, 10 (New York, 1967), 1027.
68. "The Range of Existence," *Proceedings of the Seventh Inter-American Congress of Philosophy*, 1 (Québec, 1967), 44-59.
69. "Recent Footnotes to Plato," *The Review of Metaphysics*, 20 (1967), 648-666.
70. "This Truth Sublime," *Speaking of God*, ed. Denis Dirscherl (Milwaukee, 1967), 128-156.
71. "The Starting Point of the *Prima Via*," *Franciscan Studies*, 5 (1967), 249-284. Reprinted in *St. Thomas on the Existence of God*: Collected Papers of Joseph Owens, ed. John R. Catan (Albany: State University of New York Press, 1980), 169-191.

72. Review: Felix Cleve, *The Giants of Pre-Sophistic Greek Philosophy* (The Hague,. 1965), *The New Scholasticism*, 41 (1967), 132-135.

1968

73. *An Interpretation of Existence* (Milwaukee: The Bruce Publishing Company, 1968), 153 pp.

74. *The Wisdom and Ideas of Saint Thomas Aquinas*, ed. Eugene Freeman and Joseph Owens (Fawcett World Library, Premier Books, New York, 1968), 160 pp.

75. "Nature and Ethical Norm in Aristotle," *Akten 14th International Congress of Philosophy* (Vienna, 2nd-9th Sept., 1968), 442-447. Reprinted in *Aristotle*: The Collected Papers of Joseph Owens, ed. John R. Catan (Albany: State University of New York Press, 1981), 65-68.

76. "Immobility and Existence for Aquinas," *Mediaeval Studies*, 30 (1968), 22-46.

77. "The Study of Knowledge - Natural Philosophy or Metaphysics?," *The New Scholasticism*, 42 (1968), 103-106.

78. "The Teleology of Nature in Aristotle," *The Monist*, 52 (1968), 159-173. Reprinted in *Aristotle*: The Collected Papers of Joseph Owens, ed. John R. Catan (Albany: State University of New York Press, 1981), 136-147.

79. "The Universal in *Physics* I,1," *Mélanges â la mèmoire de Charles de Konick*, ed. Lucien Zérounian (Québec: Les Presses de l'Université Laval,1968), 301-315.

80. Review: *The Cambridge History of Later Greek Philosophy and Early Medieval Philosophy*, ed. A. H. Armstrong (Cambridge, 1967), *Phoenix*, 22 (1968), 177-180.

1969

81. "Aquinas - Existential Permanence and Flux," *Mediaeval Studies*, 31 (1969), 71-92.

82. "The Aristotelian Argument for the Material Principle of Bodies," *Naturphilosophie bei Aristoteles und Theophrast*, ed. I. Düring (Heidelberg, 1969), 193-209. Reprinted in *Aristotle*: The Collected Papers of Joseph Owens, ed. John R. Catan (Albany: State University of New York Press, 1981), 122-13.

83. "The Grounds of Ethical Universality in Aristotle," *Man and World*, 2 (1969), 171-193. Reprinted in *Aristotle*: The Collected Papers of Joseph Owens, ed. John R. Catan (Albany: State University of New York Press, 1981), 148-164.

84. Review: G.E.R. Lloyd, *Aristotle: The Growth and Structure of His Thought* (Cambridge University Press, 1968), *The International Journal of Philosophy*, 9 (1969), 299-300.

1970

85. "Judgment and Truth in Aquinas," *Mediaeval Studies*, 33 (1970), 138-158. Reprinted in *St. Thomas Aquinas on the Existence of God*: Collected Papers of Joseph

Owens, ed. John R. Catan (Albany: State University of New York Press, 1980), 34-51.

86. "The Notion of Catholic Philosophy," *Antigonish Review*, 1 (1970), 112-140.

87. "Scholasticism and Metaphysics," *The Future of Metaphysics*, ed.Robert E. Wood (Chicago, 1970), 14-31.

1971

88. Reprint of *supra*, no.79 under the title, "The Universality of the Sensible in the Aristotelian Noetic," *Essays in Ancient Greek Philosophy*, ed. John P.Anton and George L. Kustas (Albany: State University of New York Press, 1971), 462-477. Reprinted in *Aristotle*: The Collected Papers of Joseph Owens, ed. John R. Catan (Albany: State University of New York Press, 1981), 59-73.

89. "God in Philosophy Today," *God,Man and Philosophy*, ed. Carl W.Grindel, (New York:St.John's University Press,1971), 39-51.

90. "Aristotle's Definition of the Soul," *Philomathes*, ed.Robert B.Palmer and Robert Hamerton-Kelly (The Hague:Martinus Nijhoff,1971), 125-145. Reprinted in *Aristotle*:The Collected Papers of Joseph Owens, ed. John R. Catan (Albany:State University of New York Press,1981), 109-121.

91. " 'Cause of Necessity'in Aquinas' *Tertia Via*," *Mediaeval Studies*,33(1971), 21-45.

92. Review: W. Charleton, *Aristotle's Physics Books I and II* (Oxford: Clarendon Press, 1970), *Phoenix*, 25 (1971), 279-282.

1972

93. "Ignorare and Existence," *The New Scholasticism*, 46 (1972), 210-219.

94. "Metaphysical Separation in Aquinas," *Mediaeval Studies*, 34 (1972), 287-306.

95. "Reality and Metaphysics," *The Review of Metaphysics*, 25 (1972), 638-658. The Presidential Address of the Metaphysical Society of America.

96. "A Non-Expendable Heritage," *Proceedings of the American Catholic Philosophical Association*, 46 (1972), 212-218. Medalist Address.

97. "Preface" to Leo Sweeney, *Infinity in the Pre-Socratics* (The Hague: Martinus Nijhoff, 1972), xvii-xix.

98. "Abstract" (*An Interpretation of Existence, supra*. no. 73), *The Monist*, 56 (1972), 144-145.

1973

99. "Aristote - Maitre de ceux qui savant," *La philosophie et les philosophes* (Montreal: Editio Bellarmin, 1973), 45-68. English version entitled "Aristotle--Teacher of Those Who Know," in *Aristotle*: The Collected Papers of Joseph Owens, ed. John R. Catan (Albany: State University of New York Press, 1981), 1-13.

100. "The Content of Existence," *Logic and Ontology*, ed. Milton Munitz (New York: New York University Press, 1973), 21-35.

101. Review: Victor Coutant, *Theophrastus, De Igne* (New York: Humanities Press, 1971), *Classical World*, 66 (1973), 468-469.

1974

102. "Realism," *The New Encyclopedia Britannica*, 15th ed. (Chicago: Encyclopedia Britannica Inc., 15, 1974), s.v. 539-543.

103. "Aquinas as Aristotelian Commentator," *Thomas Aquinas 1274-1974*: Commemorative Studies, ed. Armand Maurer (Toronto: Pontifical Institute of Mediaeval Studies, 1974). 213-238. Reprinted in *St. Thomas Aquinas on the Existence of God*: The Collected Papers of Joseph Owens, ed. John R. Catan (Albany: State University of New York Press, 1980), 1-19.

104. "Aquinas and the Five Ways," *The Monist*, 58 (1974), 16-35. Reprinted in *St. Thomas Aquinas on the Existence of God*: The Collected Papers of Joseph Owens, ed. John R. Catan (Albany: State University of New York Press, 1980), 132-141.

105. "Soul as Agent in Aquinas," *The New Scholasticism*, 48 (1974), 40-72.

106. "The Physical World of Parmenides," *Essays in Honor of Anton Charles Pegis*, ed. J. R. O'Donnell (Toronto: Pontifical Institute of Mediaeval Studies, 1974), 368-385.

107. "The Primacy of the External in Thomistic Noetics," *Église et Théologie*, 5 (1974), 189-205.

108. "Aquinas on Cognition as Existence," *Proceedings of the American Catholic Philosophical Association*, 48 (1974), 74-85.

1975

109. "Naming in Parmenides," *Kephalaion.Studies . . . offered to C. J. De Vogel*, ed. J. Mansfield and L. M. De Rijk (Assen: Van Gorcum, 1975), 16-25.

110. "Maritain's Three Concepts of Existence," *The New Scholasticism*, 49 (1975), 259-309.

111. Review: Anton-Hermann Chroust, *Aristotle*, 2 vols. (Notre Dame, Indiana: Notre Dame University Press, 1973), *The New Scholasticism*, 49 (1975), 244-246.

1976

112. "A Note on Aristotle: *De Anima* 3.4.429b9," *Phoenix*, 30 (1976), 107-118. Reprinted in *Aristotle*: The Collected Papers of Joseph Owens, ed. John R. Catan (Albany: State University of New York Press, 1981), 99-108.

113. "Aristotle: Cognition a Way of Being," *Canadian Journal of Philosophy*, 6 (1976), 1-11. Reprinted in *Aristotle*: The Collected Papers of Joseph Owens, ed. John R. Catan (Albany: State University of New York Press, 1981), 74-80.

114. "Aquinas - 'Darkness of Ignorance' in the Most Refined Knowledge of

God," *Bonaventure and Aquinas*, ed. R. W. Shahan and Francis J. Kovach (Norman: University of Oklahoma Press, 1976), 69-86.

115. "Aquinas on Knowing Existence," *The Review of Metaphysics*, 29 (1976), 670-690. Reprinted in St. *Thomas Aquinas on the Existence of God*: The Collected Papers of Joseph Owens, ed. John R. Catan (Albany: State University of New York Press, 1980), 20-33.

116. "Aristotle on Empedocles Fr. 8," *The Canadian Journal of Philosophy*, Supplementary Volume, II (1976), 87-100.

117. Review: *San Tommaso e il pensiero moderno*, ed.Pontificia Accademia di S. Tommaso d'Aquino (Roma: Citta Nuova Editrice, 1974), *The Thomist*, 40 (1976), 153-160.

118. Review: Paul Moraux, *Die Aristotelismus bei den Griechen, Classical World*, April-May (1976), 489-491.

119. Review: Franz Brentano, *On the Several Senses of Being*, trans. Rolf George (University of California Press, 1975), *The Review of Metaphysics*, 30 (1976), 122-123.

1977

120. "Aristotelian Ethics, Medicine, and the Changing Nature of Man," *Philosophical Medical Ethics*: Its Nature and Signficance, ed. S. F. Spicker and H. T. Engelhardt, Jr. (Dordrecht: D. Reidel, 1977), 127-142. Reprinted in *Aristotle*: The Collected Papers of Joseph Owens, ed. John R. Catan (Albany: State University of New York Press, 1981), 169-180.

121. "La forma aristotelica come causa del ser," *Revista de Filosofia*, 10 (México, 1977), 267-287.

122. "Jacques Maritain - Toronto Recollections," *Notes et Documents* (Institut International 'J. Maritain'), 7 (1977), 12-15.

123. "Critical Notice" on John Cooper, *Reason and Human Good in Aristotle*, *The Canadian Journal of Philosophy*, 7 (1977), 623-636.

124. Review: B. Mondin, *St. Thomas Aquinas' Philosophy in the Commentary to the Sentences* (The Hague: Martinus Nijhoff, 1975), *The Review of Metaphysics*, 30 (1977), 532-533.

125. Review: Walter Leszl, *Aristotle's Concept of Ontology, Journal of the History of Philosophy*, 15 (1977), 331-334.

126. Review: Julia Annas, *Aristotle's Metaphysics*: Books M and N, *The Review of Metaphysics*, 31 (1977), 310-311.

1978

127. *The Doctrine of Being in the Aristotelian Metaphysics*, 3rd ed. rev. (Toronto: Pontifical Institute of Mediaeval Studies, 1978), xxx-539 pp.

128. "Philosophy's Role in Thanatology," *Philosophical Aspects of Thanatology*, ed. Florence M. Hetzler and Austin H. Kutscher (New York: Arno Press, 1978), 163-170.

129. "Being in Early Western Tradition," *The Question of Being*, ed. Mervyn Sprung (University Park and London: Pennsylvania State Press, 1978), 17-30.
130. "Aristotle on God," *The Question of Being*, ed. Mervyn Sprung (University Park and London: Pennsylvania State Press, 1978), 415-442.
131. "Aristotle - Motion as Actuality of the Imperfect," *Paideia*, Special Aristotle Issue (1978), 120-132.
132. Review: Enrico Berti, *Aristotele*: Dalla dialettica alla filosofica prima, *The Review of Metaphysics*, 31 (1978), 471-472.
133. Review: Walter M. Neidl, *Thearchia*, *The International Journal of Philosophy*, 9 (1978), 124-125.
134. Review: H. Weidemann, *Metaphysik und Sprache*, *The Review of Metaphysics*, 32 (1978), 373-374.
135. Review: Harry A. Wolfson, *Studies in the History of Philosophy and Religion*, Volume II, ed. Isadore Twersky and George H. Williams (Harvard University Press, 1977), *International Journal for Philosophy of Religion*, 9 (1978), 260-261.

1979

136. "Value and Person in Aquinas," *Atti del Congresso Internazionale Tommaso d'Aquino nel suo VII centenario* (Naples, 1979), 56-62.
137. "The Relation of God to World in the *Metaphysics*," *Études sur la Métaphysique d'Aristote*. Actes du VI Symposium aristotelicum, 1978, Cerisy-la-Salle (Normandie), (Paris: J. Vrin, 1979), 207-228.
138. *The Philosophical Tradition of St. Michael's College, Toronto* (Toronto: University of St. Michael's College Archives, 1979), 40 pp.
139. "Existence as Predicated," *The New Scholasticism*, 53 (1979), 480-485.
140. "Knowledge and Katabasis in Parmenides," *The Monist*, 62 (1979), 15-29.
141. Review: *Images of Man in Ancient and Medieval Thought*. Studio Gerardo Verbeke ab amicis et collegis dicata. ed. F. Bossier, et al. *Archiv für Geschichte der Philosophie*, 61 Band (1979), Heft, I, pp. 112-115.
142. Review: Werner Marx, *Introduction to Aristotle's Theory of Being as Being*, trans. Robert S. Schine (The Hague: Martinus Nijhoff, 1977), *Classical World*, 73 (1979), 190.
143. Review: Karl Brinkmann, *Aristoteles; allgemeine und spezielle Metaphysik* (Berlin: Walter De Gruyter, 1979, Peripatoi, BD.12), *The Review of Metaphysics*, 33 (1979), 414-416.

1980

144. "Diversificata in Diversis - Aquinas, In I Sent., Prol. 1, 2," *Scholastique--certitude et recherche*, en hommage à Louis Régis, ed. Ernest Jóos (Montréal: Editions Bellarmin, 1980), 113-129.
145. "Existence and the Subject of Metaphysics," *Science et Esprit*, 32 (1980), 255-260.

146. "Form and Cognition in Aristotle," *Ancient Philosophy*, 1 (1980), 17-28.
147. "La filosofia cristiana de la 'Aeterni Patris'," *Revista de Filosofia*, 13 (México, 1980), 229-246.
148. "An Appreciation of Brand Blanschard's Views on Catholicism," *The Philosophy of Brand Blanshard*, ed. Paul A. Schilpp (La Salle: Open Court, 1980), 1015-1039.
149. Review: Angelo Capecci, *Struttura e fine. La logica della teleologia aristotelica* (L'Aquila: L. U. Japardi, 1978), *The Review of Metaphysics*, 33 (1980), 622-623.
150. "Foreword" in *St. Thomas Aquinas on the Existence of God*: The Collected Papers of Joseph Owens, ed. John R. Catan (Albany: State University of New York Press, 1980), vii-viii.
151. "Foreword" in Giovanni Reale, *The Concept of First Philosophy and the Unity of the Metaphysics*, trans. John R. Catan (Albany: State University of New York Press, 1980), xv-xvi.
152. "*Quandoque* and *Aliquando* in Aquinas' *Tertia Via*," The New Scholasticism, 54 (1980), 447-475.

1981

153. *Aquinas on Being and Thing* (Niagara, New York: Niagara University Press, 1981), 33 pp.
154. "Stages and Distinction in De Ente: A Rejoinder," *The Thomist*, 45 (1981) 99-123.
155. "The Future of Thomistic Metaphysics," *One Hundred Years of Thomism*, ed. Victor B. Brezik C.S.B. (Center for Thomistic Studies, University of St. Thomas, Houston, Texas, 1981) 142-161.
156. "Wesen und Realdistinktion bei Thomas von Aquin," trans. Wenzel Peters in *Thomas von Aquin*, ed. Klaus Bernath, II (Darmstadt: Wissenschaftliche Buchgesellschaft, 1981), 239-265 (Translation of number 49 *supira*).
157. "Metaphysische Trennung bei Thomas von Aquin," trans. Wenzel Peters in *Thomas von Aquin*, ed. Klaus Bernath, II (Darmstadt: Wissenschaftliche Buchgesellschaft, 1981), 339-365 (Translation of number 94 *supra*).

Bibliographical Data

The following is a list of the articles that are included in this book in the order of their appearance, with the pertinent bibliographical information concerning their original publication.

1. "Aristote—Maitre de ceux qui savant," *La philosophie et les philosophes*, (Montreal:Bellarmin and Desclée, Paris-Tournai,1973) translated from English by Bernard and Roger Carriere, pp.45-68. The English version is hitherto unpublished in English and is that of Father Owens.

2. "Aristotle on Categories," *The Review of Metaphysics*,14 (1960), 73-90.

3. "The Aristotelian Conception of the Sciences," *International Philosophical Quarterly*, 4 (1964),200-216.

4. "Matter and Predication in Aristotle," *The Concept of Matter* ed.Ernan McMullin, (Notre Dame,Indiana:Notre Dame University Press,1963),79-93.

5. "The Grounds of Universality in Aristotle," *The American Philosophical Quarterly*,3 (1966),162-169.

6. "The Universality of the Sensible in the Aristotelian Noetic," *Essays in Ancient Greek Philosophy*, ed. John P.Anton and George L.Kustas,(Albany:State University of New York Press,1971),462-477. Reprinted from *Mélanges à la mémoire de Charles de Koninck*, ed. Lucien Zérounian,(Québec:Les Presses de l'Université Laval,1968),301-315.

7. "Aristotle—Cognition a Way of Being," *Canadian Journal of Philosophy*,6 (1976),1-11.

8. "Aristotelian Soul as Cognitive of Sensibles, Intelligibles and Self," *Ancient and Medieval Philosophies of the Soul*, ed. Parvitz Morewedge (*Eidos Press*) forthcoming.

9. "A Note on Aristotle, de Anima 3.4.429b9," *Phoenix* 30 (1976),107-118.

10. "Aristotle's Definition of the Soul," *Philomathes*, ed. Robert B.Palmer and Robert Hamerton-Kelly (The Hague:Martinus Nijhoff,1971),125-145.

11. "Aristotelian Argument for the Material Principle of Bodies," *Naturphilosophie bei Aristoteles und Theophrast*, ed. I.Düring (Heidelberg, 1969), 193-209.

12. "Teleology of Nature in Aristotle," *The Monist*, 52 (1968),159-173.

13. "The Grounds of Ethical Universality in Aristotle," *Man and World*, 2 (1969), 171-193.

14. "Nature and Ethical Norm in Aristotle," *Akten 14th International Congress of Philosophy*, Vienna, 2nd-9th of September,1968, 442-447.

15. "Aristotelian Ethics,Medicine, and the Changing Nature of Man," *Philosophical Medical Ethics*:Its Nature and Significance, ed. S.F.Spicker and H.T.Engelhardt (Dordrecht-Holland:D.Reidel Publishing Company, 1977), 127-142.

The Reverend Joseph Owens C.Ss.R., M.S.D.

Joseph Owens was born on April 17, 1908, in St. John, New Brunswick, Canada. He was the son of Louis Michael and Josephine (Quinn) Owens. As a young man he attended St. Mary's College, Brockville (1922-1927) and St. Anne's College, Montreal, Québec, Canada (1928-30). He was professed at St. John, New Brunswick into the Redemptorist Order on August 2, 1928. He completed his theological training for the priesthood at St. Alphonsus Seminary, Woodstock, Ontario, Canada (1930-34).

Father Owens was ordained a priest in 1933 and served as a parish priest at St. Joseph's Church, Moose Jaw, Saskatchewan, Canada (1934-35). He was then assigned to St. Patrick's Church, Toronto (1935-36). His teaching career began with a position as instructor in philosophy at St. Alphonsus Seminary, Woodstock, Ontario, Canada (1936-40), but was interrupted during the war years (1940-1944) by an assignment to Maria-Hilf Church, Tomslake, British Columbia, Canada. He returned to teaching at St. Alphonsus Seminary in 1948, and received the degree of Doctor in Medieval Studies (M.S.D.) from the Pontifical Institute of Mediaeval Studies at the University of Toronto in 1949. He was the first to be so honored. His doctoral dissertation entitled *The Doctrine of Being in the Aristotelian Metaphysics* was published in 1951 by the Pontifical Institute of Mediaeval Studies with an introduction by Etienne Gilson. In 1953-4 he was Instructor in Medieval Moral Doctrine at the Accademia Alfonsiana, Rome, Italy and in 1954 he taught at Assumption University of Windsor, Windsor, Ontario, Canada (now the University of Windsor).

In 1954 Father Owens was invited to join the staff of the Pontifical Institute of Mediaeval Studies in the University of Toronto, Toronto, Ontario, Canada. He also held an appointment in the Graduate Faculty of the School of Graduate Studies of the University of Toronto. He was appointed Professor in 1960.

Father Owens has been active in professional societies as well as receiving recognition in various awards and honors. He was President of the American Catholic Philosophical Association in 1965-66, as well as President of the Metaphysical Society of America in 1971-72 and councillor in 1965-67. He was also a member of the Steering Committee of the International Metaphysical Society and the President of the Society for Ancient Greek Philosophy in 1971-72.

The Royal Society of Canada honored him by enrolling him as a Fellow of the Society. He is also a member of the Catholic Commission on Intellectual and Cultural Affairs. Father Owens is on the editorial board of several philosophical journals such as *The Monist*, *Mediaeval Studies*, and *The New Scholasticism*. He has recently retired from the Faculty of the School of Graduate Studies in the University of Toronto, Canada, and was awarded the status of Professor Emeritus of the University of Toronto as well as Emeritus Fellow of the Pontifical Institute of Mediaeval Studies, Toronto, Ontario, Canada where he continues to supervise Ph.D. theses and to publish the results of his philosophical research.

JRC

Index of Names

A page number followed by a "n." is a reference to the notes at the back of the volume, all other page numbers are to the text.

Index of Platonic and Aristotelian Texts Cited in the Texts and Notes